D1114640

Writing Winning
Business Proposals

Writing Winning Business Proposals

Your Guide to Landing the Client, Making the Sale, Persuading the Boss

Richard C. Freed
Shervin Freed
Joseph D. Romano

McGraw-Hill, Inc.

New York   San Francisco   Washington, D.C.   Auckland   Bogotá
Caracas   Lisbon   London   Madrid   Mexico City   Milan
Montreal   New Delhi   San Juan   Singapore
Sydney   Tokyo   Toronto

Library of Congress Cataloging-in-Publication Data

Freed, Richard C.
　　Writing winning business proposals : your guide to landing the
client, making the sale, persuading the boss / Richard C. Freed,
Shervin Freed, Joseph D. Romano
　　　　p.　　cm.
　　Includes index.
　　ISBN 0-07-021924-9.–ISBN 0-07-021925-7 (pbk.)
　　1. Proposal writing in business.　2. Business report writing.
I. Freed, Shervin.　II. Romano, Joseph D.　III. Title
HF5718.5.F74　1995
808′.06665–dc20　　　　　　　　　　　　　　　　94-38099
　　　　　　　　　　　　　　　　　　　　　　　CIP

1 2 3 4 5 6 7 8 9 0　DOC/DOC　9 0 9 8 7 6 5 4　(HC)
1 2 3 4 5 6 7 8 9 0　DOC/DOC　9 0 9 8 7 6 5 4　(PBK)

ISBN 0-07-021924-9 (HC)
ISBN 0-07-021925-7 (PBK)

*The sponsoring editor for this book was Betsy Brown, the editing supervisor was
Fred Dahl, and the production supervisor was Suzanne W. B. Rapcavage. It was
set in Baskerville by Inkwell Publishing Services.*

Printed and bound by R. R. Donnelley & Sons Company.

McGraw-Hill books are available at special quantity discounts to use as
premiums and sales promotions, or for use in corporate training programs.
For more information, please write to the Director of Special Sales,
McGraw-Hill, Inc., 11 West 19th Street, New York, NY 10011. Or contact
your local bookstore.

 This book is printed on recycled, acid-free paper containing a minimum of 50% recycled de-inked fiber.

Contents

Preface   xi

Introduction   **1**

Part 1. Proposal Logics   **9**

1. Understanding Generic Structure Logic   **11**

The Slots in a Proposal's Generic Structure   12
Slots Speaking to Slots   13
Slots Are Not Necessarily Sections   14
All Slots Should Be Filled or Accounted For   14
Chapter 1 Review: Understanding Generic Structure Logic   16
Work Session 1: Proposal Opportunity at the ABC Company, a Division of
   Consolidated Industries   17

2. Understanding the Baseline Logic   **18**

The Three Kinds of Current Situations, Desired Results, Benefits, and
   Objectives   20
Assessing the Baseline Logic's Alignment   22
Aligning the Project Objective and the Desired Result   22
Aligning the Benefits with the Objectives and the Desired Result   26
Testing the Baseline Logic   28
Aligning the Current Situation and Benefits   31
The Relationship Between the Generic Structure Slots, the Baseline Logic,
   and Your Proposed Project   36

Chapter 2 Review: Understanding the Baseline Logic   38
Work Session 2: Constructing the Baseline Logic for the Situation at
   ABC   39

3. Using a Measurable Results Orientation   49

Measurable Results Orientation: The Insight Project   50
Measurable Results Orientation: The Planning Project   51
Measurable Results Orientation: The Implementation Project   53
Chapter 3 Review: Using a Measurable Results Orientation   55
Work Session 3: Applying a Measurable Results Orientation for ABC   55

4. Constructing a Logical Methodology—The Pyramid Principle   56

Using Pyramid Logic   57
Step 1: Clearly Identify the Objective(s), Based on the Overriding
   Question(s)   63
Step 2: Place Each Objective atop a Pyramid and Order the *Actions*
   Necessary to Achieve It   64
Step 3: Sequence the Actions   67
Step 4: Identify and Integrate the *Activities* Necessary for Planning and
   Communicating Your Proposed Actions   68
The Pyramid and the Baseline Logic Worksheet   70
Chapter 4 Review: Constructing a Logical Methodology   73
Work Session 4: Developing the Pyramid for ABC   74

Part 2. Proposal Psychologics   79

5. Analyzing the Buyers   81

The Four Buying Roles   82
A Fifth Buying Role   86
Beyond $S_1\text{-}S_2\text{-}B$ 88
Chapter 5 Review: Analyzing the Buyers   91
Work Session 5: Identifying Buyer Roles and Generating Benefits for
   ABC   91

6. Selecting and Developing Themes—Determining What to Weave in Your Web of Persuasion   97

What Themes Are   99
Where Themes Come From   100
Selecting the Themes   105
Developing the Themes   106
Chapter 6 Review: Selecting and Developing Themes   108
Work Session 6: Identifying Hot Buttons and Evaluation Criteria,
   Countering the Competition, and Developing the Themes for ABC   110

Part 3. Proposal Preparation 121

7. Writing the Situation and Objectives Slots 123

The Story/S_1 Component   124
The Questions Component   127
The Needs Component   130
The Closing/S_2 Component   131
The Questions Component Is Modular   132
The Situation Slot and Competitive Advantage   134
Chapter 7 Review: Writing the Situation and Objectives Slots   135
Work Session 7: Writing the Situation and Objectives Slots for ABC   136

8. Writing the Methods Slot 142

PIP   142
PIP at the Task Level   144
PIP at the Methods Slot Level   145
Chapter 8 Review: Writing the Methods Slot   150
Work Session 8: Writing the Methods Slot for ABC   151

9. Interlude: Focusing on Persuasion 158

Determining the Level of Persuasiveness   160
P–Slots and Themes   163
Chapter 9 Review: Focusing on Persuasion   165

10. Writing the Qualifications Slot 166

Your Qualifications Section Needs to Be an Argument   168
Typical Qualifications Sections Don't Present an Argument   169
Use Your Themes Development Worksheet to Structure Your
   Argument   170
Chapter 10 Review: Writing the Qualifications Slot   172
Work Session 9: Writing the Qualifications Slot for ABC   173

11. Writing the Benefits Section 177

The Kinds of Benefits   178
The Function of the Benefits Slot   180
The Content of the Benefits *Section* (Work Session 10)   180
Chapter 11 Review: Writing the Benefits Section   187

12. Summary—The Proposal Development Process 188

Appendix A: Paramount Consulting's Proposal Opportunity at the ABC Company: A Case Study 197

Appendix B: Worksheets   **210**

Appendix C: Paramount's Proposal Letter to the ABC Company   **222**

**Appendix D: Internal Proposals (Make Certain They're
Not Reports)**   **243**

**Appendix E: A Few Comments About Writing Effective
Sentences (and Paragraphs)**   **250**

Glossary   261

Index   264

Preface

This book is written for businesspeople who prepare proposals (and for businesspeople who evaluate them). If you are a consultant who owns your own business or who works for a firm of two or two thousand, if you are an internal consultant who sells services to your own organization, if you are a business executive who sells ideas to your management, you will benefit greatly from this book.

If you are like most people, you probably find selling your services or ideas in a proposal both unenjoyable and difficult. Your proposals not only take too long to prepare, they are often written when you least want to write them (at night or during weekends) because during the day you are occupied with everything else that you would rather do instead: conducting projects, furthering relationships, developing people. Proposal writing often seems like extra work, extra effort to get work so that you can be successful in your intensely competitive business.

Perhaps equally frustrating is the margin of difference, the margin of victory, between winning and losing. Hundreds of people consulting in the private sector have said the same thing: on a 100-point scale, the difference between winning and coming in second is often minuscule: 2 to 5 points. The public sector is similar. For a recent proposal to manage a $30 million project for a U.S. government agency, the difference between the winner and an also-ran was 5 points out of 1000 ...$\frac{1}{2}$ of 1 percent!

What accounts for this difference? Sometimes it's price, of course. Sometimes, your particular methodology or your qualifications. But all too often, it's something much less tangible and rarely part of the evalua-

tion criteria, whether those criteria are written down or in the buyers'*
heads. That something has to do with relationships, with the buyer's *feeling* that you are *right*, that you *understand*, that the two of you are *compatible*. Of course price is frequently a consideration, and so is expertise.
But someone is always or can always be less costly, and the world is full of
experts. Price and expertise get you in the running, but they don't assure
that you're anything more than an also-ran. The goal of this book is to get
you the additional 2 to 5 points necessary to win.

One doesn't write a book like this in isolation. Over the course of many
years on this effort, I have numerous people to thank: the hundreds of
consultants from A. T. Kearney's North American, European, and Asian
offices who have helped me test and refine the concepts, as well as those
consultants from Eicher Consultancy in New Delhi and KPMG Peat
Marwick in Chicago, who were helpful in providing opportunities to test
my initial concepts. I also wish to thank the many graduate students at
Iowa State University who have served as a laboratory to develop my ideas,
as well as the university itself, which provided release time so that the project could be completed. In particular, I wish to thank Caroline Calkins-Heine and Heleen Moerland of A. T. Kearney for some of the ideas presented in Chap. 4, and I would especially like to thank Barbara Minto
whose pioneering work in what she describes as the "Pyramid Principle"
forms the conceptual basis for Chap. 4 as well as the discussion in Chap.
10 and Appendix E.

Richard Freed
Ames, Iowa

---

*The term "buyer" refers to decision makers or decision influencers—i.e., those people
who must agree that you are the right choice to support them in a proposed project.
Therefore, a buyer is your potential client, whether that person exists within or outside your
organization.

Writing Winning
Business Proposals

Introduction

I am your potential client, and I'd like to introduce myself. Whether you are a consultant (either on your own or working for a consulting firm), an internal consultant, or a project-oriented employee working within my own firm, I am a reader of your proposal or a viewer of your proposal presentation. You are trying to sell me a service, and I will decide, singly or with others, whether you, someone else, or no one will get the work you desire. Likewise, if you are an employee with an idea to sell, I am also a reader of your proposal or a viewer of your proposal presentation. You are trying to sell me an idea, and I will decide, singly or with others, whether it is valid or workable or serviceable or fundable. In all of these cases, your job is to persuade me to engage you.

Regardless of your situation, your relationship with me is far different from my relationship to you. You are courting me; I am testing you. You are wooing me; I am assessing you—your abilities, insights, perceptiveness, personal characteristics, and desire to support me. I know what you want from me—my agreement that your service or idea is worthwhile and, in many cases, more worthwhile than someone else's. But I'm not so certain that you know where I'm coming from or what I want from you. So I'll tell you.

If you're an outsider, engaging you as a consultant (at least initially) is often viewed by me and my colleagues as a sign of weakness. If I am at all typical of other potential clients I know, many of us share this perception. In my mind, hiring you frequently indicates, or at least suggests, my inability to do my job entirely by myself or within my organization. I know all the reasons why outside support makes sense and should add value. However, at the same time, when I'm really honest with myself, I'm not excited by the prospect of engaging you. Rather, I'm feeling worried, threatened, impatient, and even at times suspicious.

1

I'm worried by the implication that potential changes you propose will indicate that I haven't been doing my job, or at least not doing it as well as I should. I'm threatened by the possibility of losing control to you, the outsider, and how this could make my position—my power base—vulnerable within my organization. I'm impatient because I've tried for some time to address this issue we're discussing, didn't seek outside support when the symptoms initially occurred, and now have a need for rapid response. I'm suspicious of your ability to help me because I've been burned before, have heard all your promises, and have compared them to the eventual results. You all talk a good game. Not all of you perform as well as you talk. So when I discuss my situation with you, I want you to understand me and what makes my situation unique. It may not be unique to you, but it is to me. I'm looking for assurance that your involvement will make me and my organization significantly better and more competitive.

Therefore, if you are a consultant I believe that your responsiveness and interest in the proposal-development stage indicate the kind of service you'll provide if you're selected. As a result, I want you to demonstrate your desire to serve me, your knowledge of my organization and industry, your understanding of my priorities, and your ability to listen, to challenge, and to understand my situation, my needs, and my desired benefits. I want you to prepare thoroughly for your meetings with me, go out of your way to show me how good you are, be specific about how you will help me, share your knowledge and experience from similar situations, and make me feel that this proposed project is important to you and your firm. I want you to begin providing "service" early in the process by offering advice, ideas, and perspective, even if I don't request them.

When I do make a request, especially one that is obviously a test of your responsiveness, I want you to respond quickly and thoroughly. In short, during the early stages of our courtship, I want to learn and I want you to establish a sound relationship by providing value. I want you to act as if my situation is the most important one you are dealing with. You offer a professional service, and I need to know that you'll serve me professionally—that is, provide value for my proposed expenditure.

If you do all that, especially over time as we develop a closer relationship, you might not even have to write a proposal, and, of course, you really don't want to. Proposals take a lot of time, often a huge investment in time. And let's be honest: Even when they're well written, proposals frequently don't win jobs as much as they clinch or lose them.

But the plain truth is that we don't always have a close relationship and you can't always sell a job up front. Therefore you need to write a proposal, and therefore you might as well learn to write a good one. Hence this book. I've written it because I and other potential clients like me have read and heard hundreds of your proposals, and although a few are outstanding, most of them aren't. Many offend with "cut and paste" boiler-plate, miss important opportunities to provide value, suffer from poor logic and organization, focus more on you than on me and my organization, and look unprofessional on the page. Although some do a few things well, some don't do much well at all. All can be improved, and I guarantee that I can help you improve them.

I'm not saying your proposal will always win. That I can't guarantee. But I do promise that you'll prepare better proposals—because you'll think more strategically about how to write and present them. Getting you to think and write more strategically, particularly from my point of view, is one of the goals of this book.

So what do I as a potential client, either outside or within your organization, want from your proposal? Nothing that should surprise you. From my perspective, I want to feel that you can best meet my objectives and achieve my desired results from engaging you. Therefore, I desire:

- Agreement on my question—i.e., on the specific question or questions that must be answered to move my organization from our current situation to our desired result.

- A clear understanding of the benefits I will receive by your answering that question—benefits I will gain by the end of the proposed project and beyond.

- Clarity on how you propose to answer the question and the way we will work together as you do so.

- Confidence in and comfort with you and your proposed team.

- Return on my investment versus my actual and/or anticipated benefits.

To help you address these desires, I've developed the proven proposal development process summarized in Exhibit I.1. Although preparing effective and persuasive proposals involves far more than the process illustrates (and this book covers much more than the process itself), the following five steps will provide you with a roadmap for the journey we'll take through much of this book.

1. *Understand the baseline logic.* Every proposal situation involves a discrepancy between where I and my organization are and where we want to be—between, that is, our current situation (S_1) and our desired result (S_2). The project or ideas you propose will achieve or get us closer to achieving that desired result and therefore begin to or entirely remove that discrepancy. Consequently, benefits (B) will accrue to us. At its fundamental level, your proposal must clearly express the relationship between my current situation, my desired result, and the benefits of my achieving that result. I call this the proposal's *baseline logic,* represented by the formula

$S_1 \rightarrow S_2 \rightarrow B$. Your proposal (and your project, if you win) stands little chance of success if these elements aren't clearly identified, logically related, and agreed to. I discuss this relationship in Chap. 2.

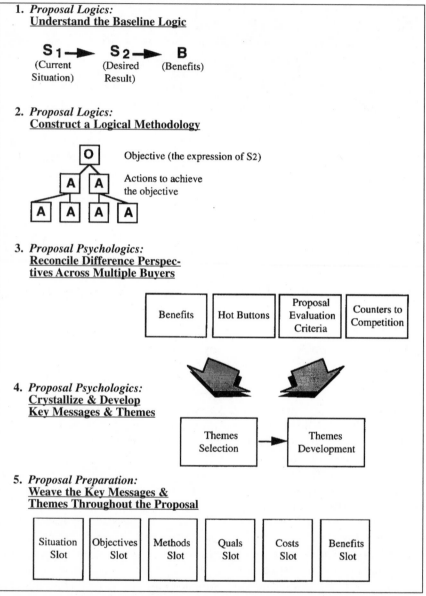

Exhibit I.1. Proposal development process.

2. *Construct a logical methodology.* To move me from S_1 to S_2, your document or projection proposes a series of actions, a method of approach, that must clearly and logically communicate how you'll help me and my organization achieve our objective and desired result. In Chap. 4 I show you how to build a pyramid, a logical framework, that will help you organize and sequence the actions necessary to achieve our objective.

Part 1 of this book, then, focuses on what I call the "logics" of proposals: the logical relationship between the current situation, desired result, and benefits; and the logically constructed methodology you will use to help remove the discrepancy between where I and my organization are and where we want to be.

Understanding proposal logics, however, may get you only part of the additional 2–5 points you need to win, since I and others buy for psychological as well as for logical reasons. Accordingly, Part 2 focuses on what I call the "psychologics" of proposals. The next two steps in my proposal development process address these psychologics.

3. *Reconcile different perspectives across multiple buyers. Writing Winning Business Proposals* assumes that most of your proposal situations involve what is called a "complex sale." A complex sale exists when you sell to multiple buyers, each of whom may play a different role in evaluating your proposal. Each may have a different perception—sometimes slight, sometimes significant—of the problem or opportunity and of the benefits that will accrue to the organization, collectively, and to them, individually, from solving or realizing it.

Too often, proposals are unsuccessful because proposers assume they are selling to organizations rather than to individuals. Although an organization can be in a problematic situation, different people within the organization often have different points of view of the current situation. What to one person is eroding profits might be a lack of productivity to a second and poor customer service to a third. Each person, in short, has a different agenda, a different critical issue, or at least a different slant on the issue that must be considered. I'll help you explore these persons as individuals who play different roles on the proposal evaluation committee and have different buying criteria. I discuss these roles in Chap. 5.

Once you've understood the individual players in the selling situation, you need to create a mosaic, a collage, to understand their similarities and differences. A successful proposal has to address these differences in one document or in one presentation. Addressing different perceptions is a major challenge. You need, for example, to know the buyers' hot buttons: their individual desires and concerns that must be addressed during the project. You need to understand the benefits that will accrue to each, once the proposed objectives are achieved. But, just as important, you need to understand how each buyer's hot buttons complement or conflict with the desires of other buyers. In Chap. 6 I discuss these matters as well as proposal evaluation criteria and counters to the competition.

4. *Crystallize and develop key proposal messages and themes.* To be most effective, your proposal (spoken or written) needs to communicate several essential messages that clearly differentiate it from the competitors' and that convince me and the other buyers that you have heard and understood the issues from our respective points of view. These messages, which characterize our story and our needs, are called *themes.* They come from your analysis of our individual hot buttons and our collective evaluation criteria and from your counters to the competition. Once you have identified your themes and developed them, you will have generated most of the persuasive content to incorporate into your proposal. In Chap. 6 I discuss themes in detail.

5. *Weave the messages and themes throughout your proposal.* All the strategy just discussed must be applied, of course, and the chapters in Part 3 address this application. Just as Beethoven repeated his musical themes throughout his symphonies, you want to "play" your themes throughout your proposal. By weaving your web of persuasion, you can communicate why you, and not somebody else, can best support me to achieve my desired result. In Chap. 8 I discuss the important concept of "persuasion slots," those parts of your proposal that contain your themes. Subsequent chapters discuss major parts of the proposal where you discuss your understanding of my situation, your proposed method for addressing it, the benefits to the buyers of your doing so, and the like.

Each of this book's chapters introduces you to important concepts and strategies, which are then applied in a work session. I've written the work sessions from your point of view, so that you can see how the strategies are applied as you develop your proposal step by step. That is, the work sessions (which are based on an extensive case) allow you to experience and practice the concepts laid out step by step in the chapter preceding it.

Before we begin our journey together, I have to let you in on a little secret. *There are no rules for writing; there are only strategies.* No rules. Not even that subjects and verbs should always agree. Not even that sentences (like this and the previous two) shouldn't be fragments.

Rule-bound writers are limited writers. Having been told by some eighth-grade English teacher (mine was particularly forgettable) never to begin a sentence with "but," they never do. "*But* why not do so?" I ask, if the situation suggests that you should. Consequently, rule-bound writers have fewer options to choose from, fewer possibilities to consider, fewer arrows in their quiver or weapons in their arsenal. You are no longer in the eighth grade. Your challenge now is to persuade me, your potential client, using all the tools and techniques at your disposal.

Writing always involves choice, always decisions among options, and the more options you consider, the better your chance of selecting the most appropriate one for a given situation. Even the rule-bound writer has made a decision, but what I call a "nondecision decision," an unconsidered one. I'll show you how to make better decisions, considered ones. And remember that what worked well in one situation will not necessarily work in another. Even if the questions are identical. Even if the industry issues are identical. If preparing winning proposals were that easy, there'd be no need for this book.

I'm willing to teach you, if you're willing to learn. I challenge you to think hard about the concepts presented. Some of them will make almost immediate sense because they will provide guidelines for what you already know, and these frameworks will allow you to use your knowledge more consistently and effectively. Other concepts will be more difficult to master, because proposals are difficult to master. I've spent over 15 years trying to master this beast called proposals. I'm closer to doing so than I used to be, and if you work with me, I'll help you get far closer than you've ever been.

Let our journey begin!

Part 1

Proposal Logics

One thing amazes and even at times upsets me about your proposals. Although you are obviously well educated and intelligent, your documents and presentations do not often logically convey your ideas. I can comprehend a well thought logical argument about my situation and how you might help me to improve it, but only if you present that argument in a clear and logical framework.

At the beginning of Part 1, I give you that framework. Then I share my desire for your having and communicating an orientation toward measurable, substantive results in whatever type of support you might propose to provide to me and my organization. Finally, I discuss how to construct a logical methodology that will answer my question, meet my objective, and therefore move me and my organization from our current situation to our desired result. You're writing your proposal because we have this gap, and your methodology must clearly and logically explain how you propose to bridge it. Because of your expertise, you know *how* to bridge that gap. But based on the hundreds of proposals I've evaluated, I can only conclude that you don't know how to *communicate* that knowledge to *me,* clearly and logically. But, you will by the end of Part 1.

1
Understanding Generic Structure Logic

Like most people, I like stories. So let me begin by telling you a very short story, after which I'll ask you several questions:

"Paula was hungry. After she entered and ordered a pastrami sandwich, it was served to her quickly, so she left the waitress a big tip."

- Where was Paula?
- What did she eat?
- Who made the sandwich?
- Who took the order?
- Who served the sandwich?
- Why did Paula leave a big tip?

How is it that you could answer those questions rather easily, even though nothing in the story *explicitly* provides the information necessary for your answers? Because you have a schema for the concept of "Restaurant."

Schemas are knowledge structures that you have stored in your memory as patterns, as analytical frameworks. Schemas represent generic concepts, like *Restaurant* or *Airplane* or *House*. Each schema has "slots" that exist in a network of relations. Your schema for *Restaurant* may have slots for "Ordering," "Eating," "Tipping," and "Paying." Your schema for *House* may contain slots for "Family Room," "Kitchen," "Living Room," and

"Bathroom." Slots for "Dark Room" and "Home Office" are also possible, but probably not for "Boardroom" or "Conference Room" since such spaces are not typically found in residences. Therefore, you don't *expect* to find a boardroom or a conference room in someone's house.

You also have schemas for different kinds of texts, and these schemas create expectations. In a novel, for example, you expect character and plot and setting. In a particular type of novel, like a spy novel, you may expect that the hero will be betrayed and captured, only to escape and triumph. In a eulogy, you expect some account of the deceased person's character and accomplishments; in a personal letter, some account of your friend's life and feelings; in a sermon, some moral based upon a religious belief. If the sermon consisted solely of an analysis of price-earnings ratios or bills of materials or various strategies for penetrating new markets, your expectations would be denied and you'd be suspicious of the speaker's competence and reliability, maybe even his or her sanity.

Proposals and other business documents also carry with them schemas and sets of expectations. If I requested you to deliver a proposal to me, I'd be surprised if the document contained findings, conclusions, and recommendations. These are "slots" I'd expect in a report, not a proposal.* Potential clients like me, then, have certain expectations, and as a writer, you're at some risk if you don't meet them. If your reader is in a proposal-reading situation, you'd better deliver a document that fits your reader's proposal-schema, and not the schema for a report or a eulogy or a novel.

Like a schema, a proposal also has slots, and these slots make up what I call a proposal's generic structure. No matter how different one proposal may be from another, something generic makes them both proposals, and that "something" is their generic structure.

The Slots in a Proposal's Generic Structure

Most of your proposal opportunities exist because I, your potential client, have an unsolved problem or an unrealized opportunity. Therefore, your primary task is to convince me, both logically and psychologically, that you can help me solve my problem or realize my opportunity and, in competitive situations, that you'll do it better than anyone else.

---

*A great many people and a great many textbooks on writing confuse proposals, which propose a method for answering a question, and internal recommendation reports, which provide an answer to that question. That's why I've written Appendix D, which discusses these two different kinds of documents and gives you some pointers on writing reports.

Your entire proposal needs to communicate that message in one seam-less argument (which may happen to be divided into sections or even volumes for my convenience). Your argument is suggested by the following propositions, each of which is preceded by the proposal slot that contains it. (See Exhibit 1.1.)

Slot	Proposition
Situation	This is our understanding of your problem or opportunity.
Objectives	Given that problem or opportunity, these are our objectives for solving or realizing it.
Methods	Given those objectives, these are the methods we will use to achieve them.
Qualifications	Given those methods, these are our qualifications for performing them.
Costs	Given those qualifications and methods, this is how much it will cost.
Benefits	Given our efforts and their associated costs, these are the benefits or value that you will receive.

Exhibit 1.1. The generic structure of proposals.

Slots Speaking to Slots

Although the preceding statements might suggest that your proposal's argument flows only one way—from top to bottom—the argument should be so tight that the logic also can flow from bottom to top:

> These are the *benefits* or value you will receive
> considering the *costs* you will incur
> given our *qualifications*
> for performing these *methods*
> that will achieve these *objectives*
> and therefore improve your *situation.*

In a tightly written or spoken proposal, every generic structure slot "speaks" to all the others. No slot exists in isolation: each contributes to your communicating the proposal's primary message. In later chapters, I'll show you specific techniques for assuring that each slot in your proposal speaks to every other one.

Slots Are Not
Necessarily Sections

You've probably noticed that I've been referring to OBJECTIVES, METHODS, BENEFITS, etc. as "slots," even though many proposals might designate those parts of the proposal by using section headings of the same name.* I've been calling these elements slots rather than sections because in any given proposal it is possible that:

- *No slot could be used as a section heading.* That's because you don't use headings in your document or because your headings are different from the slot names. The situation slot could be called "Background" or "Business Issues" or "Our Understanding of Your Situation." The methods slot could be named "Approach" or "Methodology" or "Study Strategy."

- *Two or more slots could be combined into one section.* You could combine SITUATION and OBJECTIVES into one section. Or OBJECTIVES and METHODS.

- *One slot could be split into two or more sections.* METHODS could be divided among "Approach," "Workplan," and "Deliverables." QUALIFICATIONS could be split among "Project Organization," "Qualifications," "References," and "Resumes."

All Slots Should Be Filled or
Accounted For

Every proposal you write or speak contains six slots, but these slots are not necessarily organized into corresponding sections or presented in any predetermined or fixed order. Nevertheless, whether they are combined, split, or not named at all, each slot should be filled or accounted for. On some occasions, you don't have to fill slots in the proposal *document* because they've already been "filled" in prior discussions with me, your potential client, and therefore accounted for during the proposal *process*. We all know that proposal development itself is often only one part of the selling process, and everything that occurs before the actual document is submitted affects the proposal's content, organization, tone, and the like.†

---

*From here on I will use small caps to designate generic structure slots. That is, I'll refer to the methods *slot* either by calling it that or by writing it in small caps: METHODS. I'll refer to the methods *section* either by calling it that or by writing "Methods."

†In fact, your proposal might not even take the form of a product (e.g., a document or a presentation). That is, many "proposals" consist solely of the *process* of convincing me that you are the right person and yours is the right firm to provide the services I need. That process could end, not with a written document or a presentation, but with a simple handshake.

If before you submit the proposal you have already convinced me that you thoroughly understand my problem or opportunity, then you've already filled the situation slot, and may not need to fill it in the proposal. If you and your team have previously done a good deal of commendable work for me, then you've filled the qualifications slot, and loading the document with resumes and references may be not only unnecessary but unstrategic and, perhaps, even annoying. Remember, there are no rules, only strategies. And effective strategies are driven by my situation, by the context of the selling process.

*   *   *

By understanding the schema for "house," you know what kind of rooms can exist in a house: therefore, you expect rooms like a kitchen, a bathroom, a bedroom, and so on. You also have some sense of the relationship among those rooms, and to some degree their placement. For example, in a two-story house you would expect a first-floor kitchen; in a two-story house with only one bath, you might expect a second-floor bathroom; in a house with more than one bath, you'd not be surprised to find the second one adjoined to a master bedroom.

Similarly, by understanding generic structure—the schema for proposals—you understand an important logical element of proposals. You know that proposals, to be proposals, also have certain kinds of rooms or slots, and you know the relationship among those rooms. You know, for example, that one slot explains the problem or opportunity, another explains a method for solving the problem or capitalizing on the opportunity, and yet another argues the benefits of doing so.

Throughout much of this book, I will build upon the concept of generic structure. In fact, the next chapter will focus on the three proposal slots—SITUATION, OBJECTIVES, and BENEFITS—that make up what I call "the baseline logic."

⇨ Chapter 1 Review:
Understanding Generic Structure Logic

1. All proposals have the same generic structure, which contains the following six slots:
   - *Situation:* What is the problem or opportunity?
   - *Objectives:* Given that problem or opportunity, what are your objectives for solving or realizing it?
   - *Methods:* Given those objectives, how will you achieve them?
   - *Qualifications:* Given those methods, how are you qualified to achieve them?
   - *Costs:* Given the methods and qualifications, how much will it cost?
   - *Benefits:* Given those costs, what benefits and/or value will accrue?

2. Generic structure is *not* a matter of organization. That is, a proposal is not necessarily sequenced according to the slots as they are ordered.

3. The slots do not necessarily correspond to sections. One section could contain two or more slots. A single slot could be distributed among two or more sections.

4. All slots should be filled, either in the proposal presentation or document, or in pre-proposal meetings or prior working relationships.

Work Session 1: Proposal Opportunity at the ABC Company, a Division of Consolidated Industries

```
                        MEMORANDUM

To:      You, the Reader
From:    Me, Your Potential Client
SUBJECT: WORK SESSION 1


  Before I, Your Potential Client, take you to the next
chapter, I need to introduce you to this first of 10 work
sessions that will help you think about and apply the con-
cepts discussed throughout this book. Fortunately, you
won't have to do the work; the work sessions take you
through the paces. You only have to pretend to watch your-
self work and think about what you're doing. It won't be
this simple in the real world, but understanding these
work sessions will make it far easier.


  Each of the work sessions is based on the ABC Case in
Appendix A, which you should read for this session. Please
do not be concerned if the case relates to a business sit-
uation unfamiliar to you. Understanding the technical
aspects of the situation is not a prerequisite to your
understanding the strategies used in subsequent work ses-
sions to prepare a winning proposal. In subsequent chap-
ters, I will refer to the work sessions and the proposal
that gets structured piece by piece throughout them. So
you can't skip these sessions; to internalize the con-
cepts, you need to read the work sessions in order.


  You may not always agree with the analyses in the work
sessions or with what "you" decide to include or not to
include in the proposal. In fact, I encourage you to dis-
agree, to consider other alternatives, perhaps even bet-
ter strategies. But please, let's not debate the techni-
cal aspects of the case. I've simplified it somewhat for
the purpose of this book, which is to discuss proposal
strategy and development, not all the technical aspects of
the ABC situation.


  Remember, there is no Right Answer, no rules, only some
possible guidelines and a set of possible alternatives at
every juncture. Some alternatives may be better than oth-
ers, depending on your analysis of the specific selling
situation, its history, its magnitude and importance, your
relationship or lack of relationship with the buying com-
mittee, and other situational factors discussed through-
out this book.
```

2
Understanding the Baseline Logic

A lot of people (and I'm one of them) think that too many proposals try to make the simple complex, when in fact what I and many other buyers want them to do is to make the complex simple. So let me simplify what proposals do, or at least what I'd like them to do from my perspective. Let's concentrate on just three things (which, we'll see at the end of this chapter, are related to three of the generic structure slots—SITUATION, OBJECTIVES, and BENEFITS). Exhibit 2.1 depicts your proposed project in a nutshell.

In the beginning is my organization, which is in a condition, a current "state of health," a current situation (S_1). This current situation is what is happening today. Perhaps we don't like this situation because we have a problem that needs solving. Or perhaps we would like another situation better because we have an opportunity that we might capitalize on. In either case we desire to change. Or we might be uncertain about whether we like or should like our current situation, and we'd like to know whether or not we ought to like it or dislike it.

In each of these cases, an actual or possible discrepancy exists between where we are and where we want to be. Therefore, you propose a project at the end of which we will have closed the gap and be in a different, improved state, call it S_2, which is what I call my desired result. At that point, our problem will be solved (or on its way to a solution), or our opportunity will be realized (or at least closer to its realization), or we will know whether or not we have a problem or an opportunity. In each case we will have or know something more than we had or knew. And we will be better off because of it; we will benefit and gain value from reaching our desired result, S_2, by the end of your proposed engagement.

I am here, I want to be over there, and I'll benefit when I get there. That simple idea needs to function as the baseline of your proposal—and of

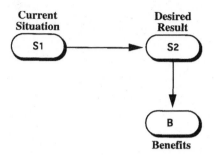

Exhibit 2.1. The baseline logic.

your thinking about your proposal to me. That idea has a logic to it, a fundamental logic, a *baseline* logic. And that idea, that baseline logic, needs to drive the argument of your proposal: "You are here, and we understand that 'here' is or might not be desirable. You want to be somewhere else instead, which is more desirable; once we help you to that somewhere else, you will enjoy the benefits of being there."

Although all this certainly isn't rocket science, only a minority of proposal writers understand this logic, and far fewer know how to test for and apply it. Most proposals are illogical at their core because the writers don't understand the baseline logic, and even when they do, they don't know how to clearly convey that understanding to me. They don't know how to take advantage of that logic to increase the persuasiveness of their presentations and documents. This baseline logic—or, if you prefer, this problem definition or analytical framework—is the basis for a meaningful and persuasive exchange of ideas.

Here, I should express two cautionary notes. First, there are times when I, your potential client, am not clear about this baseline logic. I'm not clear about my current situation or about where I want to be at the end of your proposed project. When this occurs, and you do not help me to achieve clarity, you and I are in a potential lose-lose situation. In this situation, you will probably write a proposal without clear objectives, without clearly defining my desired result, S_2, at the end of your project. I might even accept that proposal, but we might both pay a price, often a significant price, during the engagement. You may not satisfy me, possibly incur a cost overrun, and not develop the long-lasting relationship we both desire. To avoid this situation and to ensure that your proposal is fundamentally sound, the rest of this chapter will build on the concept of the baseline logic, show you how to test for it, and demonstrate how you can use it to your advantage.

The second cautionary note: Although I remarked at the beginning of this chapter that I want you to make the complex simple, I have to admit that the relatively simple concept of the baseline logic is not often easy to understand. Accordingly, this is *not* an easy chapter. At times the reading will be laborious. Sometimes it will even appear redundant, because I want constantly to reinforce important points that will help you use the baseline logic to:

- Challenge the depth of my thinking
- Clarify my overriding question
- Clarify your project's objective
- Articulate and generate benefits
- Communicate a measurable results orientation
- Construct your methodology
- Define the magnitude of your effort
- Identify your necessary qualifications
- Make better go/no go decisions

These substantial benefits will accrue to you only after you have mastered the concept of the baseline logic. But mastery of anything is difficult. So hang in there: I'm going to give you the key that unlocks the mystery of proposals.

The Three Kinds of Current Situations, Desired Results, Benefits, and Objectives

As shown in Exhibit 2.2, my current situation (as well as my desired result) can be one of only three conditions. These are the three possible S_1 situations that can serve as a starting point for your efforts:

1. I and my organization don't know if we should change, because we *lack insight* about our situation.

2. We know we should change but we don't know how, because we do *have insight* but not a plan of action.

3. We know we should change and we know how, because we *have a plan,* but we need help to implement it.

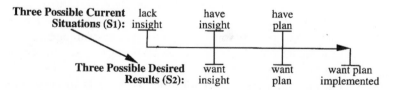

Exhibit 2.2. The three possible current situations and desired results.

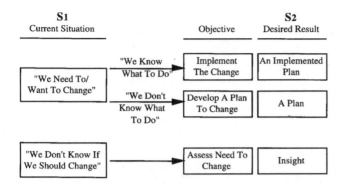

Exhibit 2.3. The relationship among current situations, objectives, and desired results.

As Exhibit 2.3 illustrates, each of these three possible S_1 conditions corresponds to one of three project objectives and desired results.

Each of these desired results is related to one of three projects you could propose: insight, planning, or implementation. In an Insight Project (at the bottom of Exhibit 2.3), I don't know if my organization should change, so I might desire a competitive assessment or an identification of potential opportunities. Market surveys, benchmarking studies, and audits fall into this category. Actions that identify this type of project's objective would include words like "assess," "compare," "determine," "evaluate," "understand," and "identify." You provide me insight, which has value because it makes me and my organization smarter and provides a basis for learning whether or not we need to change.

In a Planning Project, I already know that I need to change but don't know how, so I might desire a plan detailing how my organization should change. Your project's objective would begin with words like "develop," "determine," "define," or "recommend."

In an Implementation Project, I know that I want to change and I know what to do because I have a plan, but I need additional resources or expertise to implement the change. Therefore, your project's objective would be "to implement" or "to increase or improve" or "to decrease or reduce" some specific operational parameter by definable measures.

As you know, real life is never simple: A single engagement might involve two or more of the three types of projects. That is, for example, a single project might have objectives that reflect two desired results: a plan and an implemented plan. The achievement of these objectives will produce the results I am paying you for, and these results will be valuable and beneficial to me and my organization. (See Exhibit 2.4.)

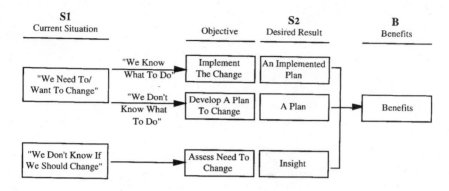

Exhibit 2.4. The relationship among current situations, objectives, desired results, and benefits.

Assessing the Baseline Logic's Alignment

It's essential that you understand the baseline logic and the three kinds of projects that fit within it. Everything else in Part 1 of this book (and a good deal of Part 2) depends on this understanding, which provides the foundation you will need to add the two to five points necessary to win. To assure that your foundation is solid (and that my thinking is clear), you need to answer the three important alignment questions shown in Exhibit 2.5. While all this might look complicated, it really isn't. I'll discuss each of these alignments in the next section.

Aligning the Project Objective and the Desired Result

To align your proposed objective with my desired result, you need to consider the journey on which you will be taking me. (See Exhibit 2.6.) The top three steps are the three possible S_1 states we've already discussed: (1) my organization and I lack the insight necessary to know if we should change; (2) we have the necessary insight and therefore know that we should change, but we don't know how; or (3) we have a plan to change but need help to implement it. The bottom three steps correspond to the three possible S_2 results we desire as an outcome of your assistance: insight, a plan, and/or an implemented plan.

   Which and how many objectives your project will have depends on where I am on the continuum and where I want to be at the end of your proposed engagement. (By the way, I know that the baseline is not technically a continuum, but I can't find a better word to describe the concept.) If your efforts will move me from one step to the next, the project will have only

1. Is the objective aligned with S_2?

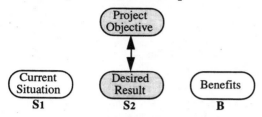

2. Are the benefits aligned with the objective and S_2?

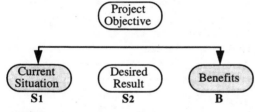

3. Are the benefits aligned with S_1?

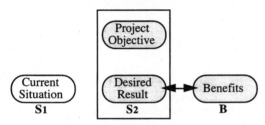

Exhibit 2.5. The three kinds of alignments.

one objective. For example, assume that my S_1 state is characterized by lack of insight—I don't know if we should enter a particular market. Assume that my desired result is to gain such insight. In this instance, you would move me one step along the continuum, and therefore your study would have only one objective: to provide insight. As Exhibit 2.7 illustrates, there are three possible combinations of S_1 and S_2 states that involve a movement of one step and therefore require only one overriding objective.

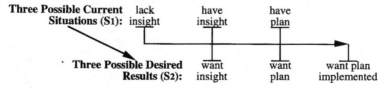

Exhibit 2.6. The baseline logic continuum.

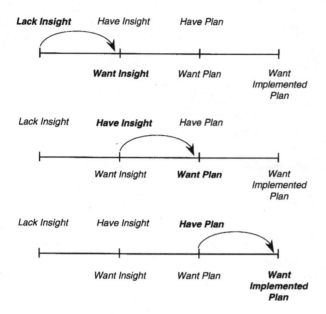

Exhibit 2.7. Projects with one objective.

In some cases, I might want your efforts to move me two or more steps along the continuum. Assume again, for example, that my current situation is characterized by lack of insight—I don't know if we should enter a particular market. My desired result, however, might involve more than just insight—I might also want a plan for entering my target market. In this instance, you will move me two steps along the continuum, and therefore your project will have two objectives. First, you will determine the feasibility of entering the market; second, if entry appears attractive, you will develop a plan for doing so. Here, then, you would propose a two-step project, and a single overriding objective would govern each step. As Exhibit 2.8 illustrates, there are three possible combinations of S_1 and S_2 that involve a movement of two or three steps.

Your proposal's objectives express the major outcomes of your project. Therefore, they must clearly indicate which step or steps along the continuum you will take me. As you'll see in Chap. 4, this clarity is essential if your proposal is to have a logical base on which to build your methodology.

While all this might appear pretty simple, let me reinforce the point that I, your potential client, don't always make it easy for you. I am often unclear in my own mind about what we are trying to do, and therefore might unintentionally confuse you. But we're not here to debate right and

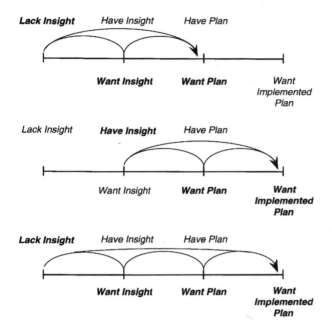

Exhibit 2.8. Projects with two or three objectives.

wrong. And we're not here to become better mind readers. We're here to get agreement on the specific issues to be addressed so that your services will be of greatest value to me and my organization.

Let's take the ABC case as an example. Many experienced consultants would believe that ABC's problem requires a combination study: insight and planning. These consultants would argue that ABC might not need to add capacity because new equipment, better utilization of current space, outsourcing, and the like could allow ABC to produce enough product to meet demand. These consultants would believe, therefore, that two over-riding questions should drive the ABC study: Does ABC in fact need to add capacity? (That's the insight piece.) If so, how best should the company do so? (That's the planning piece.)

Note the decision point here. If the answer to the first question is "No," then the second question becomes moot. If the answer to the first question is "Yes," then the second question needs to be addressed. Combination studies typically have such decision points, which occur after the first overriding question is answered and before the second is addressed. (I'll explain more about overriding questions in Chap. 4.)

Based upon my reading of the case, I don't believe that ABC is asking both questions, only the latter; and if I were the potential client at ABC,

I'd be surprised by a proposal that contained a two-phase study. I might even be suspicious, suspecting that the consultants were trying to sell me more than I'd asked for. Of course, the consultants could be correct in their assessment that I need both insight and a plan. If that's the case, however, they'd better convince me before submitting the proposal. If they don't, then my perception of my desired result will not be aligned with theirs.

Those who have had the greatest success with me—both during the proposal process and while conducting the actual project—have made certain that clear alignment exists between my perception of my desired result or results and their own.

Aligning the Benefits with the Objectives and the Desired Result

Once you have defined the distance on the continuum between S_1 and S_2, you know how many overriding objectives your project will have:

> if $S_1 \rightarrow S_2$ = one step, you will have one overriding objective
>
> if $S_1 \rightarrow S_2$ = two steps, you will have two overriding objectives
>
> if $S_1 \rightarrow S_2$ = three steps, you will have three overriding objectives

Once the project's objective or objectives have been achieved, benefits will accrue. Benefits are the value, improvements, gains—all the good things—that occur to me and my organization as a result of newly acquired insight, a newly acquired plan, and/or an implemented plan. Therefore, the benefits must be aligned with both the desired result and the project's objective(s).

Let me offer you two examples of misalignment between the benefits and the objective/desired result. Assume that I know that my customer service levels are too low to be competitive. That's my current situation, my S_1 state. What I have is insight; I know I have a problem. What I don't have, but desire, is a plan for acting on that insight.

Therefore, my desired result, S_2, is to have a plan for improving customer service, and your objective would be related to developing that improvement plan. The benefits to me in this effort would *not* be those advantages accruing from achieving improved levels of customer service. My desired result, at least for now, at the end of this engagement, is *not* to improve my customer service but to learn how to do so. Therefore, the benefits to me of your support are those advantages related to my *having* the plan you propose to develop. Those benefits, of course, could be considerable. At the beginning of your involvement, I had a problem that I didn't know how to fix. At the end of your efforts, I have a plan for fixing it. I now know how to improve the levels of my organization's customer service.

All this might sound pretty simple and straightforward. But in proposal situation after proposal situation, I have asked for a plan (e.g., to improve customer service) only to get a proposal filled with benefits related to *improved* customer service. This is a benefit I'd receive only after the plan were implemented. The problem, then, is that the proposers haven't aligned the benefits with their single overriding objective: to develop a plan.

Now, as we'll see in the next chapter, your proposal could, and probably should, discuss the benefits related to subsequent implementation, especially if you can estimate those benefits. For example: "Subsequent to implementation, we expect your customer service to improve by x percent, thereby enabling you to do good things A, B, and C." But if those implementation benefits are the only ones you discuss, you are missing significant opportunities to persuade me of the advantages of *your* developing the plan itself. These advantages—learning what we need to do better or faster, assessing our current organization's capabilities, selling the capital requirements to corporate management, evaluating our probability of success, training our people—provide me and my organization with significant benefits. With this plan, we can compare our options, decide to implement, wait, or whatever else may be appropriate given our resources and all the other plans we are considering in areas beyond the one you are helping us with.

Here's a second example of misalignment. Again assume that I know that my customer service is less effective than necessary. Again, what I have is insight. In this case, however, assume that what I desire is an implemented plan that actually improves my customer service.

Therefore, your project's objectives (note the plural) need to be related both to developing that plan and to implementing it. Likewise, the benefits you express need to be those related both to my having the kind of plan you develop *and* to having that plan implemented. Again and again, in proposal situations like this one, the proposers indicate only the benefits of having the plan implemented. What they fail to realize, or at least to communicate to me, is that the quality of the implementation often depends on the quality of the plan. Therefore, they miss important opportunities to persuade. They fail to indicate the benefits aligned with their first objective: developing the plan itself.

Testing the Baseline Logic

To this point I've told you about two kinds of alignment within the baseline logic: the alignment of the objective(s) with the desired result(s), S_2; and the alignment of the benefits with the objective(s) and the desired result(s). To make certain that I've been clear, I'd like you to evaluate the alignment of the baseline logic in the following six situations. Each table takes information from a different proposal I've had presented to me. Each table summarizes the current situation, the desired result, and the benefits as they were defined in the proposal. Below the S_1 description, I've indicated which of three steps on the continuum is being described; below the S_2 description, which of three desired results is being described; below the benefits description, which objectives the benefits relate to.

I've placed an "x" in each of the three columns, indicating my interpretation of the writer's description. By comparing the items indicated by an "x" in each column, you should easily be able to detect misalignments. The bottom of each table explains whether the baseline logic is aligned or misaligned.

1. Aligned or Misaligned?

Project objective: compare Sales and Marketing's effectiveness with competition		
S_1 (Current situation)	S_2 (Desired result)	B (Benefits)
A leading small appliance manufacturer with a large, direct sales organization calling on retail outlets doesn't know if its sales and marketing organization is as effective as competitors'.	Knowledge of the level of effectiveness of Sales and Marketing as compared to competitors.	The magnitude of the gap and level of urgency to improve the sales force's effectiveness.
They have: x no insight ■ insight ■ a plan	They want: x insight ■ plan ■ implemented plan	They'll receive: x insight benefits ■ plan benefits ■ implementation benefits

Answer: Aligned. The organization desires to move one step on the continuum, from no insight to insight. Accordingly, there is one objective, related to insight. The benefits are related to insight.

2. Aligned or Misaligned?

Project objective: profile market dynamics and success factors necessary for successful entry		
S_1 (Current situation)	S_2 (Desired result)	B (Benefits)
A manufacturer of automotive products selling mainly to original equipment manufacturers is uncertain about its ability to market its products through repair shops and about competitors' strategies, capabilities, and vulnerabilities.	Identification of market dynamics, customer service requirements, and opportunities to increase sales to the aftermarket.	Revenue growth from $9 million to over $70 million in 7 years in this new market.
They have: ✗ no insight ■ insight ■ a plan	They want: ✗ insight ■ plan ■ implemented plan	They'll receive: ■ insight benefits ■ plan benefits ✗ implementation benefits

Answer: Misaligned. The organization desires to move one step on the continuum, from no insight to insight. Accordingly, there is one objective, related to insight. The benefits, however, are related to implementation.

3. Aligned or Misaligned?

Project objective: develop a marketing and logistics plan to improve competitive position		
S_1 (Current situation)	S_2 (Desired result)	B (Benefits)
A large paperback book publisher has problems related to its complex distribution system, including high warehousing and transportation costs.	A new marketing and logistics strategy to achieve competitive advantage.	Significantly higher revenues, cost savings of approximately 20% and logistics linked throughout the organization.
They have: ■ no insight ✗ insight ■ a plan	They want: ■ insight ✗ plan ■ implemented plan	They'll receive: ■ insight benefits ■ plan benefits ✗ implementation benefits

Answer: Misaligned. The organization desires to move one step on the continuum, from insight to plan. Accordingly, there is one objective, related to developing a plan. The benefits, however, are not those related to having a plan; they are related to the plan's subsequent implementation.

4. Aligned or Misaligned?

Project objective: develop a facilities strategy related to product quality

S_1 (Current situation)	S_2 (Desired result)	B (Benefits)
A metals processor anticipating a plant capacity constraint within the near future knows that higher product quality expected in some key markets is not attainable from existing facilities.	A strategic plan for building a new facility with the capability of improving the quality of the product.	The specification of required resources will allow the comparison of the proposed action with other strategic options.
They have: ■ no insight ✗ insight ■ a plan	They want: ■ insight ✗ plan ■ implemented plan	They'll receive: ■ insight benefits ✗ plan benefits ■ implementation benefits

Answer: Aligned. The organization desires to move one step on the continuum, from insight to plan. Accordingly, there is one objective, related to developing a plan. The benefits are related to having one.

5. Aligned or Misaligned?

Project objectives: develop and implement a plan to improve competitiveness

S_1 (Current situation)	S_2 (Desired result)	B (Benefits)
A large agricultural products company has not adjusted to changes in its livestock and agricultural markets, having an obsolete strategy, organization, and financial control system.	A plan and an implemented plan to achieve competitive advantage and increased financial returns.	Increased market share, $2 million in improvements already gained, and $3 million in additional improvements to be realized one year.
They have: ■ no insight ✗ insight ■ a plan	They want: ■ insight ✗ plan ✗ implemented plan	They'll receive: ■ insight benefits ■ plan benefits ✗ implementation benefits

Answer: Misaligned. The organization desires to move two steps on the continuum, from insight through planing to implementation. Accordingly, there are two objectives: one related to developing a plan and another related to implementing it. The benefits, however, are related to implementation only. The benefits should also include those related to having a plan.

6. Aligned or Misaligned?

Project objectives: assess "fit" with North American market and develop and implement a plan for entering		
S_1 (Current situation)	S_2 (Desired result)	B (Benefits)
A major European manufacturer wants to acquire a North American company but doesn't understand NA market dynamics, segmentation, and distribution channels.	Insight about the market, as well as a plan and an implemented plan to enter that market as a first step to become a dominant global player.	A specific positioning and entry strategy in the NA market.
They have: ɀ no insight ■ insight ■ a plan	They want: ɀ insight ɀ plan ɀ implemented plan	They'll receive: ■ insight benefits ɀ plan benefits ■ implementation benefits

Answer: Misaligned. A rare project, indeed, in that the organization desires to move three steps on the continuum, from no insight (about the market it desires to enter) all the way to implementation (i.e., to *being* in the market). Accordingly, there are three objectives: one related to providing insight, another related to developing a plan based on that insight, and a third related to implementing that plan just developed. The benefits, however, are related only to having a plan, and these benefits aren't benefits at all: they are really the second objective. Also included should be benefits related to having insight and having the plan implemented. These are critical because benefits at these points may be important at key management decision points during the project.

To this point I've shown you how to ask two important questions regarding the alignment of the baseline logic:

1. Is the objective(s) aligned with S_2?

2. Are the benefits aligned with the objective(s) and S_2?

In the work session at the end of this chapter, you'll be able to watch "yourself" fill out a Baseline Logic Worksheet for the proposal to the ABC Company. There again, you'll be able to test for the alignments we've been discussing so far, as well as for one further alignment—between S_1 and B.

Aligning the Current Situation and Benefits

Now you need to answer one more question: Are the benefits aligned with my current situation, S_1? By answering this question, you will not only assure alignment, you will also be able to generate additional possible benefits and additional possible problems that characterize and broaden your understanding of my current situation.

Assume, for example, that my current situation could be described as an ineffective organizational structure. I have that insight, and I'm thinking about engaging you to develop and implement a plan for improving my organizational effectiveness. As you are considering my situation, you jot down some notes in three columns that look something like this:

Column 1 Current Situation	Column 2 Plan Benefits	Column 3 Implemented Plan Benefits
ineffective organizational structure	cross-functional teams will be used during plan development, creating better communication across functions	increased operational effectiveness and customer responsiveness

Your plan, you've decided, will be beneficial to me because it will involve teams from various parts of my organization working together during development, and your implemented plan will be beneficial because it will provide a structure that will increase operational effectiveness and customer responsiveness. Assuming that cross-functional teams would indeed be beneficial to me, the alignment looks good.

What you can do now is to use the power of the baseline logic to increase your depth of understanding of my situation by using the information in the columns. To do so, you keep asking yourself, "What is the effect of this problem" or "What is the effect of this benefit?" "What does or might it lead to?" As you look at column one, you decide that an ineffective organizational structure could lead to lowered morale, which could lead to higher turnover, which could lead to increased costs related to hiring and training. As you look at column two, you decide that a plan using cross-functional teams could lead to increased teamwork across functions, which could increase the shared knowledge across organizational functions and help to break down functional "silos." As you look at column three, you decide that increased operational effectiveness and customer responsiveness could lead to lowered costs, which in turn could lead to increased market share.

At this point, all these effects are "might-be's." They might be problems within my organization or benefits that might accrue to my organization, and they might not. As you have further conversations with me, however, you can ask me to test their validity and applicability. You should be able to find out, if you ask. In any event, your three columns might now look like this:

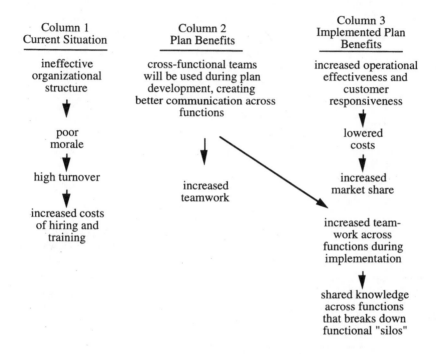

Column 1 Current Situation	Column 2 Plan Benefits	Column 3 Implemented Plan Benefits

By spending just a few minutes, you could probably fill several pages of problems and benefits. Look at what you've done. You have caused me to define more precisely my current situation and the potential benefits from improving it. You have added value in the proposal preparation process by logically building on my initial thinking. Cause and effect, effect and cause all tied together into a logical framework.

But let's remember how you got to where you are. Your first list included one item in each column. Then you checked for alignment. Then you expanded the list to include additional items. Now you need to check for alignment again. For every problem in column 1, you want to include a related benefit in columns 2 and/or 3. For every benefit in columns 2 or 3, you want to include a "problem" in column 1. You decide to focus on the last two items in the third column. What "problems" in my current situation might be associated with increased teamwork across functions and with shared knowledge across functions that break down functional silos? The answer is shown by the two dashed arrows:

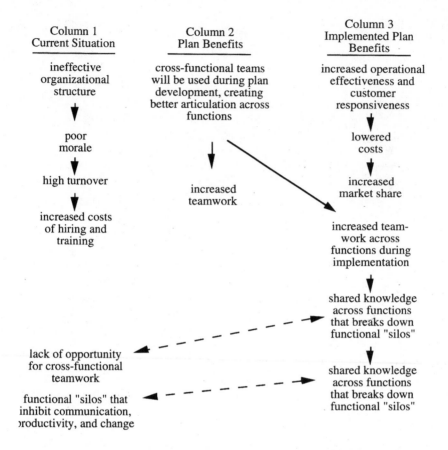

Column 1 Current Situation	Column 2 Plan Benefits	Column 3 Implemented Plan Benefits
ineffective organizational structure	cross-functional teams will be used during plan development, creating better articulation across functions	increased operational effectiveness and customer responsiveness
poor morale		lowered costs
high turnover	increased teamwork	increased market share
increased costs of hiring and training		increased team- work across functions during implementation
		shared knowledge across functions that breaks down functional "silos"
lack of opportunity for cross-functional teamwork		
functional "silos" that inhibit communication, productivity, and change		shared knowledge across functions that breaks down functional "silos"

I call these two additions, not "problems" but rather "lack of benefits" (Lack B). They are not the primary reason why I'm thinking about engaging you, but they might be important aspects of my current situation, which involves more than just a problem or opportunity. It also includes a lack of benefits. That is, I want to reach S_2 because being there is inherently beneficial; *and* I do not want to be at S_1 because certain aspects of that situation are not beneficial. The current situation is undesirable, not only because it includes an unsolved problem or an unrealized opportunity, but also because it lacks benefits. This lack of benefits is so much a part of the current situation that I include it in the baseline logic (Exhibit 2.9). Therefore, as you consider your proposal's baseline logic, you want to make certain that benefits are aligned both with S_1 and with Lack B.

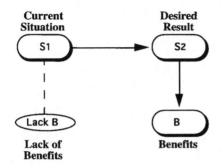

Exhibit 2.9. The baseline logic, with "Lack B."

As you can see, by checking the alignment of S_1 and B, you can generate a good deal of additional content to be used in your situation and benefits slots. That is, you can use the alignment of S_1 and B as a powerful *discovery* process to deepen your understanding of my problem or opportunity and the benefits that would accrue from your helping me solve or realize it. Just as important, the benefits you decide to include in your proposal will look all the more "beneficial" if they are compared to "Lack B":

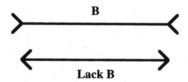

Which line is longer? Well, I'm certain you know that they are of equal length, but B seems longer. So too, your discussion of benefits will "seem longer," "show greater depth of understanding," by your including a discussion of "Lack B."

I can summarize this whole discussion of the baseline logic with Exhibit 2.10. I want you to answer my question: "Why should I consider using your services?" "Because," you should explain, "you (the potential client) are experiencing a problem or opportunity and a lack of benefits. That's your reality and my starting point." Then, I want you to answer my question: "What will this project accomplish?" "Move you," you should respond, "from your current situation to something better. That's your desire and our objective." Finally, I want you to answer the question: "What will happen after you complete this project?" "Benefits will accrue," you should say. "If you engage us, these are the outputs we both want to achieve."

Potential Client's Questions	Your Answer	
"Why should I consider using your services?"	"You are experiencing a problem or opportunity and a lack of benefits. This is your reality and my starting point."	(S1) (Lack B)
"What will this project accomplish?"	"It will move you from your current situation to something better. This is your desire and my study's objective."	(S1) → (S2)
"What will happen after you complete this project?"	"You will benefit from achieving your desired result."	(B)

Exhibit 2.10. The baseline logic—summary.

The Relationship Between the Generic Structure Slots, the Baseline Logic, and Your Proposed Project

Now, after this lengthy discussion of the baseline logic, we're ready to integrate what you've learned in this chapter with what you learned in the previous one. In Chap. 1, you saw that a proposal, because it is a proposal, has certain slots: SITUATION, OBJECTIVES, METHODS, QUALIFICATIONS, COSTS, and BENEFITS. In this chapter, we have been discussing the logical relationship of three of these slots: SITUATION (S_1) → OBJECTIVES (which are related to reaching my desired result, S_2) → BENEFITS (B). That is:

- S_1, *my current condition, is something I want to change.* You communicate your understanding of that condition in your proposal's situation slot.

- S_2, *my desired result, is the outcome that will be produced at the end of your support. That desired result is expressed by your project's objectives.* That is, your objectives define what I and my organization will have when your efforts are complete: insight, a plan, and/or an implemented plan. You communicate those objectives in your proposal's objectives slot.

- *The achievement of that desired result is beneficial to me and my organization.* You communicate those benefits in your benefits slot.

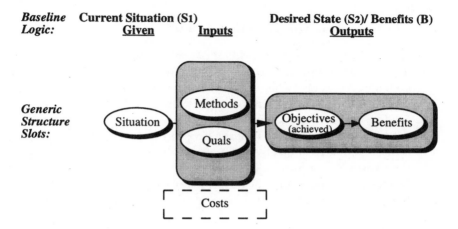

Exhibit 2.11. The relationship between the generic structure slots and the project.

In Exhibit 2.11 you can see that the baseline logic is related to my situation as it currently exists ("given") and to my situation as it will exist at the end of your project ("outputs").

To get me from S_1 to S_2, your efforts will require several inputs. These inputs are related to METHODS, QUALIFICATIONS, and COSTS:

- *The desired result (and your project's objectives) is achieved by applying your methods.* You communicate your methods in the methods slot.
- *The desired result (and your project's objectives) is achieved by the performance of your staff, supported by the resources and the experience of your firm.* You communicate your team's abilities and your firm's capabilities in the qualifications slot.
- *The desired result (and your project's objectives) is achieved because of the money I will pay you.* You indicate the project's costs in the costs slot.

Chap. 4 will discuss how to construct a logical methodology that will convince me that you can move me along the continuum from S_1 to S_2. Before we can turn to methodologies, however, I need to discuss in the next chapter other matters related to objectives. And before we turn to that chapter, I want you to get some practice in applying your understanding of the baseline logic in the work session that follows.

⇨ Chapter 2 Review
Understanding the Baseline Logic

1. Proposals contain a baseline logic expressed by $S_1 \to S_2 \to B$:
   - S_1 refers to the current situation. That situation always involves a discrepancy between "what is" and "what could be." Therefore, S_1 is characterized by a problem or opportunity *and* by a lack of benefits (Lack *B*). S_1 is discussed in the situation slot.
   - S_2 refers to the endpoint(s) of the project or phases of the project. S_2 is discussed in the objectives slot, since your project's objective(s) are the expression of S_2.
   - *B* refers to the benefits that accrue from achieving the desired result. Benefits are discussed in the benefits slot.

2. The desired result(s) expressed by the proposal's objective(s) can be one or more of the following:
   - Insight (e.g., audits, market research, or benchmarking projects)
     Potential client says: "We don't know if we should change."
   - Plan
     Potential client says: "We want to change but don't know how."
   - Implementation
     Potential client says: "We want to change and know how, but we need help to do so."

   Note: If the project combines two or more of the previous elements (e.g., insight and planning), a clear decision point will exist necessitating a phased study.

3. To test the alignment of the elements within the baseline logic:
   - Be certain that the project objective(s) are aligned with S_2.
     if $S_1 \to S_2$ = one step, you will have one overriding objective
     if $S_1 \to S_2$ = two steps, you will have two overriding objectives
     if $S_1 \to S_2$ = three steps, you will have three overriding objectives
   - Be certain that the benefits are aligned with both S_2 and the project's objective(s).
   - Be certain that S_1 and *B* are aligned.

Work Session 2: Constructing the Baseline Logic for the Situation at ABC

You approach the subject of your proposal's baseline logic with a good deal of care because you know that it provides the foundation for your entire proposal and because you also know that you can use its alignment to help you think more strategically about ABC's current situation, desired result, and potential benefits. Everything else in your proposal will be built on this foundation and mistakes in thinking and understanding at this point will have dire consequences later. Similarly, good strategy and thinking at this point will pay great dividends later on (extending even to the project's execution after you win). To ensure that you construct a logical baseline, you use the Baseline Logic Worksheet shown in Appendix B, completing each of its three pages.

The Baseline Logic Worksheet: Completing Page 1

The first page of the worksheet asks you to identify the kind of project, the potential client's overriding question(s), and the specific objective(s).

ABC, you believe, has insight about their current situation—they know they have a production capacity problem, and they desire a plan to address that problem. On the face of it, then, it would appear that you will be proposing a planning study. However, you're not certain that ABC has the *right* insight. For example, although they do have a sales forecast—and one in which VP of Marketing Marcia Collins has considerable confidence— you believe that any forecast must be validated, since it provides the basis for all further analysis. A validated forecast might reveal that ABC doesn't need quite as much capacity as they now believe or that the timing is sooner or later than now anticipated. Furthermore, although Gilmore's inspection of the main manufacturing facility revealed good housekeeping and excellent equipment, your experience tells you that various marginal improvements at that facility (and perhaps at the satellite facilities) could provide some additional capacity, perhaps without their having to invest in bricks and mortar so soon. Finally, there's the issue of outsourcing. At present, ABC appears to manufacture most of its components, rather than relying on outside suppliers to provide them. Various buy scenarios could also provide capacity that ABC does not now enjoy, and eliminate or certainly delay the need for additional capacity.

In short, this might be a classic insight and planning study. Like all such combination studies, this one could involve clear phasing, a clear "go/no go" decision point at the end of the insight piece. That is, the first phase of the study might supply ABC with the insight it needs to determine whether it indeed needs additional capacity.

On the other hand, you don't believe that you could sell an insight and planning study to ABC or that ABC senses a decision point. All the buyers seem to believe that additional capacity is necessary, although the amount and timing is uncertain. More specifically, Collins would certainly object to an insight study and, depending on her influence, so might others. So you decide to characterize this opportunity as a planning study. It will certainly have an insight piece (e.g., on validating Collins' forecast) but it will have only one objective: to develop a plan. Therefore, because there will be no decision point after validating the forecast, you decide to call the project what in your mind ABC believes it to be: a study to develop a plan for increasing production capacity. Accordingly, the first page of your Baseline Logic Worksheet looks like Exhibit 2.12.

The Baseline Logic Worksheet: Completing Pages 2 and 3

The instructions for pages 2 and 3 ask you to follow a 10-step process during which you need to list what you know about ABC's situation and potential benefits, expand on that knowledge, align what you've expanded on, and then repeat the process for as long as it provides you additional insight and value. These are the ten steps:

List   1. In the column "Current Situation," list the relevant problems.

         2. Within the relevant benefits categories, list as many benefits as possible.

Expand 3. For each problem identified, list the problem's effect and the effects of that effect. Draw arrows that show the causal relationship between problems and effects and between effects and their effects.

         4. For each benefit identified, try to list a beneficial effect and the effects of that effect. Draw arrows that show the causal relationship between benefits and effects and between effects and their effects.

Align   5. Draw a double-headed arrow between each problem in the column "Current Situation" and its related benefit in one of the benefits columns.

         6. In the column "Current Situation," locate each problem unconnected to a benefit. In a benefits column, try to create a benefit related to each unconnected problem. Draw double-headed arrows to make the connections.

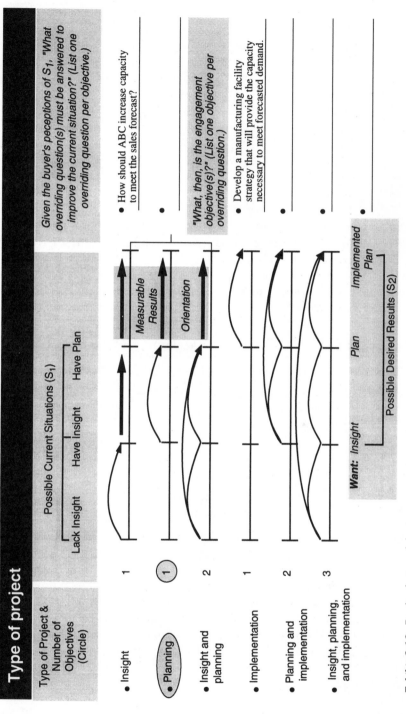

Exhibit 2.12. Baseline logic worksheet, page one.

7. In the "benefits" columns, locate each benefit unconnected to a problem. In the column "Current Situation," try to identify a problem related to each unconnected benefit. Draw double-headed arrows to make the connections.

Repeat 8. Repeat Step 3 for the newly created problems.

9. Repeat Step 4 for the newly created benefits.

10. Continue the process until you reach a point of diminishing returns.

Completing Steps 1 and 2 ("List")

Step 1 asks you to list the relevant problems at ABC. Step 2 requests you to list information within the relevant benefits columns. In this case those columns include "Plan Benefits," because your objective is to develop a plan, and "Implementation Benefits." The latter will allow you to exercise a measurable results orientation (discussed in the next chapter). Thus far, your list looks like this:

Current Situation	Benefits of Having Plan	Benefits of Implementated Plan
ABC has been successful because of good quality, low costs, and high service, but forecasts show that future demand will outstrip capacity in just a few years.	The right "road map" for providing additional, needed capacity to ensure meeting objectives related to cost, quality, and service.	More cost-effective operations. Improved product quality. Improved service levels.
	An operations strategy that optimizes landed cost and customer service.	
	Internal agreement on on expansion plan.	
	Convincing, thorough, and credible request to Consolidated.	

You believe that once the study's objective is achieved and the desired result is realized, ABC will benefit by having a "road map" for providing additional capacity to ensure that their business objectives related to costs, quality, and service will be met. The road map, agreed to by various constituencies within ABC, will contain an operations strategy to optimize landed cost and customer service. The whole package will form a convincing, thorough, and credible request to Consolidated. These benefits, it seems to you, are well aligned with the objective and S_2. Once this plan is implemented, you feel confident that costs, quality, and service will, in fact, improve.

Completing Steps 3 and 4 ("Expand")

Steps 3 and 4 ask you to expand on what you have by thinking of and then list the various effects of the problems and benefits you've identified, and then to consider the effects of these effects. You also need to draw arrows that connect the problems and benefits to their related effects. For example, in the third column you have benefits related to cost, quality, and service. Improvements in these areas would no doubt help ABC maintain or increase market share. So in that column you add "maintained/increased market share." After completing steps 3 and 4 your columns look like this:

Current Situation	Benefits of Having Plan	Benefits of Implemented Plan
ABC has been successful because of good quality, low costs, and high service, but forecasts show that future demand will out-strip capacity in just a few years.	The right "road map" for providing additional, needed capacity to ensure meeting objectives related to cost, quality, and service.	
Without adequate capacity, delivery performance will deteriorate, quality could suffer, and costs could rise because of overtime and schedule interruptions to meet "rush" delivery dates.	An operations strategy that optimizes landed cost and customer service. Internal agreement on an expansion plan. Convincing, thorough, and credible request to Consolidated.	More cost-effective operations. Improved product quality. Improved service levels.
Threatened ability to maintain/increase market share. Negative impact on bonuses.		Maintained/increased market share.
Utilization will soon reach maximum.		Continued good reputation of ABC at Consolidated.
Productivity levels will be difficult to maintain.		Continued autonomy vis a vis Consolidated.

Completing Steps 5, 6, and 7 ("Align")

Step 5 asks you to find where a problem in the first column is aligned with one or more benefits in the other columns. For example, in the column "Current Situation," you have written: "Threatened ability to maintain/increase market share." This problem is already well aligned with one of your benefits: "Maintained/increased market share." So you draw a double-headed arrow between them to express the alignment. You also draw a double-headed arrow connecting the one additional alignment, between the second item in column 1, which relates to service, quality, and cost, and the first group of items in column 3. Despite these two alignments, most of the items on your list are unaligned. That is, you don't have double-headed arrows that link all problems with all benefits. Therefore, your thinking is not yet complete.

Ideally, you realize, every problem in the first column should be linked to a benefit in the third column, since each problem that's relevant to your project should be solved after implementation. Accordingly, steps 6 and 7 ask you to create additional problems and benefits so that your baseline logic is completely aligned. For example, the first column has an item that indicates a problem related to productivity ("Productivity levels will be difficult to maintain"), but no related benefit exists. So you create one in column 3: "Increased productivity." After completing these three steps, your expanded list looks like this:

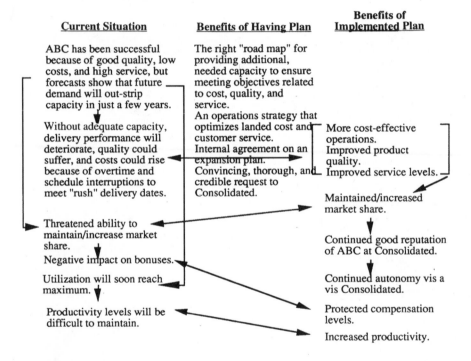

Current Situation	**Benefits of Having Plan**	**Benefits of Implemented Plan**
ABC has been successful because of good quality, low costs, and high service, but forecasts show that future demand will out-strip capacity in just a few years.	The right "road map" for providing additional, needed capacity to ensure meeting objectives related to cost, quality, and service.	
Without adequate capacity, delivery performance will deteriorate, quality could suffer, and costs could rise because of overtime and schedule interruptions to meet "rush" delivery dates.	An operations strategy that optimizes landed cost and customer service. Internal agreement on an expansion plan. Convincing, thorough, and credible request to Consolidated.	More cost-effective operations. Improved product quality. Improved service levels.
Threatened ability to maintain/increase market share.		Maintained/increased market share.
Negative impact on bonuses.		Continued good reputation of ABC at Consolidated.
Utilization will soon reach maximum.		Continued autonomy vis a vis Consolidated.
Productivity levels will be difficult to maintain.		Protected compensation levels.
		Increased productivity.

Completing Steps 8, 9, and 10 ("Repeat")

Now you have to go back and repeat the process, because you have thought of new benefits and problems. What are the effects of these? What are the effects of the effects? For example, what are the effects of "Productivity levels will be difficult to maintain"? Although you're not certain, you hypothesize that such a difficulty could sap managerial and other resources and therefore affect work on longer range, more challenging improvement projects, provide less flexibility for change, and possibly increase the frequency of using a third shift, which could increase downtime and equipment maintenance costs. Once these additional problems are listed, you align additional benefits with them.

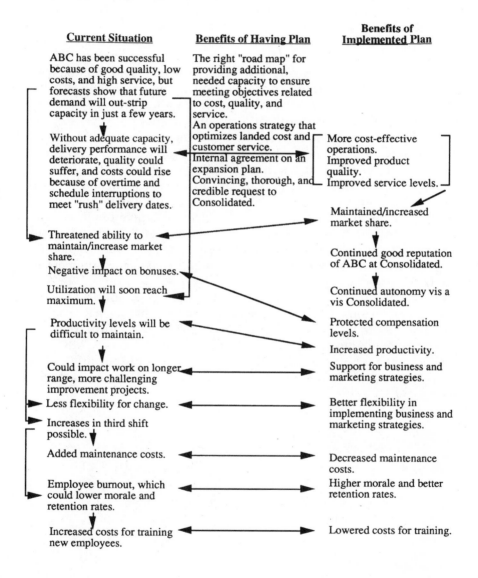

As you consider your list and the process that created it, you realize that all along you have been looking for alignment between the benefits in columns 2 and 3 and the current situation in column 1. Every time you generated a new benefit, you not only tried to determine what additional benefit might accrue from it, you also checked to make certain that something in the current situation was aligned with that benefit. Similarly, every time you generated a new problem or lack of benefits in column 1, you not only tried to determine what additional problem might result, you also checked to make certain that some benefit was aligned with it.

Although this process initially seemed time-consuming to you, you realize that it has added robustness and depth to your understanding of ABC. It has also quite likely identified information you will need to test and verify, to ensure that you perceive ABC's situation as they do.

Even with your expanded list, you know that much more could be done. For example, the fifth and sixth items in column 3 focus on ABC's relationship with Consolidated, but nothing in column one speaks to that relationship. You'll need to do something about that lack of alignment, since ABC's relationship with Consolidated is crucial. More than one person told Gilmore about ABC's needing to compete for capital funding at the "corporate trough." Your proposal should include such information, to demonstrate to ABC that you understand ABC's position vis à vis Consolidated and the need for a thorough and convincing argument to take to the parent company.

You realize that you could go on ad infinitum generating additional problems and benefits. However, you decide for now that you have enough (Exhibits 2.13 and 2.14) to show to Gilmore, who can confirm what you have or seek additional confirmation from the major players at ABC. Just as important, you feel confident that the foundation to your proposal is indeed sound and logical—and much more extensive than you had realized.

"What is the potential client's current problem/opportunity/critical issue?"

S_1

PC's Current Situation

☐ ABC has been successful because of good quality, competitive costs, and high service, but forecasts show that future demand will exceed current capacity in just a few years.

☐ Without adequate capacity, delivery performance will deteriorate, quality could suffer, and costs could rise because of overtime and schedule interruptions to meet "rush" delivery dates.

☐ Threatened ability to maintain/increase market share.

☐ Negative impact on bonuses.

☐ Productivity levels will be difficult to maintain.

☐ Could impact work on longer range, more challenging improvement projects.

☐ Less flexibility for change.

☐ Increases in third shift possible.

☐ Added maintenance costs.

☐ Employee burnout, which could lower quality, morale, and retention rates.

☐ Increased costs for training new employees.

Exhibit 2.13 Baseline logic worksheet, page 2.

S_2

PC's Desired Tangible Result if _Implementation (or Tangible Results Mindset_ if Plan and/or Insight Engagement)*

Increased capacity to meet the market forecast for the next 3-5 years

PC's Desired Result if _Plan_*

- validated market forecast
- validated market share and product mix projections
- specified current equipment and space utilization
- specified opportunities to better utilize current equipment and space
- specified opportunities for utilizing new equipment technology
- specified make vs. buy options
- specified potential factory roles and locations for increasing capacity
- an implementation plan

*Include deliverables ➤ from pyramid

B

PC's Benefits of an _Implemented Plan_

- More cost-effective operations
- Improved product quality
- Improved service levels
- Maintained/increased market share
- Continued good reputation of ABC at Consolidated
- Continued autonomy vis à vis Consolidated
- Increased productivity
- Protected compensation levels
- Support for business and marketing strategies
- Better flexibility in implementing business and marketing strategies
- Decreased relative maintenance costs
- Higher morale and better retention rates
- Decreased costs for training

PC's Benefits of a _Plan_

- The right "road map" for providing additional, needed capacity to ensure meeting objectives related to cost, quality, and service.
- An operations strategy that optimizes landed cost and customer service.
- Internal agreement on an expansion plan.
- Convincing, thorough, and credible request to Consolidated.

Exhibit 2.14 Baseline logic worksheet, page 3.

48

3
Using a Measurable Results Orientation

Let's assume for a moment that you're writing a proposal to a foundation. More than likely, the foundation's RFP (request for proposal) will ask you to state quantifiable, measurable objectives. And because your objectives are the expression of your project's intended results, the funding agency also will probably ask you to include a plan for evaluating (i.e., measuring) the project's outcome and your performance. This is standard operating procedure for foundations as well as for local and federal government agencies because, quite simply, they want some measure of assurance that their money will be well spent and will generate a return. And for multi-year projects, they want to be able to measure the results of one year's effort before funding the efforts of another. If you're like me, you find such agencies' desires reasonable and unobjectionable.

In many ways I, as a potential client, have the same desires and you shouldn't object to them. For most of the work you do for me, I want change and I'm willing to pay you to help me get it. So I might request some evidence, after your project is completed, that change has occurred; and some plan, included in your proposal, for how you will determine if change has in fact occurred.

Of course, sometimes I might not be or need to be so rigorous. I might be satisfied if the evidence is anecdotal—that is, if someone in my organization tells me that they believe change has taken place. Sometimes I might be satisfied if the evidence is personal—that is, if I myself believe that change has occurred, because things look and feel different than they did before your involvement. But sometimes this "good feeling" is not enough. I might only be satisfied with hard evidence, the numbers, objec-

49

tive rather than subjective proof of improved processes, saved money, better-served customers.

Even if I don't request such information, your providing it in your proposal could differentiate you from your competitors and thus be very persuasive. However, there is a major obstacle: *You can't propose achieving measurable results unless your project involves implementation.* Only after implementation can I expect processes to be improved, money to be saved, customers to be better served, or market share to increase. Only Implementation Projects can provide measurable results, which I define as tangible, quantifiable, demonstrable improvements in my business processes. So only in Implementation Projects can you promise such concrete results. But in Insight Projects and Planning Projects, you can provide what I call a "measurable results orientation."

Measurable Results Orientation: The Insight Project

Let's recall the three kinds of projects discussed in Chap. 2, remembering that a combination of them is not only possible but common:

My situation	Kind of project	Objectives (verbs)
"I don't know if I should change."	Insight	*To learn, assess, compare, determine whether, evaluate, understand,* or *identify*
"I know that I need to change but don't know how."	Planning	*To develop, determine how, define,* or *recommend*
"I know how to change but need help to do so."	Implementation	*To implement*—or *to increase/improve* or *decrease/reduce* some parameters by definable measures

In an Insight Project, I don't know if I should change and therefore I need insight to determine whether I really have a problem or an opportunity or whether I should maintain the status quo. I might, for example, have some questions about my manufacturing processes. They might be suitable and they might not; I don't know. Perhaps they are terribly inefficient, or perhaps they are adequate but improvable. I don't know, but I might be willing to engage you to conduct an audit or a competitive assessment to provide me with that insight. You might compare my processes

Because this is an Insight Project, the project objective expresses non-measurable results. However, note the measurable results orientation expressed in the last sentence.	**Objectives** Our project will focus on three representative product lines—specifically, Graybeard, Bluebird, and Redbeak. The objective of our project is to compare the manufacturing processes that produce these lines to those of your competitors and to the "best of the best" in other industries using these manufacturing processes. If gaps exist, we will evaluate the potential savings and other benefits of closing them.

Exhibit 3.1. Measurable results orientation—Insight Project.

with someone else's and evaluate whose are better. That insight is not a measurable result; it is not by itself a change in any of my business processes. Therefore, you can't express measurable results by the project's objective. But notice how you still might be able to provide a measurable-results *orientation* (see Exhibit 3.1). In an Insight Project, I am paying you for insight. That insight is beneficial to me and what I expect you to deliver. But you can go beyond my expectations by looking further ahead, by including an objective that, once achieved, could indicate the value to me and my organization of our acting on that insight. Therefore, your methods slot could discuss tasks related to evaluating potential savings of subsequently closing the gaps, and the benefits slot can discuss the potential value of closing them.

Measurable Results Orientation: The Planning Project

In a Planning Project, I know that I need to change but don't know how, so I desire a plan for changing. Your objective could be to define a better way of doing things and to incorporate that definition into a plan for realizing the improvement. Once again, you will not be providing me with a measurable result (a realized improvement during your engagement); I've only asked you for a plan. Therefore, measurable results can't be expressed by the objective itself, but within the objectives slot you might be able to demonstrate a measurable results orientation by estimating the value to me of eventually implementing that plan:

Objectives

Because this is a
Planning Project,
the project objective
expresses nonmea-
surable results.
However, measur-
able results, so far
as they can be
expressed at this
point, are included.
Achieving these
measurable results
could very likely be
the objective of
a subsequent
Implementation
Project.

Our project will focus on the Graybeard line
and provide a framework for improving the
other product lines. The objective of our project
is to define for Graybeard the most appropriate
manufacturing process to reduce scrap and
rework and to increase productivity. After
careful consideration, and based on our
experience, we believe that for the Graybeard
line alone, a fully implemented plan could
reasonably be expected to:

- Decrease rework from 30 to 5%
- Reduce scrap rate from 20 to 5%
- Decrease cycle time from 30 days to 10 days

Exhibit 3.2. Measurable Results Orientation—Planning Project.

The benefits slot could indicate possible savings if the plan were implemented, discuss the benefits of the measurable results for my organization as well as for me, and stress the possible realization of measurable
results (and the benefits that might accrue) even before implementation.

Given that you haven't yet completed the plan, you might ask how it is
possible to include potential measurable results. And isn't including measurable results like the preceding ones just bad business, leaving you open
to criticism (or, worse, a lawsuit) if later you can't deliver them or I can't
implement your plan successfully?

These are valid questions, so let me address them. First of all, I'm not
saying that you should include measurable results in all proposals, not
even in Implementation Projects. Second, I'm not suggesting that you can
exactly quantify the expected results (e.g., reduce cycle time from 30 days
to 10 days); you might be able to quantify within some range (e.g., a reduc-
tion of 10 to 20 days). Third, note that the quantification in the preceding
Planning example is qualified: After careful consideration, you *believe*
these are the results that could be expected *after* the new process has been
implemented. In summary, then, while you cannot promise measurable
results in all projects, you can communicate an orientation toward such
results.

Additionally, to the extent that you can identify and even implement short term, typically minor improvements during your engagements, I will be pleased. These are measurable insight or planning results, but not the primary ones or the significant ones that will accrue when the whole plan is implemented. This "low-hanging fruit" or "pay-as-you-go" orientation is good, but since it doesn't address implementing my primary result, I still consider it a measurable results orientation.

Your *orientation* toward results, your focus on trying to achieve recognizable and quantifiable change for me and my organization, tells me something about you. It tells me you are interested in my eventually receiving results rather than just another report that will sit on my shelf.

And by the way, if you in fact have all that experience listed in your boilerplated qualifications section (e.g., you have performed 40 similar studies in my industry over the last two years), I would hope that you could give me some estimate of my potential measurable results. Let's not kid each other. By including a measurable results orientation that practically considers my risks and rewards, you indicate your true qualifications to support me—far better than do most qualifications descriptions or discussions I've had to read or sit through. Save your scissors and use your brain. It will be worth the effort.

Measurable Results Orientation: The Implementation Project

In an Implementation Project, I want to change—I know what to do, but I need additional resources or expertise to actually implement the change. That change will alter my business processes, and that result can be measured. Therefore, you might wish to propose achieving an objective that will increase or decrease certain factors by definable parameters. In an Implementation Project, then, measurable results can be expressed by the objective itself:

	Objectives
An Implementation Project: The project objective itself expresses measurable results.	The objective of our project is to implement for Graybeard an optimum manufacturing process that will: ■ Decrease rework from 30 to 5% ■ Reduce scrap rate from 20 to 5% ■ Decrease cycle time from 30 to 10 days

Exhibit 3.3. Measurable results orientation—Implementation Project.

The benefits slot can focus on the benefits of achieving measurable results, not only to my organization but to me.

In each of the three examples, your project's objectives are the expression of S_2, of my organization's desired result(s), whether that result is new insight, a well-developed plan, and/or implemented actions. The achievement of these objectives will produce the results I am paying you for, and these results will be beneficial to me and my company.

⇨ Chapter 3 Review: Using a Measurable Results Orientation

1. Measurable results are tangible, quantifiable improvements in my business processes.

2. Measurable results can only occur in projects that involve implementation.

3. Therefore, insight and planning projects cannot provide measurable results, but the objectives in insight and planning proposals can express a measurable results orientation (i.e., what is likely to result after a plan is eventually implemented).

Work Session 3: Applying a Measurable Results Orientation for ABC

To apply a measurable results orientation, you know that you must try to quantify those items on page 3 of the Baseline Logic Worksheet that fall under the category "Benefits of an Implemented Plan." Some of those items, like "Continued autonomy vis à vis Consolidated," aren't necessary or even possible to quantify. Others, like "Higher morale," are probably too difficult to quantify. However, many of the items are subject to quantification or estimation, assuming that you have relevant data from ABC or from previous projects whose results have been tracked.

Therefore, you decide to get relevant data from questionnaires that had been sent to clients at various times after projects have been completed. These data track measurable improvements that could be attributed to projects completed by you or your firm. The question you want to answer is something like this: In projects similar to the one you hope to conduct at ABC, what measurable results have accrued in terms of overall cost effectiveness of operations, improved product quality and service levels, or maintained or increased market share, etc? Assuming that data are available and that you are confident that the situations have enough similarities, you plan to incorporate a range of such increases, decreases, and improvements within the proposal itself, to indicate to ABC that you, in fact, have significant experience and expertise to achieve their project's objective.

4
Constructing a Logical Methodology—The Pyramid Principle

As discussed in Chap. 3, the objectives* in your proposal express the steps along a continuum your project will take me. These steps can result in my having insight, a plan, and/or an implemented plan. The objectives are an important set of outcomes of your project, and your methodology describes how you will achieve them. It comprises a logically sequenced group of worksteps or actions that will achieve the objectives.

Unfortunately, many of the methodologies you present in your proposals don't persuade me that you will effectively achieve the project objectives. Sometimes those methodologies contain vague generalities like "Interview Management," "Gather Data," "Analyze Data," and "Report Results." These generalities provide me with very little or no insight about how, precisely, you will achieve the objectives. Other times, the methodologies contain more specific tasks, but the logical relationship between the tasks and the objectives is unclear, as is the relationship of the tasks to each other. From my perspective, it often appears that you have "cut and pasted" from past proposals to describe what you will do in this one. That's not good enough to prepare winning proposals, especially if a thoughtful, tailored methodology is one of my evaluation criteria.

---

*I should have written the word "objective(s)," since depending on whether your project takes me one step along the continuum or more than one step, your project will either achieve one overriding objective or more than one. But I'm getting tired of writing the word that way, and you're probably getting tired of reading it. So from here on I'll occasionally use the plural "objectives" even when I might also be referring to the singular. What this loses in precision it makes up for in lack of distraction.

You may believe that a compulsively logical methodology is not an important factor in my decision-making process—and sometimes that's the case. But more often than not, I believe you use this belief to rationalize your lack of effort in developing logical methodologies (and effective project workplans after you have been awarded the assignment).

Likewise, you may believe that the more detailed the methodology, the greater the chance that I will take it and apply it myself using my own resources. Yes, I'm certain this has happened, but nowhere near as frequently as you believe. Listen, I want as good a relationship with a dependable, results-oriented problem solver as you want with me. If we can develop a good level of trust, I believe that the risk to you is minimal. Moreover, if I believe that the methodology is critical, you won't win without a logical, well thought-out one.

I also suspect that you may not have a structured and rigorous way of constructing a clear and logical methodology. I do. Let me share it with you. It involves the following four steps:

1. Clearly identify the objective(s), based on my overriding question(s).

2. Place each objective atop a pyramid and order the *actions* necessary to achieve it.

3. Sequence the actions.

4. Identify and integrate the *activities* necessary for planning and communicating your proposed actions.

I'll discuss each of these steps in this chapter. But, first, because the key to completing them is a pyramid, I need to tell you what that is and how to construct one.

Using Pyramid Logic

A pyramid, according to Barbara Minto in her book *The Pyramid Principle,* is a framework for organizing ideas.* It structures a group of actions and their consequences that, taken together, produce a desired result. A pyramid is based on the assumption that sequences of actions are performed to achieve a specific result. That is, actions are not random; they are undertaken deliberately. A pyramid expresses these actions and the reason they are performed.

---

*The Pyramid Principle is a system for logical thinking and writing developed by Barbara Minto and taught to major consulting firms and other businesses around the world. For a fuller explanation of pyramid logic, see Barbara Minto, *The Pyramid Principle: Logic in Writing and Thinking.*

For example, let's say you decide to perform the following two actions. Why would you do so?

butter one side of each slice	join the buttered sides

The answer might be to make a butter sandwich, which is not necessarily a great sandwich or a culinary challenge, but a good illustration for my purposes at this point:

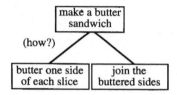

Here, we have a pyramid. It contains a single box at the top. That box expresses a result (the "ends"), in this case a butter sandwich. The boxes below it are the actions (the "means" necessary to produce that result). If you told me, in the methodology of your proposal, that one task you would undertake would be to make a butter sandwich, I might ask "How?" You would answer by naming the two steps on the lower row.

Note two things. First, the boxes are related through a logic that goes both bottom-up and top-down; second, whether you read bottom-up or top-down, the boxes always exist in a question–answer relationship. From the bottom, the lower boxes are the actions necessary to achieve the result implied by the top box to which they are joined. So, if you were building your pyramid from the bottom up, you would ask yourself, "What result would be produced from these two actions?" That answer would generate the top-level box. From the top down, the higher level box also generates a question: "How would you achieve the result implied by this action?" That answer would give you the boxes (the actions) at the lower level.

But there's always one other question involved, and it's the most important one because it provides the rationale for the whole pyramid. In our example so far, that question provides the reason for making the butter sandwich in the first place. I call this the "overriding question" because it motivates the entire pyramid.

What possible question could there be to which the top box, "make a butter sandwich," could be an answer? "What should I eat?" won't work because the answer to that question is "a butter sandwich," not "*make* a butter sandwich." "What should I do?" would work, but (as we'll see) it's really not specific enough. Here's a better one: "Given the limited number of 'resources' in my refrigerator and my desire to eat immediately, what should I do?" Answer: "Make a butter sandwich!" How? By buttering one side of each slice of bread and by placing the buttered sides together.

Now let's assume that you want more to eat than a butter sandwich, though given the limited amount of food in your refrigerator, the butter sandwich will have to serve as a main course. So instead of the box "make a butter sandwich," we substitute the box "prepare main course," and we include two other boxes on the same level:

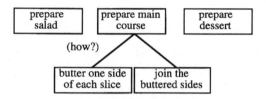

What will be the result of those three top boxes? A three-course meal. The top box, then, will again be an action that expresses that result:

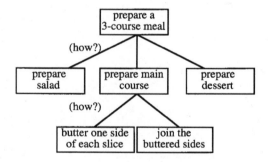

Each box needs to be an action that expresses a result because, depending on your perspective, each box is either an action or a result. Look at the box "prepare main course" in the pyramid immediately above. "Prepare main course" expresses the result of the two boxes below it. But "prepare main course" is also an action that, together with the two other actions on its level, produces the result expressed by the box above: "prepare a 3-course meal."

Let's continue building our pyramid by assuming that "prepare a 3-course meal" is only one of five actions on its level:

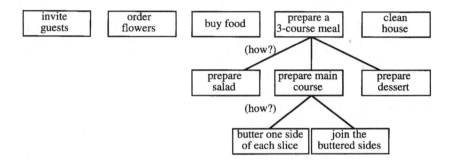

In a moment we'll try to generate a box that might express the result of those top-level actions. Before we add that box to the top of the pyramid, I hope you noticed something wrong. "Buy food" shouldn't be on what is now the top level. Why? Because it's an action that would be necessary in preparing the three-course meal. Therefore this action needs to go below that box and above the boxes related to making the salad, main course, and dessert. Because the "buy food" box can't exist on a level by itself, we therefore need another box parallel (in level and phrasing) to it:

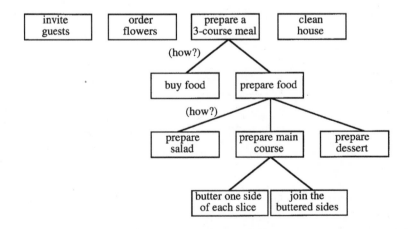

Let's call the box that would sit atop this pyramid "give a dinner party." Now if I wanted to try your patience even further, I could continue building the pyramid ever-upward. I could also continue to build it downward, since further actions could be required to explain how you butter one side of each slice of bread and join them together. What determines where you start and how far down you go? I can explain the "down" part in one sentence: As far down as you need to go so that your reader or listener no longer asks "How?" Explaining where you start will take two more paragraphs.

Assume you have a potential client to whom you've been trying to sell for some time. You have had several meetings with him and have developed a fairly sound business relationship, but as yet, you've been unable to make the sale. It so happens that he and your best friend went to school together and haven't seen each other for over 20 years. He would like to see your friend, and your friend would like to see him (and you, of course, would like to make the sale). Next week, this potential client will be in town for two days. Your overriding question is: "How can I further my relationship with him to increase the likelihood of a sale?" Your answer is to give a dinner party that he and your friend will attend (and during which, we'll assume, you won't serve butter sandwiches as a main course).

Note that three things have generated the pyramid and therefore determined where it begins. First, a problem: in this case, your not having yet made a sale. In your proposal, the problem is discussed in the situation slot. Second, an overriding question related to the problem: in this case, "How can I further my relationship with my potential client and thereby increase the likelihood of a sale?" Third, an objective, which is the answer to the overriding question: in this case, "Give a dinner party." The objective is stated in your proposal's objectives slot. It also becomes the top box in your pyramid, which gives you the logically related actions necessary to achieve that objective:

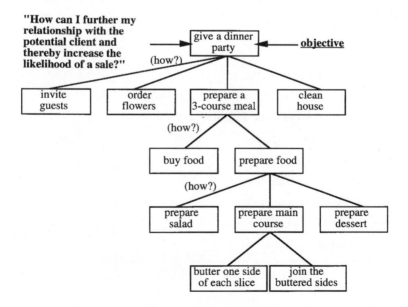

In the rest of this chapter I'll show you how all those actions under the objective form part of your proposed project's methodology. I'll also take you through the revision of a methodology of an internal proposal written to the XYZ Company, a provider of information systems. XYZ's marketing group wanted to explore the idea of offering their services to a new market, the motor freight sector, possibly in partnership with a motor carrier.

Exhibit 4.1 lists the objectives and the tasks as they first appeared in the proposal. After you've read the exhibit, I'll take you through the four-step process of constructing (in this case, revising) the methodology. Because constructing a pyramid seems complicated the first few times you try to build one, I'll repeat much of what I said when building the pyramid for giving a dinner party. In the work session at the end of this chapter, you'll have yet another opportunity to see a pyramid constructed. After that, you should be able to start building your own.

Objectives

- Develop market and competitive information to assist XYZ in determining if there is a demand for the proposed service offering, and how it could be tailored to better meet customer needs.

- Determine how the product should be marketed given customers' needs, the marketplace, and the activities of competitors.

- Identify potential actions for XYZ to be successful in this marketplace.

Tasks

- Conduct kickoff meeting.
- Identify market participants and develop questionnaires.
- Evaluate motor carriers' requirements.
- Evaluate competitors' capabilities.
- Evaluate shippers' needs.
- Review progress with top management.
- Assess overall market potential.
- Define market opportunities.
- Assess strategic alternatives.

Exhibit 4.1. The original methodology.

Step 1: Clearly Identify the Objective(s), Based on the Overriding Question(s)

Because the methodology contains the tasks you will use to achieve your project's objectives, the starting place for building your methodology has to be the objectives themselves. It makes little sense to plan a trip if you don't know where you're going, and it makes equally little sense to tell me how you're going to go about achieving what you're uncertain about accomplishing. Fortunately, I've given you some important tools for thinking about your objectives. As we've seen, they can be of only three kinds—Insight, Plan, or Implemented Plan. If yours is an Insight Project, you will have only one objective, related to insight. A Planning Project will have only one objective, related to developing a plan. An Implementation Project will also have only one objective, related to implementing a plan. Understandably, a project intended to develop a plan *and* implement it will have two objectives. So will one that combines insight with a plan.

You must know the overriding question before you can state the objective. Overriding questions occur because something in my current situation—some problem or opportunity or critical issue—has triggered the need for a different situation, a desired result. In my experience, many proposals fail to sell and many projects fail to succeed because proposers and buyers have not defined (and achieved consensus on) the overriding questions. Consider two possible overriding questions in the ABC situation discussed in Appendix A:

	First situation	Second situation
Desired result, S_2	A plan for meeting the market forecast	A plan for meeting the market forecast
Overriding question:	"How can we best *increase capacity* to meet projected product demand?"	"How can we best *supply product* to meet projected product demand?"

The desired results are the same, but the objectives will be different, because the overriding questions are different. The first objective will focus only or mostly on increasing capacity. It assumes that ABC will probably continue to make most everything it currently makes, and therefore needs the capacity to do so. The second objective will involve a different kind of project (i.e., a different methodology). That project will have to consider, for example, the feasibility of outsourcing certain components or products which ABC makes today. In this second study, no additional manufacturing capacity might be needed if increased outsourcing made sense. Without clarity and consensus about the overriding questions, consultant Gilmore could write a document proposing one kind of project, even though President Armstrong and others at ABC have a very different project in mind.

Now, back to the XYZ situation—the methodology we're trying to revise. Two overriding questions existed in this situation, one related to insight and one related to a plan. XYZ wanted to know whether or not entering the market was desirable, and if it were, the company needed a plan defining how to do so. But you'd be hard pressed to glean that information from the objectives shown in Exhibit 4.1. In fact, the objectives as originally stated don't even suggest that the study might only involve one phase—the market assessment. After all, if the market were not worth entering, XYZ wouldn't need or even want a plan for entering it. Therefore, the proposers should have revised their objectives so that the first related to insight and the second related to a plan:

- Determine if XYZ should enter the information-service market for motor carriers.

- If appropriate, determine how XYZ should enter this market.

These objectives much more clearly capture the desired results and also indicate the phased nature of the project.

Step 2: Place Each Objective atop a Pyramid and Order the *Actions* Necessary to Achieve It

In building a pyramid, you need to keep two principles in mind:

1. Each box in the pyramid is a single action that expresses a result.
2. The actions must be as specific as possible.

Each box must be a single action that expresses a result. Because all the actions in the pyramid work together to produce the objective, all are logically integrated. The integration occurs because each action on each level is part of a group of actions that produces a result at a higher level. The following exhibit depicts this condition. On the lowest level are three groups of actions. Since the logical reason for performing any group of actions is to achieve some result, each group on the lower level produces a result at the next higher level:

Actions 1, 2, and 3 are performed in some logical manner to achieve result #1. Actions 4, 5, and 6 produce result #2. And so forth.

As you construct your methodology, you must phrase these three results as actions, because they are undertaken to produce a higher-level result or group of results. At the very top of the structure (Exhibit 4.2), regardless of how many levels it contains, is always the final result: the project's objective. On every level except the lowest, each box is an action that expresses a result. Subtask 1.1 expresses the result of the two sub-subtasks below it. But Subtask 1.1 is also an action that, together with the subtasks on its level, produces a result on the next level. That next level includes the major tasks. Each of them is a result produced from the actions below. And all of them together will result in what the entire pyramid builds to— the objective of the project—because all the actions are designed to achieve that single result.

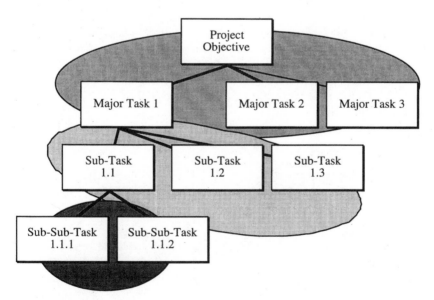

Exhibit 4.2. The objective is the top box in the pyramid.

If your project has more than one objective (if, for example, it's a combined insight and planning study, as in the proposal to XYZ) you will need to build a pyramid for each objective:

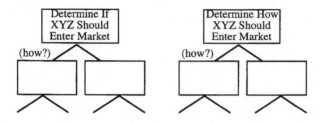

In building the pyramid, make the actions as specific as possible. In constructing your pyramid, you must try to phrase the actions as specifically as possible, because I might want to know precisely and specifically what you will accomplish. An effective technique is to test your action by rephrasing it in your mind as an actual result. For example, the result of the action "gather information" would be "gathered information." The result of "interview top management" would be "interviewed top management."

These results, I think you see, aren't very specific. They don't express a result. After you've gathered information, all you have is a bunch of information. After you've interviewed top management, all you have is a bunch of interviewed managers. Compare these nonspecific actions to "identify resources and timing required" or "specify capabilities required." These actions express specific results: "identified resources" and "specified capabilities." These are things I can see; I can visualize a list of resources or capabilities.

Now let's take a look at part of the pyramids that could have been developed by XYZ's internal consultants. I've included all of the first two levels and part of the third:

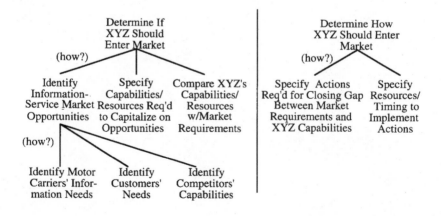

This and any well-constructed pyramid develops your ideas by way of a series of arguments. In the preceding pyramids three arguments exist, which are mutually exclusive and collectively exhaustive. First, whether or not XYZ should enter the market can be determined by three major tasks: identifying market opportunities, specifying the capabilities and resources required to capitalize on those opportunities, and comparing XYZ's capabilities and resources to the market requirements.

Second, the market opportunities can be learned by identifying three things: the motor carriers' needs for the proposed information system, the needs of the motor carriers' customers, and the capabilities of XYZ's competitors. Finally, to develop a plan for actually entering the market, XYZ needs to know (a) which actions are necessary for closing the gap between what the market demands and what XYZ can do and (b) what resources and timing are necessary to carry out those actions.

In checking the logic of your pyramid, just use the several requirements I've discussed:

- Each box must be an action that expresses a result. Therefore, each box must be phrased as specifically as possible.

- Each group of boxes on one level must produce a result on the next. That group and its result form an argument that goes something like this: "To achieve result A, action X, action Y, and action Z, and only those actions, must be performed."

- All arguments are mutually exclusive and collectively exhaustive.

Applying this pyramid technique will help you to indicate logical relationships and to identify the holes in your logic, letting you know where you have left something out.

Step 3: Sequence the Actions

Once you're satisfied with your pyramid, you can sequence the actions by using typical outline or bullet form, as I've done in Phase I below. Once again, I've taken the steps completely down to two levels and only partially, for illustrative purposes, to a third. Note now how the project is phased, with the project's objectives used, in this case, as the titles of the phases:

Phase I: Determine If XYZ Should Enter the Market

- Identify information–service market opportunities.
  - Identify motor carriers' information needs.
  - Identify customers' needs.
  - Identify competitors' capabilities.

- Specify capabilities and resources required to capitalize on market opportunities.

- Compare XYZ's capabilities and resources with market requirements.

Phase II: Determine How XYZ Should Enter the Market

- Specify actions required for closing the gap between market requirements and XYZ capabilities.

- Specify resources and timing to implement actions.

Because the outline form does not readily reveal logical relationships or logical inconsistencies (as the pyramid does), you should use the outline form only after you have constructed your pyramid.

Step 4: Identify and Integrate the *Activities* Necessary for Planning and Communicating Your Proposed Actions

In building your pyramid, you must distinguish between actions and activities. When you take in your car for repairs, you want your mechanic to perform two very different kinds of tasks. First are those actions directly related to achieving your objective of fixing or maintaining your car. These are the "hands-on" procedures to diagnose and solve the problem. Second are those kinds of tasks related to planning and communicating. These activities might involve the mechanic calling you when the car is fixed, or calling you if the problem will cost more than was originally estimated. Then, you could decide whether to have the car repaired, trade it in, or live with the problem. Both kinds of tasks—those actions necessary for achieving the objective and those activities necessary for planning and communicating—are part of the mechanic's methodology, and they're also part of yours. (See Exhibit 4.3.)

In constructing your methodology, however, you need to separate the two kinds of tasks. Only in that way can you construct a pyramid that reveals the logical set of actions that will achieve the project's objective. Although an activity like presenting a final report might be extremely important to the success of your efforts, it is crucial only in *presenting* the plan you constructed. It is not an action necessary for actually achieving the project's objective of *developing* the plan. The same holds true

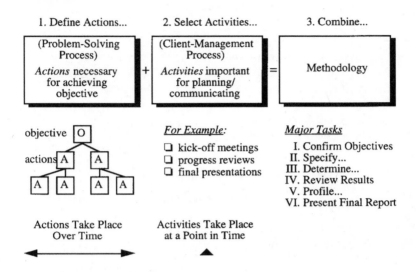

Exhibit 4.3. Methodology = actions + activities.

for other typical activities like presenting interim reports or conducting kickoff meetings. Even those activities, however, should be phrased as specifically as possible. Therefore, instead of "conduct kickoff meeting," you might phrase the activity as "confirm project objectives in a kickoff meeting."

After identifying the activities, you can sequence them in your outline, as I've done in the right-hand column of Exhibit 4.4, which compares the original methodology with part of the one we've been building by using a pyramid.

If you compare the original and the revision, I'm certain you'll agree that the latter much more clearly defines the desired results and how you will get there. The original methodology is typical of those I see, in proposal after proposal. The relationship of the tasks to the objectives is unclear, as is the relationship of the tasks to each other. The revised methodology, on the other hand, clearly reveals the project's objectives and how they will be achieved. If a logical methodology were important to me, I would surely reward you for that clarity. In my evaluation of your proposal, I would most certainly give you some of the 2–5 extra points you need to win. And even if a logical methodology weren't important to *me*, it would provide *you* the basis for a logical workplan to better help you execute the project after you've won.

Original

Objectives

- Develop market and competitive information to assist XYZ in determining if there is a demand for the proposed service offering, and how it could be tailored to better meet customer needs.

- Determine how the product should be marketed given customers' needs, the marketplace, and the activities of competitors.

- Identify potential actions for XYZ to be successful in this marketplace.

Tasks

- Conduct kickoff meeting.

- Identify market participants and develop questionnaires.

- Evaluate motor carrier requirements.

- Evaluate competitor capabilities.

- Evaluate shippers' needs.

- Review progress with top management.

- Assess overall market potential.

- Define market opportunities.

- Assess strategic alternatives.

Revised

I: Determine if XYZ should enter market

- Confirm phase I objectives in a kickoff meeting.

- Identify information–service market opportunities.

- Specify capabilities and resources required to capitalize on market opportunity.

- Compare XYZ's capabilities and resources with market requirements.

- Report phase I results, and if necessary, confirm phase II objectives.

II: Determine how XYZ should enter market

- Specify actions required for closing gap between market requirements and XYZ capabilities.

- Specify resources and timing to implement actions.

- Report phase II results.

Exhibit 4.4. The original methodology revised.

The Pyramid and the Baseline Logic Worksheet

After you have constructed your pyramid, you need to examine all boxes to determine which express a deliverable, one of four kinds of outputs suggested by the baseline logic (see Exhibit 4.5):

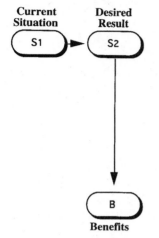

Current Situation   **Desired Result**

S1   S2

B

Benefits

1) **Deliverables:** the outputs produced during the process of achieving S_2. *Example from ABC: specifications of current equipment and space utilization.*

2) **Desired Result (S_2):** the output(s) of the project or its phases: insight, a plan, and/or an implented plan. *Example: a plan for increasing capacity.*

3) **Project Objective(s):** the expression of S_2, the desired result(s) achieved at the end of the project. *Exaample: develop a plan for increasing capacity.*

4) **Benefits:** the effects, the good things that accrue from the potential client gaining insight, having a plan, and/or implementing that plan. *Example: a thorough justification of the chosen option that provides the basis for requesting the necessary funding from Consolidated.*

Exhibit 4.5. The four kinds of outputs.

You have already recorded the last three outputs on your Baseline Logic Worksheet. After constructing your pyramid for ABC (which you'll do in this chapter's work session), you will need to add the deliverables to that worksheet. The pyramid for XYZ contains deliverables like these: defined market opportunities, defined capabilities and resources, and a comparison of capabilities and resources with market requirements.

*   *   *   *

Before you read this chapter's work session, I want to say something about workplans which, as I've hinted before, can be formed in part from your pyramid. As Exhibit 4.6 illustrates, a workplan is nothing more than your methodology sequenced over time.

Methodology

Major Tasks

I. Confirm Objectives
II. Specify...
III. Determine...
IV. Review Results
V. Profile...
VI. Present Final Report

Workplan

Major Tasks

I.
II.
III.
IV.
V.
VI.

Resources/ Accountabilities

Exhibit 4.6. Workplan = methodology sequenced over time.

In proposals, the workplan is often presented in the form of a Gantt chart that includes the actions and activities on one axis and the timing of those tasks on the other. This kind of chart is most helpful in letting me see when you expect each task to begin and end. The Gantt chart also indicates which tasks will be performed concurrently and which tasks overlap. Before you can develop your workplan, however, you need to construct a logical methodology. You'll get some practice in the following work session, which develops a pyramid for the proposal to ABC.

⇨ Chapter 4 Review: Constructing the Methodology

1. The proposal's methodology consists of actions and activities:
   - Actions are tasks necessary for achieving the project's objectives. They are necessary in the problem-solving process. These actions must express results.
   - Activities are tasks important for planning and communicating to the potential client. Activities are necessary during the client-- management process. For example: confirming the project's objectives, reporting interim results, and delivering a final report. As much as possible, these tasks should be phrased to express results.

2. Constructing the proposal's methodology requires four steps:
   - *Clearly identify the objective(s), based on the overriding question(s).* An Insight Project has only one objective—providing insight. A Planning Project has only one objective—developing a plan. An Implementation Project has only one objective—implementing a plan. A combined Insight/Planning Project has two objectives. A combined Planning/Implementation Project has two objectives.
   - *Place each objective atop a pyramid and organize the actions necessary to achieve it.* You should develop one pyramid for each objective. Every box in the pyramid contains one result. Every box on one row is connected to at least two boxes on the next lower row. These lower-row boxes are the set of actions necessary to achieve the result on the row above. These lower-row actions, however, are also results of the boxes connected to them on even lower rows. Each box in every row is a result produced by the related actions on the row below. Therefore, each box is an action expressed as a single result. The actions must be expressed as specifically as possible.
   - *Once the pyramid is constructed, list the actions in sequence.* Use indentations or standard outline form to indicate the hierarchical relationships. You have now logically organized the actions.
   - *Within that sequence, integrate the activities important for planning and communicating.* You have now constructed the methodology.

3. Once the pyramid is completed, deliverables should be identified, added to those already on the Baseline Logic Worksheet, and aligned.

Work Session 4: Developing the Pyramid for ABC

Confident that your baseline logic is well aligned, you turn your attention to the final element that provides a proposal with its logical foundation: the methodology. The methodology indicates how you plan to close the gap between the current situation, S_1, and and the desired result, S_2; it effects the transition from S_1 to S_2.

A comprehensive and logical methodology will play a significant role in convincing ABC's management that Paramount can best help them develop a plan to solve their capacity problem. That you know. Because you also know that manufacturing strategy isn't one of your own strengths, you suggest to Gilmore that he assign some of the firm's functional specialists to work with you to develop the methodology. Gilmore quickly acts on your suggestion and joins the group himself.

Defining the Overriding Question and Objective

The group's first task is to define ABC's overriding question. As you expected, they differ about what the overriding question should be. Some believe it should be phrased like this: "How can ABC best provide product to meet forecasted demand?" Proponents of this question suggest that internal resources and capital investment can be conserved by having more operations, especially low value-added ones, performed by outside suppliers.

Others believe the question should focus not on product supply but on capacity: "How should ABC increase capacity to meet the sales forecast?" Both you and Gilmore argue for this question. Gilmore explains to the group that ABC's President Armstrong gave him the clear impression that ABC preferred to have closer control of its manufacturing processes by performing most of its major operations within its own facilities. As a result of Gilmore's counsel, the group agrees that the project's objective should be this: "Develop a manufacturing facility strategy that will provide the capacity necessary to meet forecasted demand." Of course, this question should be tested with ABC's management.

Building the Pyramid

After about two hours the group completes a first and a second draft (Exhibits 4.7 and 4.8) of the pyramid for ABC:

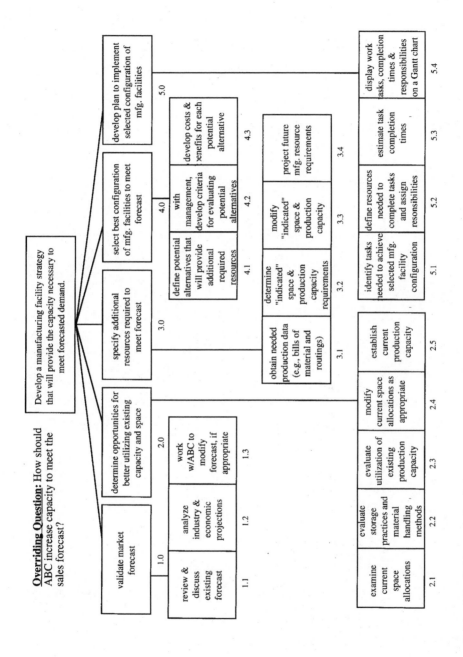

Overriding Question: How should ABC increase capacity to meet the sales forecast?

Develop a manufacturing facility strategy that will provide the capacity necessary to meet forecasted demand.

validate market forecast	1.0	
review & discuss existing forecast	1.1	
analyze industry & economic projections	1.2	
work w/ABC to modify forecast, if appropriate	1.3	

determine opportunities for better utilizing existing capacity and space	2.0	
examine current space allocations	2.1	
evaluate storage practices and material handling methods	2.2	
evaluate utilization of existing production capacity	2.3	
modify current space allocations as appropriate	2.4	
establish current production capacity	2.5	

specify additional resources required to meet forecast	3.0	
obtain needed production data (e.g., bills of material and routings)	3.1	
determine "indicated" space & production capacity requirements	3.2	
modify "indicated" space & production capacity	3.3	
project future mfg. resource requirements	3.4	

select best configuration of mfg. facilities to meet forecast	4.0	
define potential alternatives that will provide additional required resources	4.1	
with management, develop criteria for evaluating potential alternatives	4.2	
develop costs & benefits for each potential alternative	4.3	

develop plan to implement selected configuration of mfg. facilities	5.0	
identify tasks needed to achieve selected mfg. facility configuration	5.1	
define resources needed to complete tasks and assign resonsibilities	5.2	
estimate task completion times	5.3	
display work tasks, completion times & responsibilities on a Gantt chart	5.4	

Exhibit 4.7. ABC Pyramid—first draft.

75

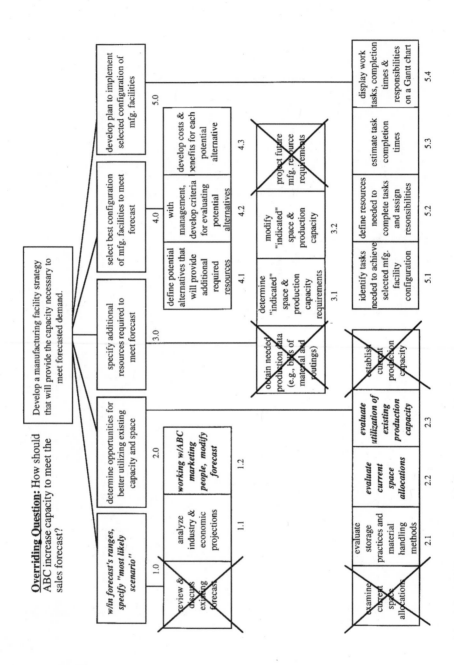

Overriding Question: How should ABC increase capacity to meet the sales forecast?

Develop a manufacturing facility strategy that will provide the capacity necessary to meet forecasted demand.

w/in forecast's ranges, specify "most likely scenario"
1.0

determine opportunities for better utilizing existing capacity and space
2.0

specify additional resources required to meet forecast
3.0

select best configuration of mfg. facilities to meet forecast
4.0

develop plan to implement selected configuration of mfg. facilities
5.0

review & discuss existing forecast
1.1

analyze industry & economic projections
1.1

working w/ABC marketing people, modify forecast
1.2

examine current space allocations
2.1

evaluate storage practices and material handling methods
2.1

evaluate current space allocations
2.2

evaluate utilization of existing production capacity
2.3

establish current production capacity

obtain needed production data (e.g., bills of material and routings)
3.0

determine "indicated" space & production capacity requirements
3.1

modify "indicated" space & production capacity
3.2

project future mfg. resource requirements

define potential alternatives that will provide additional required resources
4.1

with management, develop criteria for evaluating potential alternatives
4.2

develop costs & benefits for each potential alternative
4.3

identify tasks needed to achieve selected mfg. facility configuration
5.1

define resources needed to complete tasks and assign responsibilities
5.2

estimate task completion times
5.3

display work tasks, completion times & responsibilities on a Gantt chart
5.4

Exhibit 4.8. ABC Pyramid—second draft.

As you look over the x'd-out and italicized boxes in the second draft, you see clearly why various changes were made and still need to be made. For example, various x'd-out boxes didn't survive the second draft because they don't express a result. Cases in point include "review and discuss existing forecast," "examine current space allocations," and "obtain needed production data." The results implied by these tasks include a reviewed forecast, examined space allocations, and obtained data. These implied results just aren't as specific as they should be. You can't visualize them, as you could with specifications or comparisons or definitions.

Other boxes in the second draft are problematic in another way: they aren't necessary for achieving the result implied in the box above them. Task 1.2 ("modify forecast") is a case in point: it expresses the same result as the box above it. These "mistakes" confirm to you the power of the pyramid in constructing a logical argument for your methodology: the pyramid clearly displays gaps and errors in logic and helps you, more quickly and effectively than you could otherwise, to generate a third draft, shown in Exhibit 4.9. Even this draft, you recognize the next day, has some problems, but you are satisfied that it is good enough for now. It will provide you with the guts of your methodology and the building blocks for your methods section. It also generates some additional deliverables that you record on your Baseline Logic Worksheet.

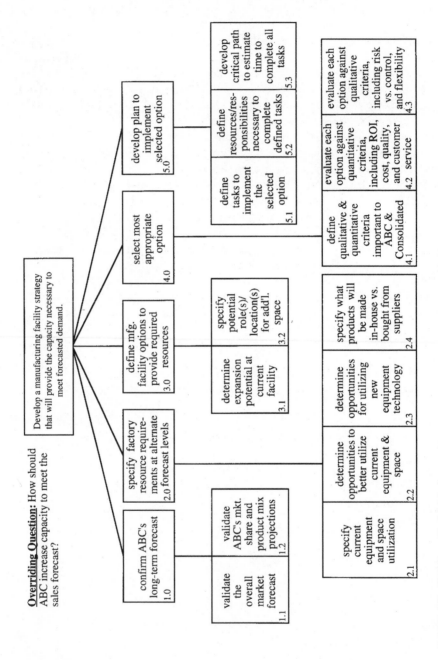

Overriding Question: How should ABC increase capacity to meet the sales forecast?

Develop a manufacturing facility strategy that will provide the capacity necessary to meet forecasted demand.

confirm ABC's long-term forecast
1.0

specify factory resource requirements at alternate forecast levels
2.0

define mfg. facility options to provide required resources
3.0

select most appropriate option
4.0

develop plan to implement selected option
5.0

validate the overall market forecast
1.1

validate ABC's mkt. share and product mix projections
1.2

specify current equipment and space utilization
2.1

determine opportunities to better utilize current equipment & space
2.2

determine opportunities for utilizing new equipment technology
2.3

specify what products will be made in-house vs. bought from suppliers
2.4

determine expansion potential at current facility
3.1

specify potential role(s)/ location(s) for add'l. space
3.2

define qualitative & quantitative criteria important to ABC & Consolidated
4.1

evaluate each option against quantitative criteria, including ROI, cost, quality, and customer service
4.2

evaluate each option against qualitative criteria, including risk vs. control, and flexibility
4.3

define tasks to implement the selected option
5.1

define resources/responsibilities necessary to complete defined tasks
5.2

develop critical path to estimate time to complete all tasks
5.3

Exhibit 4.9. ABC Pyramid—third draft.

Part 2

Proposal Psychologics

Now that you've completed Part 1, on proposal logics, you may believe that your more logical presentations and proposals will win far more often. They might. But logics only provide you the base—the necessary, but not the sufficient—because I buy for psychological as well as for logical reasons. I want to feel comfortable with you, to trust you, to sense with confidence that you understand my situation, my risks, and perhaps most important of all, my potential rewards—the benefits I will receive from the project you propose.

So your task now becomes combining the logical with the psychological, combining your *analysis* of my situation and what you will do to support me with how I *feel* about you. I want to be confident about your ability to deliver on your promises to meet my objectives. I want a relationship, based on trust and founded on rapport.

Therefore in Part 2, I assume that your logics are in place and that relationships or psychologics are now critical to your success. Accordingly, I show you how to align yourself with me and the other members of the buying committee and how to position yourself, favorably, against the competition. Finally, I show you how to use that alignment and positioning to develop themes—important messages that you will weave throughout your document or presentation to make me say, "Yes, these people have listened to and understood us; they appreciate our risks, and they have articulated our rewards."

5

Analyzing the Buyers

Generic structure, as we discussed in Chap. 1, primarily relates to the logic of proposals. Unless you're selling equations to a logician or theories to a scientist, however, logic is rarely enough. That's why you'll have to use more than logic. You'll have to give me, your potential client, more than technical expertise or a logically constructed methodology, more than elegant sounding resumes or qualifications statements that I know look pretty much the same in every proposal you prepare. You'll have to convince me that I want to work with you.

Think about what you offer to me: you often don't know what you're going to make (i.e., what you'll deliver to me) until you make it. You operate more like a medical doctor than a mechanical engineer. The engineer designs a bridge to span a river, while the doctor creates, tests, and recreates hypotheses to discover something unknown, something hidden, and perhaps not agreed to. Accordingly, to choose you as my "doctor" I need to develop trust that you, your team, and your firm can address my uncertainty, my often ill-defined, even illogical current situation. In such cases, attitude or "bedside manner" is just as important as expertise.

You see, although you may think we know each other well, we don't—certainly not during our initial meetings. I don't know or likely trust you completely or appreciate your complex personality. And you, certainly, don't know me completely or how I will respond in a given situation. In some situations I become extremely analytical, seeking a lot of evidence, asking a lot of questions, and behaving methodically and systematically. This orientation toward information and reasoned, rational analysis may be based on the risk or magnitude of a potential decision I must make. In this situation, I might desire a detailed method of approach (perhaps even your sharing of your pyramid logic).

In a different situation, I become more concerned about people and their relationships within my organization. This more supportive orientation is one I often take during implementation projects where I must convince others in my organization to change. In this situation, therefore, I might desire your sensitivity, your care for the personal and developmental concerns of me and others.

At yet other times, especially when I'm dealing with a future issue, one that is often ill-defined, I become more concerned with ideas and hypotheses and creativity. This orientation leads me to rely heavily on intuition and feelings. Therefore, I might desire from you a more conceptual and open-ended orientation.

Finally, in yet other situations I become more assertive, more oriented to action, more desirous of control. I might adopt this directive or controlling orientation when I sense urgency and the need for rapid change or forceful response. I become more task-oriented, more insistent on getting something accomplished quickly. Therefore, I might desire from you a certain assertiveness, a proactive orientation.

So even if you think you know me, because you've seen me operate in one kind of situation, you might be surprised at my response in another situation. Your task is to make reasonable and educated guesses about the nature of my likely response so that you in turn can respond to my situation and convince me that you understand my organization's problems or opportunities and that we can work together.

Additionally, if I'm not the only one making the buying decision (which is almost always the case), you also need to know my colleagues on the evaluation committee and how they perceive the situation, and what they like and don't like about the scope and range of potential solutions, as well as their relationship to me, and mine to them. Would you be surprised to hear that we may even see the situation differently, have different selection criteria, and even different biases? Well, more often than not, we do.

The Four Buying Roles

Let me recommend a book to you that isn't at all about writing but is about selling (and that's what your proposal process needs to do: sell). The book, *Strategic Selling,** contains a powerful method for analyzing the

*Robert M. Miller and Stephen E. Heiman. *Strategic Selling.* Reno, NV: Miller Heiman, Inc. (1987).

members on a buying team. Each of these individuals, in what Miller and Heiman call a "complex sale" (i.e., one with multiple decision influencers), plays *one or more* roles: economic buyer, user buyer, technical buyer, or coach.

The economic buyer (only one exists in most selling opportunities) has direct access to and control of the budget, discretionary use of these funds, and veto power over the sale. This buyer's focus is primarily on the bottom line and on the impact the sale will have on the organization. Exhibit 5.1, briefly summarized and adapted, is Miller and Heiman's description of the economic buyer.

I have played the role of economic buyer, and I have also been a user buyer, focusing primarily on the project's potential day-to-day effect on my own area of responsibility or organization. If I am a user buyer, you'd better not ignore me if you want a long-term relationship. If you by chance sell an initial project and circumvent me, I might sabotage subsequent projects or even hinder acceptance and implementation during the initial one. That's because your project will have a direct impact on my job performance and on those I manage. If I'm a user buyer (see Exhibit 5.2), you'd better convince me that the winds of change are pleasant, or if they're not, that the hurricane will at least clear out a lot of unwanted dust and debris, leaving me as one of the survivors.

Role:	To give final approval to buy
Focus:	Concerned with bottom line and overall impact on the organization. Such as: ■ Strategic position ■ Profitability ■ Competitiveness ■ Productivity ■ Market growth ■ Budget fit ■ Cash flow ■ Meeting business goals/objectives
Number:	Only one per sale (but may be one set of people, like a board or a committee)
Characteristics:	Has discretionary use of funds Can release these monies Has veto power
Primary question:	"What will be the overall performance improvement and return on this consulting investment?"

Exhibit 5.1. The economic buyer.

Role:	To judge impact on operational performance
Focus:	Adequacy and practicality of proposed solution General effects on the potentially affected organizational units
Number:	Often several
Characteristics:	Will be directly affected by the project Will often have a subjective response to the proposal Is very important for implementation and for continuing relationships
Primary question:	"How will the project affect my job and those I manage?"

Exhibit 5.2. The user buyer.

I might also be a technical buyer (Exhibit 5.3), who primarily judges the measurable and quantifiable aspects of your proposal. If so, I'm a gatekeeper, making recommendations to the other groups of buyers. As a technical buyer, I can't accept your proposal, but I can play a decisive role in eliminating you from further consideration.

Role:	To screen out
Focus:	Concerned with measurable, quantifiable aspects related to this proposal situation. Such as: ■ ROI ■ Match of specifications ■ Price ■ Adequacy of technical solution
Number:	Often several or many
Characteristics:	Judges proposal by measurable, quantifiable aspects Acts as gatekeeper Makes recommendations Can't say "yes"; can say "no"
Primary question:	"Do the proposed approach and qualifications meet our specifications?"

Exhibit 5.3. The technical buyer.

The fourth buying role is the coach, an individual (or individuals) that you hope to find and develop to help you make the sale. The coach can exist within my potential client company, within your own firm, or outside both. It's highly desirable to have a coach or coaches on the buying team. It's ideal if one of your coaches is the economic buyer.

Why do you need a coach? Well, sometimes you don't. But often you do, probably more often than you realize. You see, sometimes I don't fully trust you. I don't know you well enough for you to have earned my trust. In fact, if you're a consultant, as I stated earlier, I often would prefer not having you or other consultants around, asking me a lot of time-consuming questions, prying into my affairs. You are an outsider, and I would prefer that you stay that way. I wish that I didn't need you and that I could resolve my own organization's issues. But even though I *might* need you (you still have to convince me), I'm not likely to reveal everything. I might not believe that what you need to know from me is actually worth your knowing. Even those things I'm reluctant to tell, you might forget to ask, and you might not have another opportunity to do so. Or, you may never even have the opportunity to meet me at all, because I'm too busy to see you, or I judge you too unimportant to see.

This is where your coach (or coaches) comes in. The coach may be able to arrange introductions with me or with other buyers on my team, identify buyers that you have overlooked or would not normally be able to identify, elaborate on our evaluation criteria, provide advice and counsel about selling strategies and maybe even the competition, and in general act as guide and confidant during the selling process. Although coaches can often help you indirectly, by arranging introductions and providing intelligence, sometimes (as an experienced consultant and friend of mine explains) they can actually help you sell. "A young fellow," as my friend tells the story,

> who is an internal consultant for a company I was trying to sell invited us in in a competitive situation to talk about inventory. We had a long meeting with him and then a long second meeting, and then we had to write a proposal to go with him to his boss.
>
> I hate that kind of situation. We never met his boss; all we knew was that his boss is a hard-charging, young, very creative guy who, like all the other top people at XYZ, shot up in the organization. And I said, "Does he like presentations, or does he like written documents?" The internal consultant said, "He gets annoyed at too many words and things; he likes creative presentations."
>
> So I put together a presentation with about 25 pages, a little flip chart thing that I would put on the boss's desk, so I was totally in con-

trol. It was mostly cartoons and all kinds of wild stuff, a lot of meaning and very few words. The last cartoon showed a boat with the captain leaning over the bow. On the captain were the words "XYZ Management." In front of the boat were a bunch of icebergs. On the tops of the icebergs, I wrote things like "reduce inventory" or "cut inventory costs," and on the bottoms phrases like "destroy customer confidence." At the very top of the cartoon I wrote, "Our objective is to steer you through these icebergs, avoid some of them, go right through others because they are so small that they don't make any difference, and show you where to set dynamite charges to get rid of the really bad ones."

Now the internal consultant asked me for a copy of all this in advance, so I sent him a letter, giving him the philosophy of what we were trying to do and so forth, and word by word I explained that whole last cartoon.

At the meeting, I flipped through the charts and when I came to the last one, I said, "It's sort of like icebergs," and then paused. Suddenly, the internal consultant said, "Yes, as a matter of fact ..". and he just took over, independently quoting right from my little personal letter to him, which really was the proposal. Now, he looked smart. His boss liked it, and we got the job. If he wouldn't have said anything, I would have kept talking. But we made him part of the creative team without soliciting it. He could be part of our team, which he wanted to be; he could be smart in front of his boss, and be selling to his boss.*

Coaches (at least in their coaching role) are interested in the strokes or recognition or visibility they will get from helping you make a successful sale and thus initiating a project that proves valuable. They will gain recognition or visibility, get strokes, or be seen as problem solvers if they have played a part in your selection and were therefore instrumental in helping to choose the right firm that eliminated pain or capitalized on opportunity and therefore allowed results to be delivered and benefits to accrue. (See Exhibit 5.4.)

A Fifth Buying Role

Would you believe that I might not select you even if your firm scored the highest number of points on our evaluation scale? Even though you would "beat" the second-place finisher by 2 to 5 points, you (and not they) would place second; they (and not you) would win. In almost all such situations, you will lose because a fifth buying role—the ratifier—strongly prefers someone else.

---

*Glenn J Broadhead and Richard C. Freed. *The Variables of Composition: Process and Product in a Business Setting.* Carbondale, IL: Southern Illinois University Press (1986), pp. 52–53.

Role:	To act as guide for this proposal opportunity
Focus:	Your success with this opportunity
Number:	Develop at least one, in your or the buyer's firm, or outside both
Can be found:	In your or the potential client's firm or outside both (could be a member of the Board of Directors)
Characteristics:	Wants you to win and therefore provides/interprets information about the potential client's environment, such as: ■ Current situation ■ Competition ■ Other buyers ■ Benefits, individual and ■ Hot buttons collective ■ Evaluation criteria
Primary question: "How can we pull this off?"	

Exhibit 5.4. The coach.

A ratifier doesn't exist in all selling situations, and when he does, he isn't an official member of the selection committee. The ratifier is, however, consulted by the economic buyer to approve or bless the selection committee's decision. In the ABC situation, for example, there might be a ratifier at Consolidated, an individual from whom President Armstrong would normally seek approval before selecting a consulting firm. Even if Paramount Consulting were ranked highest by ABC, Armstrong might want to have that choice blessed by the ratifier. And the ratifier could say no—because he has a poor opinion of Paramount, because he has a better opinion of one of the other competitors, or simply because he wants to play it safe by going with a higher profile or better-known firm. If the ratifier refuses to bless ABC's decision, the selection committee might very well have to continue its deliberations.

In his role to bless the recommendation of the economic buyer, the ratifier wants to be certain that the proposed project (and the proposers themselves) meets his broader political and/or personal objectives and desires. As such, he is most concerned about the potential cultural or environmental conflicts within the organization. He wants to know, as Exhibit 5.5 shows, whether the project or proposers will cause conflicts with his colleagues, with his organization's culture and its constituencies, or with other projects then being or soon to be undertaken.

Role:	To bless the recommendation of the economic buyer
Focus:	Concerned with potential cultural/environmental conflicts in the organization, such as: ■ Conflicts with colleagues ■ Conflicts with corporate culture ■ Conflicts with constituencies ■ Total resource availability/allocation ■ Conflicts with other programs
Number:	If exists, usually only one in corporate organizations; sometimes several in governmental organizations
Can be found:	Higher up in the organization
Characteristics:	■ Ratifies the recommendation ■ Often at the highest levels of the organization ■ Acts as gatekeeper ■ Has veto power
Primary question:	"Will this project and these proposers meet my broader 'political' and/or personal objectives?"

Exhibit 5.5. The ratifier.

Beyond $S_1 \to S_2 \to B$

Note that in using the various categories of buyers, Miller and Heiman aren't talking about individual people but about *roles* people on the selection committee play during the selling situation. An economic buyer, regardless of who he is personally, individually, is always concerned about your proposed project's bottom-line impact on the organization; therefore, he focuses on ROI or good budget fit or increased productivity. A user buyer, regardless of title, is always concerned about your service's day-to-day impact on her department's operation; therefore, she may focus on the ease and effectiveness of implementation or on improved efficiency.

The real significance of these different orientations is that individuals playing each of the roles will expect different kinds of benefits than will others playing a different role. Allow me to emphasize this last point. Because you, I, and everyone else buys because of benefits, you must recognize that we have different expectations about how we will each benefit from your proposed approach and results. We aren't really buying your product or service; we are buying what that product or service delivers—benefits.

Because of these differences, the formula for the baseline logic that I used in Chap. 2 to express the engagement process,

S_1 (current situation) $\rightarrow S_2$ (desired result) $\rightarrow B$ (benefits)

is inadequate. It would be adequate only if you were selling to a one-person buying team with that single individual playing all buying roles. Because this situation almost never occurs, the formula is oversimplified and must be expanded as depicted in Exhibit 5.6. This second formulation is much more realistic (and strategic) because of these three truths:

- *Truth 1. The perception of* S_1, *our current situation, varies by buyer and is conditioned by buying role.*
  Never assume a group-wide or firm-wide perception of the current situation. S_1 refers to *individual* pain, uncertainty, or opportunity. The difference between my personal perception of S_1 and S_2 is the distance *I* must go to eliminate *my* pain or realize *my* opportunity. The distance my fellow buying committee members must travel is likely very different, because they start from a different point, have a different orientation, and travel a different terrain.
  Our individual perceptions of S_1 will be different because, obviously, we are different people with different needs, desires, responsibilities, and perspectives. What might be a problem in customer service to one person might be a problem in sales effectiveness to another. What to one person might be perceived as increased inefficiency might to me be eroding profits.

- *Truth 2.* Regardless of individual perceptions of the current situation, *definable agreed-upon results,* S_2, *will eliminate everyone's perception of* S_1.

- *Truth 3.* Although the desired result may be agreed upon by all members of the buying committee, *the perceived benefits accruing from achieving* S_2 *vary by buyer and by buying role.*

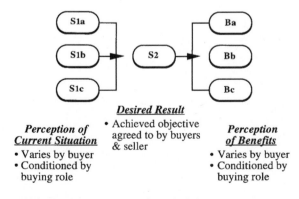

Exhibit 5.6. The baseline logic, for multiple buyers.

If S_1 is an ineffective information system and S_2 the implementation of an effective one, the user buyer might benefit from increased versatility and efficiency; the economic buyer from increased efficiency, yes, but primarily as it impacts profitability; the technical buyer from obtaining more sophisticated state-of-the-art capability and functionality.

In Chap. 6, I'll begin to show you how to convince me and each of the other buyers that you and your firm are better, more convincing, and more responsive than anyone else. This persuasion will take you a giant step toward gaining the 2 to 5 points that make the difference between winning and, well, just your time to prepare a losing proposal. Before that, you need to read the following work session, which not only indicates the buying roles played by individuals on ABC's selection committee, but also identifies benefits that will accrue to each once the plan is developed and after it's implemented.

⇨ Chapter 5 Review: Analyzing the Buyers

To begin to analyze the buyers:

1. Classify the members of the buying team according to the role or roles each will play in making the decision. A single buyer can play more than one of the four possible buying roles: economic, user, technical, coach.

2. Identify each buyer's perception of S_1, the current situation, remembering that that perception will be conditioned by buying role, position in the organization, and personality.

3. Identify for each buyer the individual benefits that will accrue from achieving S_2, remembering that those benefits will be conditioned by the buyer's role and position in the organization.

4. If at all possible, develop at least one coach, considering all potential sources.

Work Session 5: Identifying Buyer Roles and Generating Benefits for ABC

In your previous work sessions, you've focused on the "logics" of the selling situation: the logical relationship among the current situation, S_1, the desired result, S_2, and the benefits, B, that will accrue; and on the logical methodology that will ensure ABC's transition from its current situation to its desired result. The "logics" necessarily focus on the ABC organization collectively. You're not selling, however, to an organization but to people within it, people who will evaluate your proposal through the lenses of their own perceptions, desires, and needs. Now, therefore, you must begin to focus on the individuals on the consultant selection committee.

These are some of your thoughts as you review your notes from the initial meeting with ABC's consultant selection committee and carefully study Gilmore's interview notes from his follow-up visit. You consult your Baseline Logic Worksheet to review the current situation and desired result (from a collective, corporate point of view); then, you complete a Benefits Worksheet on which you identify the various buyers, their buying roles, and the benefits *each* will enjoy from having a plan for increasing capacity, as well as from having that plan implemented.

Ray Armstrong, President

You believe that Ray Armstrong is presently the economic buyer because he will give final approval for the study. However, you realize, if

Armstrong has a budget threshold beyond which he would have to gain approval from Consolidated, then someone at Consolidated would be the economic buyer if your or your competitors' proposed fees exceed that limit. Not recalling any discussion of this matter and not finding such discussion in your colleague's notes, you decide to take up this issue with Gilmore.

Armstrong appears pleased with ABC's past and present performance. Success has been heavily dependent on the ability of manufacturing to produce at low cost, with high quality and with a high degree of responsiveness to the needs of ABC's customers. However, Armstrong's warning bells are now ringing because the division's performance will probably deteriorate dramatically within the next few years when, as marketing's forecasts show, product demand will significantly exceed current manufacturing capacity.

Armstrong has two other concerns, you believe. One is that ABC must decide quickly on the amount and type of capacity needed because lead times for additional building and/or manufacturing equipment are quite long (perhaps 6 to 12 months). A second concern is that however ABC decides to provide additional capacity, its plan must be thoroughly documented and justified. The plan must be understandable, logical, and convincing to Consolidated, which will have to evaluate the return on investment and provide capital funding for the expansion.

Armstrong desires that the consultant's study quickly show ABC how to provide the capacity it needs by defining the amount and type of capacity required, identifying and evaluating various alternatives for providing that capacity, and documenting the results of their analysis in a report and possible presentation that will convince Consolidated of the need for and the viability of the additional capacity.

When S_2 is reached, Armstrong believes he will have a "roadmap" that will show ABC how to get where it wants to be and a report that will help convince Consolidated to release the necessary funds. To date, Armstrong has a good reputation with the parent company, and he would like to keep that reputation, you believe, for at least two reasons: first, to increase his chances of getting future requests approved, and second, possibly, to increase the likelihood of his own career advancement. You have no hard evidence in this regard, but your research about his employment history indicates that Armstrong's ambitions could take him higher than the presidency of the ABC division. For these reasons, the outcomes of your potential study will be critically important to Armstrong.

Norm Williams, VP Operations

You clearly see Norm Williams as a user buyer because he has overall responsibility for manufacturing operations and the study will recommend the best alternative for increasing capacity. Your notes indicate that Williams has concerns about adding that capacity at the present site because the available space may not be adequate for expansion. Furthermore, even if sufficient space were available, Williams believes ABC would be vulnerable by having the great majority of manufacturing resources centralized at one location. Williams also suggested the possibility of adding capacity at the satellite sites, although he expressed some doubt that all of ABC's expansion needs could be provided there. Recognizing the wide range of possible expansion alternatives and the capital-intensive nature of the proposed project, Williams knows that they need a thorough and convincing study.

As VP of Operations, Williams has the responsibility for producing quality products at competitive costs and for meeting customer delivery requirements in a timely manner. With inadequate capacity, delivery performance will deteriorate, quality could suffer, and costs could rise because of overtime and schedule interruptions to meet "rush" delivery dates.

Williams' expectations from the study are rather straightforward: He wants the consultant's analysis to produce a well-documented, convincing plan for providing additional capacity. For him, achieving S_2 means that he and his manufacturing team will have a comprehensive plan for providing the additional capacity in the most advantageous manner.

Marcia Collins, VP Marketing

You conclude that Marcia Collins is a technical buyer because she wants to make certain that the study methodology uses customer-service levels as a criterion for selecting and evaluating the expansion alternatives. By doing so, Collins believes that customer service must be maintained or improved after additional capacity is implemented. She will undoubtedly also play the role of user buyer because the results of the study will most certainly affect her marketing function and her desire to gain market share.

At present, Collins is anxious to see that additional manufacturing capacity is provided to remedy the shortfall that her forecasts predict in just a few years. Without that additional capacity, service levels will deteriorate. She also believes that capacity should not be added at the present site for two reasons: first, because of the shift in product demand away from ABC's present location in the Midwest; second (and in this she agrees with Williams) because with most of the manufacturing resources in one location, ABC could risk its hard-won reputation should there be a catastrophe or labor stoppage that disrupts production at that location.

Therefore, Collins not only wants the selected consulting team to develop and evaluate various alternatives for adding manufacturing capacity; she would prefer that the team's recommendation would enhance (or, at minimum, not diminish) current service levels. If service levels are used as an evaluation criterion, Collins is confident that the recommended alternative will enable ABC to serve its customers better and contribute to the division's financial and market performance and, consequently, to her own compensation and career advancement.

Paul Morrison, Industrial Engineer

Paul Morrison, you conclude, will also play two buying roles. He's a technical buyer because he will be concerned with the thoroughness and rigor of the proposed methodology. Morrison believes these qualities will be necessary to address the complex issues involved in selecting the best alternative. Given that he developed the in-house distribution model, he will likely focus on those parts of the methodology that focus on logistics, landed cost, and service levels. He's also a user buyer because he will undoubtedly lead the ABC project team that will use the study's results to plan for and implement the new capacity plan. If your study were to result in ABC's building a new factory, Morrison could also become plant manager at that site.

Morrison has expressed several concerns about the current situation (S_1). First, although everyone seems to agree that additional capacity is needed, no one has attempted to quantify the amount or its timing. Second, some individuals, he believes, may be pushing their own agendas, thereby advocating expansion alternatives that could be better for themselves than for ABC. Finally, and related to the previous point, he doesn't believe that the present site will support the additional manufacturing capacity needed (though adding at the present site would be advantageous to others, particularly Metzger).

Morrison expects the study to produce specific results: to define the precise amount of capacity necessary to meet the forecast, to evaluate thoroughly the alternatives both quantitatively and qualitatively, and to produce a recommendation that will enable ABC to provide capacity effectively and expeditiously.

Frank Metzger, Plant Manager

You conclude that Frank Metzger is also both a user and a technical buyer. As plant manager with intimate knowledge of ABC's manufacturing operation, he will certainly be part of the project team that uses the results of the consultant's study to plan and implement the additional capacity. In his technical buyer role, he will likely examine the methodology closely to determine that it gives adequate consideration to adding capacity at the current facility.

Metzger is concerned that his operations are already approaching capacity and that as demand continues to grow he will be forced to operate uneconomically (e.g., with excessive overtime, minimum time to maintain equipment, and premium freight costs). Like others, he agrees that ABC badly needs additional manufacturing capacity.

Metzger is looking forward to reviewing the consulting team's quantification of ABC's need for capacity. He is hopeful, however, that the amount of capacity indicated is such that most if not all can be accommodated at the existing site, particularly if newer manufacturing technology is utilized. As a result, his managerial responsibilities would increase and he would be able to promote some of his supervisors, who have supported him and performed well in the past.

Examining Your Notes: What's Missing?

In examining your detailed notes on each buyer, you now know what you know and, just as importantly, what you don't know. For example, none of the buyers, according to your determination, can be considered a coach. This makes you uneasy, given that the situation is competitive and that at least two of your competitors have done previous (and, apparently, good) work for ABC. Those firms could very well have special access to people and intelligence at ABC that you do not and perhaps will not have. According to Norm Williams, Paramount had been recommended to ABC. That's what he told Gilmore. But as far as you know, Gilmore didn't find out who the recommender was. That person could very well be (or turned into) a coach. You decide to discuss this matter also with Gilmore.

Your completed Benefits Worksheet (Exhibit 5.7) lists each buyer and his or her respective buying roles, as well as the benefits that could accrue to each by having a plan and subsequently having that plan implemented. In completing the worksheet, you focus on unique benefits to each individual, rather than on the overall corporate or collective benefits you included on the Baseline Logic Worksheet.

	Buyer/Title	Buyer Role(s) E	U	T	C	Benefits From Insight or Plan	Measurable Benefits From Implemented Plan
1	Ray Armstrong, President	✓				The right roadmap to take ABC where he wants it to go.	More cost-effective operations.
						The beginnings of a sound internal team with an appreciation of different functional disciplines and broad knowledge of company operations, encouraging diversity and different perspectives.	Success for division and employees.
							Continued good reputation of ABC and him.
						Improved ability to compete for capital funding.	
2	Norm Williams, VP Operations		✓			Will have "road map" showing how ABC should provide additional, needed capacity in most advantageous manner. This will assure his success in being able to meet cost, quality, and service performance objectives.	Successful implementation will protect compensation levels and ensure continued autonomy from Consolidated.
3	Marcia Collins, VP Marketing		✓	✓		An effective plan for increasing capacity, developed with an objective of maintaining or improving current levels of service.	Adequate capacity, in the right place, to ensure current or better levels of service.
						Service levels will be an important criterion and thus proper consideration will be given to a separate, new facility.	
4	Paul Morrison, Chief Industrial Engineer		✓	✓		Opportunity to show analytical capability using his model.	Right amount and right type of added capacity in right location to support business and marketing strategies and to satisfy demand.
						Resolution of troubling number of alternatives for expanding capacity.	Perhaps added prestige/responsibility of leading teams to implement selected plan at new sites.
5	Frank Metzger, Plant Manager		✓	✓		A plan that includes increasing capacity, either wholly or in part, at the current site.	Assuming increased capacity at current site, ability to promote well-deserving supervisors and to maintain control.

Exhibit 5.7. Benefits worksheet.

6

Selecting and Developing Themes— Determining What to Weave in Your Web of Persuasion

In Chap. 5, I indicated that if you're going to write a fully responsive proposal to me, your potential client, you need to do more than meet my buying team's requirements related to the analytical and technical aspects— the "logics"—of your proposed support. You also need to respond to the "psychologics" of our situation, to us, to our individual and group concerns, desires, and needs. I'm not devaluing expertise here. I want it. But you're not the only expert around. Your expertise is necessary, but it alone is usually not sufficient. So what else do I want?

In addition to expertise, I want a relationship, built on trust, founded on chemistry and rapport, characterized by understanding and assurance. Although I want to be confident in your technical abilities, I also want to be confident of your willingness to serve me, to put me first, to be there when I need you, to answer questions neither of us anticipated during the proposal process. That's a tall order, but I'm willing to reward you now and perhaps in the future for filling it.

Let me give you a good example of what I mean. I was once a vice president at RST, one of the world's largest industrial companies. We were introducing a new organizational concept in all our domestic and foreign factories, an effort that would be extraordinarily complex, involve massive change in the organization, and require a high level of rapport between us and the consultants. We were looking for outside support to work together with us in an ill-defined situation to detect problems, resolve issues, and implement solutions that neither of us could anticipate. The risk was potentially high, the rewards potentially higher. Nobody had tried this sort of thing before and, obviously, no consultant had ever tried to help do it.

None of this, of course, was lost on the consultant who wrote the winning proposal. Here's the first major section of that proposal letter. Study it carefully, and you'll see what I mean.

Our Understanding of Your Situation

During the past few weeks, we appreciated being included in the evolution of your thinking on this difficult project and our potential involvement to help implement your ABC Cost Concept. This letter concisely describes how we can help you successfully accelerate the worldwide integration.

Over the years, RST has managed its manufacturing on a plant-by-plant basis. As a result, similar and related products were produced using different methods and technology in different locations. For this reason, costs and quality often varied. To reduce variability and costs, you are in the process of establishing integration centers to be responsible for products or related component groups wherever they are manufactured. In other words, each center will be responsible for developing products at the lowest cost and at high quality in order to "optimize" results.

Each center will be responsible for total worldwide volume for its selected products and for developing a common manufacturing process to improve technology utilization and reduce overhead. In this way, each center will balance design, manufacturing, use of automation, and scheduling. It will become involved early in the product design effort to set design ground rules to ensure optimum production. Furthermore, it will consolidate worldwide throughput, yields, defect control, costs, inventory, turnaround time, etc., for its product or component responsibility.

Implementation of this concept will be extremely complex. This complexity was emphasized when we reviewed the matrix of centers and locations. Indeed, changes in coordination, measurement and evaluation systems, training, motivation, organizational structure, communications, and control will be significant.

Yet, the breadth of these changes is only the first complicating factor. Next is the exceptional magnitude of the change, in terms of the number of plants involved, the varieties of locations and countries, and the depth of change to your traditional manufacturing style.

In addition, the speed with which the integration will be implemented leaves little opportunity for error. Furthermore, the introduction of the ABC Cost Concept provides an additional complication of significantly higher volumes to your organization, which is traditionally accustomed to low-volume production.

Finally, no precedent exists for such a complex change except perhaps that which occurred in your own marketing organization.

What this passage has that so many proposals lack is the theme of this chapter, which is THEMES:

The

Highlighted

Essential

Messages that

Express the character of my

Story

What Themes Are

Themes are the *highlighted* messages of your proposal because they are repeated, and gain force and emphasis through their repetition. They are *essential* because they come from your understanding my and the other buyers' concerns, desires, and needs. Therefore, themes *express my story* and that of the other buyers.

The writer of the RST proposal knew (and knew that I knew) that the effort would be extraordinarily complex, would involve massive change in my organization, and would require a high level of rapport between the consultants and my people as we all worked together to detect problems, resolve issues, and recommend solutions in a situation that was ill-defined, to put it mildly. Recognizing that these three ideas (complexity, change, and working together) were key issues to be addressed during the proposed project, he used them (and others) as themes throughout the document.

In the first sentence, he subtly suggests three of the themes we will discuss here:

> ...we appreciated being included in the evolution [i.e., "change"] of your thinking on this difficult project ["complexity"] and our potential involvement ["working together"].

After narrating the past, present, and future of the improved operating concept in the next three paragraphs, he concentrates on two of the themes, beginning in paragraph four. From there on he uses "complex," "change," and related words 10 times and heightens the effect through parallelism ("breadth of these changes," "exceptional magnitude of the change," "depth of the change"). He also uses many "additive" transitions

("Indeed," "Yet," "Next," "In addition," and "Finally") to create a crescendo effect. The flourish comes in the last sentence, which is signaled by "Finally," underscored in importance by "no precedent exists," and concluded by a phrase—"complex change"—that uses both themes together.

The writer doesn't pretend that the task is less than arduous or that he has performed numerous studies similar to this one. Rather, he recognizes my concerns (my story) and makes them his own. He knows that I'm anxious and that my coworkers are anxious, and he even intentionally writes the section to *make* me anxious, to make me recall my anxiety and the high risk involved. But at precisely the right point, in that last sentence, he compliments my organization by suggesting that if any firm can weather the coming storm, it is RST. Well, maybe RST. "Perhaps" RST. Despite the compliment, he implies that we cannot do it alone; despite our considerable resources and expertise, additional support and abilities are crucial. That support is underscored by the document's next heading (which I haven't printed). "How We Can Work Together" begins the methods slot, and it continues the proposal's third theme, "working together."

By selecting and playing the right themes, then, the proposal writer demonstrates to me that he understands far more than just the logics of my situation. By the time I finish reading the first section of his proposal, he has reinforced these qualities I saw in him during our several hours of preproposal discussions: his sensitivity to the complexity of human organizations (including mine) and the cultural shocks resulting from change; his ability to work with me and my people constructively and competently to implement change. As a result, he increases his and his organization's credibility. He makes me an accepting rather than an objecting or rejecting reader, one much more inclined to agree with his proposal's later discussions of objectives, methods, qualifications, and costs. And those discussions, like this one, are certainly not boilerplate, nor were they written by a junior "just-happened-to-be-available" consultant who never met me. Clearly, the writer developed his themes specifically for my situation.

Where Themes Come From

You're not selling in a vacuum, but rather in response to my specific situation. That situation is conditioned by what the buyers, individually and collectively, on the one hand, and your competitors, on the other, bring to it. Therefore, you must (1) address the *individual* needs and desires of me and the other buyers, (2) respond to our *collective* needs and desires, and (3) counter your competition. These three actions provide you with the three sources themes come from: hot buttons, evaluation criteria, and counters to the competition. (See Exhibit 6.1.)

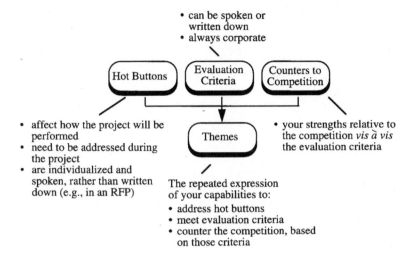

Exhibit 6.1. Where themes come from.

Hot buttons are needs and desires of single individuals that have an impact on how the project will be conducted. They are almost always psychologically oriented and process oriented. Hot buttons, therefore, have to be addressed during the project—by the way you conduct it and by how you conduct yourself. In the RST excerpt, complexity happened to be one of my hot buttons. I was concerned about the complex nature of the project, about all the possible pitfalls, including those I could see and those that I couldn't see at the time but knew would present themselves. Complexity, then, wasn't a result of the study, but it was an issue that had to be strategically addressed during the study. So the writer built into his proposal's methodology specific tasks for managing the study's complexity. And he conditioned my response to that methodology by convincing me, in his proposal's opening section, that he understood the complex nature of our undertaking.

Addressing hot buttons is extremely important in selling your services because your recognizing and acting on my hot buttons significantly helps to build the trust and chemistry that are essential to a good business relationship. And using hot buttons offers you a further advantage: they help you generate additional benefits for your proposal. The following little stories suggest how.

Several years ago, my spouse and I had our house remodeled by a contractor we would never hire again. Their expertise or craftsmanship wasn't at issue—they did a fine job at what we hired them to do. The way they did it, however, caused us unnecessary time, frustration, and anger.

In a word, they were slobs. They tracked mud inside, failed to control the dirt and dust, and even left cigarette butts on the floor. As a consequence, my spouse and I returned from work every evening with more work to do: mopping, vacuuming, and, most strenuous of all, controlling our tempers. The problem wasn't with the "what" (their expertise), but with the "how" (the application). Were we to remodel our house again, the contractors bidding on the job would be confronted with our unmistakable hot button—call it "neatness" or "cleanliness" or just plain "consideration."

Note that two effects would occur if the contractors would have addressed that hot button, neither of which involves their *technical* approach to solving our problem. First, they would alter how they work for us (assuming, of course, that they weren't already paragons of neatness). Second, we would benefit from that alteration. We would be saved both time and aggravation.

Here's another, but similar situation. You know how to drive your car, and you know a bit about how your car works, but you don't know very much at all about how to fix it. So when your car doesn't work, you take it to someone with the expertise you lack. As in some situations where you have little expertise and someone else has a great deal, you have little control and feel quite helpless. Knowledge is power, and in this case you have very little of either. When you pay the bill and the expert tells you the problem wasn't the relatively inexpensive fan belt but the much more expensive starter or alternator, you have no way of evaluating that claim, no way of knowing for certain whether or not you're being "taken." Worse, even if you're not being taken, you have no way of knowing that you're not. So when you take your car to a mechanic, you have a hot button—call it "lack of trust" or "desire for honesty" or "need for clear communication."

Again, note that if your hot button would have been addressed, two effects would have occurred, neither of which involves the mechanic's technical approach to solving your problem. First, the mechanic would have to change how he works with you (for example, by calling you for approval if the solution turned out to be different from or more expensive than what you anticipated, or by returning to you the damaged part, or by clearly showing you how or why the part was damaged). Second, you would benefit from that change. You would feel better. You'd be less anxious or apprehensive and more certain, not that the car got fixed but that what was *wrong* got fixed.

I can think of three morals from these two stories:

- *Moral 1:* Those without expertise who have to work with those who have it are frequently cautious, uncertain, and untrusting.

If I'm thinking about having you do a project for me, I'm doing so because you probably have knowledge, skills, or experience that I lack. Because what you tell me will be based on the knowledge that I lack and that you have, I don't have the proper framework to evaluate the veracity of your claims.

- *Moral 2:* If I have a hot button and you choose to address it, you will have to work with me in a certain way. Addressing hot buttons always affects how you conduct your project.

- *Moral 3:* If you do indeed address my hot button, I will benefit. Because my hot button reflects one of my needs, desires, or concerns, I will have that need, desire, or concern satisfied or addressed if you respond to that hot button during the project.

Consequently, for every hot button you identify, you should generate at least one benefit that accrues from your addressing it. Take, for example, one of ABC President Armstrong's possible hot buttons discussed in the work session of this chapter: "teaching/training." A solid teaching/training component in the project could be beneficial to him. It could help produce for Armstrong the beginnings of a more competent internal team, one that appreciates different functional disciplines and has a broader, multidisciplined view rather than a parochial orientation toward company operations.

Both hot buttons and *evaluation criteria* are used by me and others, consciously and unconsciously, to judge your proposal. Whereas hot buttons are always individual considerations, evaluation criteria are collective considerations—that is, shared and agreed-upon. While most hot buttons have emotional content (involving individual needs and desires), evaluation criteria have more technical content (involving requirements, specifications, and the like).

That said, it's important to note that one category of hot buttons does have technical content: those hot buttons of technical buyers. Marcia Collins, the VP of Marketing at ABC, has a hot button (conditioned by her technical buyer role) related to "maintaining or improving service levels." In preparing your proposal to ABC, you would certainly want to include the impact on service level as a hot button. But unless the focus on service level is shared by all members of the buying committee, it isn't likely to be one of the group's evaluation criteria.

Though evaluation criteria are corporate and may be written down in an RFP, they are not always specified in a section of the RFP that lists and sometimes weights the criteria to be used in evaluating the proposal. The following three "criteria" were essential to consider in a recent proposal to manage a hazardous waste program, even though the criteria did not appear in a lengthy RFP:

National consistency: To demonstrate our commitment to accomplishing national goals, consistency in approaches used to set priorities is essential in a decentralized program. The strategic management framework identifies key areas where national consistency is needed to ensure that we are achieving progress in meeting national goals.

Flexibility: Flexibility in setting program priorities is key to regions and states closest to environmental needs. The strategic management framework must preserve regional and state flexibility while assuring progress toward national goals.

Trade-offs: We cannot implement the entire agenda at once. Strategic management planning recognizes the need for trade-offs. We all must articulate these trade-offs and ensure that we make informed and defensible decisions about the resulting environmental and programmatic impacts.

The previous list wasn't called criteria at all, but "Principles governing strategic management of the program." However, these "principles" were used in evaluating the proposal. And the proposers certainly could have used themes like "consistency" and "flexibility" to increase the persuasiveness of their document.

Counters to the competition are those selling points that allow you to differentiate yourself from the known or likely competition's approaches or expertise. If you are a small engineering consulting firm bidding against a larger, more diverse competitor (for example, a broad-line management consulting firm) you might try to claim that your narrower focus and your size are strengths. That is, your project, you might argue, involves an engineering problem requiring nothing more than an engineering solution, especially by an organization whose relatively small client base allows for better, more client-oriented service. Of course, the larger firm would argue quite differently. Similarly, if you headed a team of in-house professionals proposing a particular study and if management were thinking of soliciting outside bids for the same study, you would likely need to argue that your team's greater familiarity with your own organization and its situation were highly advantageous and beneficial.

In generating counters to the competition, however, you must also consider this as well: *counters to the competition need to relate to the evaluation criteria.* Assume yours is an international consulting firm with 25 offices around the world and that the competitor is a "single-shingle" outfit—one consultant, perhaps a university professor, operating out of a home office. Your large firm with strategically placed offices offers you little or no competitive advantage unless your size and location are meaningful for the proposed project—that is, unless the evaluation criteria make them meaningful.

Selecting the Themes

Themes therefore come from three potential sources: hot buttons, evaluation criteria, and counters to the competition. However, not all hot buttons, evaluation criteria, and counters to the competition should become themes. Themes are your *highlighted* essential messages, and they can only be highlighted, like the italicized word in this sentence, if other things are not. You want themes to be the figure and not the ground, so you need to select them well and use them sparingly. The following selection criteria in Exhibit 6.2 will be helpful.

To see how these criteria can be applied, let's consider ABC again. The hot button "urgency" has considerable breadth: many on the buying committee have alluded to it in some manner. Capacity will soon be exceeded and, before that condition arises, a plan must be developed and implemented. Moreover, Consolidated must bless whatever plan is developed and fund it, and then ABC must implement it. Building a new facility (if that's part of the plan) will take considerable time. So "urgency" is a potential theme, and it takes on added importance because it leverages other potential themes. Paramount is prepared to do the study immediately and, perhaps, to commit substantial resources to complete it. Given their smaller sizes, the local engineering firms may not be able to react so quickly or to have the necessary staff to apply. So "urgency" has both breadth and leverage. It is relevant to most of the buyers, and it intersects with other themes related to counters to the competition.

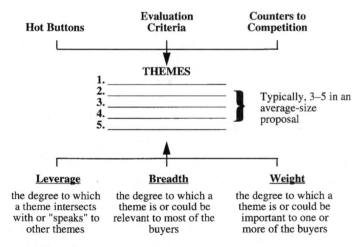

Exhibit 6.2. Criteria for selecting themes.

"Comprehensiveness" satisfies all three criteria: it has weight (there's good reason for comprehensiveness, given the necessity of persuading Consolidated to approve funding), breadth (several members of the selection committee expressed this hot button), and leverage ("comprehensiveness," as you'll see in this chapter's work session, shows up on both the Hot Buttons Worksheet and the Competition Worksheet).

Selecting your themes is a dynamic and creative process because the themes you end up with will not necessarily be phrased the same or even be the same as one or more of the hot buttons, evaluation criteria, or counters to the competition. Some of your themes will be combinations or transmutations of these.

One likely combination exists in the ABC situation. "Service levels" has considerable weight as Marcia Collins' hot button, but it doesn't appear to have considerable breadth. Morrison's hot button (which happens to be "well-defined and agreed-upon evaluation criteria") offers the same problem: it carries weight with Morrison but (as far as is known) not with others on the selection committee. Therefore, it may have little breadth. To increase the breadth of both, they could be combined. When you discuss Morrison's desire for well-defined and agreed-upon evaluation criteria, you could use service levels as an example of the kind of criteria that the study will employ. Then you would have a potential theme with both weight and breadth that appeals to multiple buyers.

The hazardous waste example discussed previously offers an example of a possible transmutation. "National consistency" and "flexibility" were two of the principles established to govern the program, and these two principles would seem incompatible and perhaps even contradictory. But a new theme could emerge from these two—call it "balance." That is, a salable quality of the proposers could be the ability to understand the national need for consistency but to remain flexible by *balancing* that need in light of the states' and regions' local circumstances. This theme of balance also leverages with the third principle listed: "trade-offs."

Developing the Themes

The Themes Development Worksheet, shown partially in Exhibit 6.3 (also see Appendix B), allows you to develop much of the persuasive content you will employ both during the proposal process and in the proposal itself. Using this worksheet, you can create a web of persuasion throughout your communication. The worksheet uses the generic-structure logic you're already familiar with:

Given my organization's situation, these are the methods, out of a universe of possible methods, that you will use to solve our problem or realize our opportunity. Given those methods, these are your qualifications for conducting them. Given those methods and qualifications, these are the benefits we will receive from your solving our problem or realizing our opportunity.

This logic can be applied to each of your proposal's themes. Assume that one of your themes is "well-defined and agreed-upon evaluation criteria." What you have to do is to write a claim or proposition or assertion—provide some evidence related to the theme—that is appropriate for each of the cells. For example:

Theme	Situation (express as potential client needs)	Methods	Qualifications	Benefits
Well-defined and agreed-upon evaluation criteria	Because of the many and varied proposed expansion options, ABC needs well-defined and agreed-upon criteria for evaluating these options.	Early in the study, we will conduct strategy sessions with all relevant interest areas within both ABC and Consolidated to establish the proper criteria and gain consensus on them.	Our proposed team understands the range of criteria that might be important to use and is adept at facilitating discussions to secure group consensus.	Because the final decision will be based on agreed-upon criteria, the selected option will be best accepted by ABC and Consolidated personnel with diverse agendas.

Exhibit 6.3. Themes Development Worksheet.

The idea here is not to come up with the exact sentences that will find their way into the proposal, but with the ideas or propositions that will later be formed precisely to support your argument.

In a completely filled out worksheet, the argument gets developed both horizontally and vertically. From left to right, the worksheet spins a web of persuasion related to your theme. By filling major proposal slots with that theme, you demonstrate your responsiveness to that hot button in four different ways: first, that you understand its existence and my desire to address it; second, that your approach is designed to consider it; third, that you are qualified to act on it; and fourth, that I will benefit by your acting on it.

When the worksheet is expanded to contain several themes, then an argument would also begin to be developed vertically for several of the proposal's major slots. For example, a completed worksheet would supply you with several good reasons for why you have designed your approach as you have and for why you believe you are best qualified to conduct it.

In the following work session, you'll see clearly how this can be applied when you fill out a Themes Development Worksheet relevant to the opportunity at ABC. This worksheet is very important: it supplies a substantial amount of the persuasive content that will help you when you prepare your proposal. You will also be filling out worksheets related to hot buttons, evaluation criteria, and counters to the competition. I should note that you will probably find that filling out these worksheets is time consuming. However, over time as you gain experience, I guarantee that you will write the proposal itself much more quickly and persuasively. Additionally, on those occasions when others help you prepare your proposal, these and the other worksheets provide an excellent method for communicating a consistent message to your team.

⇨ Chapter 6 Review:
Selecting and Developing Themes

1. *Identifying themes.* Themes are the repeated expression of your abilities and capabilities to address hot buttons, meet evaluation criteria, and counter the competition:
   - *Hot buttons* are needs and desires of individual buyers. They will have an effect on the project and must be addressed during the project. Hot buttons almost always have emotional content.
   - *Evaluation criteria* are collective needs and desires of the buyers. They are often written down. Evaluation criteria typically have technical content.
   - *Counters to the competition* are your strengths relative to the competition vis à vis the specific evaluation criteria for this proposal opportunity.

2. *Selecting themes.* Three criteria can be used to select themes:
   - *Breadth:* the degree to which the theme is or could be relevant to most of the buyers.
   - *Weight:* the degree to which the theme is or could be important to one or more of the buyers.
   - *Leverage:* the degree to which the theme intersects with or "speaks" to other themes.

3. *Developing themes.* Themes spin a web of persuasion throughout the proposal if they are developed using the Themes Development Worksheet, which uses four proposal slots (see also Exhibit 6.4).

- SITUATION: given the problem or opportunity, what is needed by the potential client, related to this theme?
- METHODS: given that need, how will the project be configured, related to this theme?
- QUALIFICATIONS: given those methods, how are you qualified to perform them, related to this theme?
- BENEFITS: given those methods and qualifications, what benefits will accrue, related to this theme?

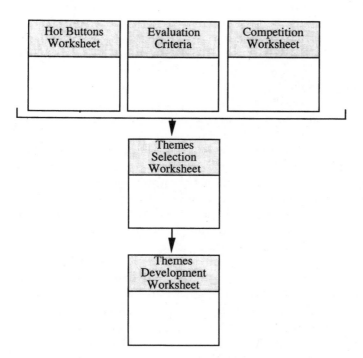

Exhibit 6.4. Identifying, selecting, and developing the themes.

Work Session 6: Identifying Hot Buttons and Evaluation Criteria, Countering the Competition, and Developing the Themes for ABC

Identifying Hot Buttons

You know that hot buttons involve the buying team members' expectations during the project and therefore they have to be addressed by the way you and your team conduct the project. You also know, because consultant Gilmore has told you and because you've seen it over and again in discussions with Gilmore and in his notes, that one of the hot buttons is *thoroughness*. Armstrong said the study needs to be "thorough and convincing." Williams said the same. Morrison hinted the same. Given these repetitions—hardly coincidental, you believe—it's quite likely that President Armstrong first sang the tune and that the others joined in the harmony.

That tune probably sounds good to the others, but for different reasons based on their buying roles and even their personalities. For Armstrong, thoroughness is a means by which he can achieve his goal of remaining competitive and convincing Consolidated to provide the capital funding. So thoroughness to him has an economic buyer, bottom-line meaning. For Morrison, however, because he's a technical buyer and because of his background and temperament, thoroughness may mean something quite different: perhaps the logical rigor required in a project of some complexity, a project whose alternatives are being advocated, he believes, without an analytical basis. The various bases, according to Morrison, need to be thoroughly and convincingly examined, ideally using his distribution model.

So as you develop your hot buttons, you try to remember that the roles individuals play influence their expectations and thus the hot buttons themselves and how they are construed. You also realize that detecting hot buttons is something of an art because you're not necessarily dealing with hard data but with feelings, desires, perceptions, and hidden agendas. You have to try to get below the obvious and into the personalities, the psychologics. Hot buttons almost always have emotional content.

For example, Armstrong said something to Morrison, who remarked about it—almost as an afterthought—to Gilmore. You had missed it when the two of you discussed his meetings, as well as the first two times you went through Gilmore's notes, but this time it struck you as possibly important. Armstrong had encouraged Morrison and his project team to develop the in-house distribution model because he had been convinced that doing the project in house was both feasible and cost-effective.

Armstrong also believed "that the project would provide a beneficial learning experience, so he gave his approval to proceed."

Armstrong, it appears, not only desires professional development but actively supports it. And, it strikes you, he has a good many managers who need it. Collins, for example, appears to know little of the operations outside of marketing. She certainly knows little of manufacturing, a point she readily admitted to Gilmore. Most likely, manufacturing and marketing don't talk very much to each other, even though what the one produces the other must sell and even though the selling itself and the customer service that goes along with it must rely on accurate production schedules, cycle-time projections, and the like. Metzger, it appears, is in a similar position, knowing much about manufacturing but little about marketing.

So if Armstrong is into *teaching/training* (that's how you decide to phrase this potential hot button, although *professional development* or *staff development* are other options), maybe you can find a way to build teaching, training, and teambuilding into your methodology.

You're particularly sensitive to this hot button because of the recent experience of one of your colleagues. He had bid on but lost a proposal to a competitor. Following up, he called the company to try to determine why the engagement had been given to another. The winning firm, he was told, had included a significant training component in their methodology. In response, your colleague remarked that no one he interviewed had said anything about a training component. Every bidder, came the reply, was told the same thing. Perhaps every bidder was. Perhaps your colleague had missed a hot button that his competitor had detected and capitalized on. Perhaps the competitor was more adept at reading between the lines and getting below the surface.

As you turn to your Hot Buttons Worksheet, you try to keep four things in mind. First, hot buttons aren't always explicitly stated. In searching for them, you should examine not only what was said but also what was unsaid, or said between the lines, or just below the surface. You're looking for the psychological, the emotional, not just the logical. Second, hot buttons can be conditioned by the buyer's role. For example, cost-related matters are likely hot buttons of an economic buyer or of a chief financial officer playing a technical buyer. Third, to make it easier to convert them into themes, you should try to designate hot buttons by key words or short phrases, like *thoroughness* or *complexity* or *involvement/respect*. Finally, for every hot button you detect, you should generate a benefit that will accrue by your addressing that hot button during the project. The likelihood of these benefits accruing often sways a buyer toward one competitor versus another. Your completed Hot Buttons Worksheet looks like Exhibit 6.5.

Hot Buttons		
Buyer	Buyer's Hot Buttons	"What desires/concerns of each buyer must be addressed during this project?" Benefits to Each Buyer From Addressing Their Hot Buttons
Armstrong	**Comprehensiveness:** "A sound, comprehensive study is critical to the future of ABC." **Urgency:** wants to "initiate the study quickly." **Thoroughness:** the study should be "thorough and convincing." **ROI/Bottom Line:** the study must be "well-documented, with ROI clearly defined," since Consolidated will closely scrutinize the request. **Teaching/Training:** According to Morrison, Armstrong's into internal development, providing learning experiences to management.	Report will be thorough and comprehensive and well-documented; and because directed to Consolidated, it will respond to urgency and therefore improve ability to compete for capital funding. The beginnings of a sound internal team with an appreciation of different functional disciplines and broad knowledge of company operations, encouraging diversity and different perspectives.
Williams	**Thoroughness:** In developing, evaluating, and recommending expansion alternatives, consultants must be "thorough and convincing" because major capital investment will be required.	Credibility from leading development of a plan accepted by Consolidated.
Collins	**Service Levels:** considering changing markets and sales distribution patterns. **Risk:** concerned about natural disasters, etc., if capacity is at one site.	Service levels and risk will be important criteria and thus proper consideration should be given to a separate, new facility.
Morrison	**Thoroughness/Logical Rigor/Complexity:** study must be done right. Complicated situation because alternatives being advocated w/out basis. Evaluations must be based on agreed-upon criteria. **Involvement/Respect?:** might desire active role in study, perhaps using his distribution model.	Perhaps added prestige/responsibility of leading teams to implement selected plan at new sites.
Metzger	**Consideration of his preferred option:** expanding capacity at the current site.	Assuming increased capacity at current site, ability to promote well-deserving supervisors and to maintain control.

Exhibit 6.5. Hot Buttons Worksheet.

Identifying Evaluation Criteria

Here, you are troubled. So far as you can tell, Gilmore identified no evaluation criteria during his discussions with ABC. True, the technical buyers have hot buttons that they, *singly,* will use to evaluate the proposal. But no shared evaluation criteria exist—at least none that you know of. And Gilmore, as far as you know, didn't ask about them. This fact has two ramifications. First, you cannot fill out the Evaluation Criteria Worksheet (Exhibit 6.6); second, because your counters to the competition need to be articulated in relation to these criteria, you must consider suspect everything you list on the Competition Worksheet. Because you haven't identified the evaluation criteria, you could be at a significant competitive disadvantage, especially since ABC has had good experience with one or more of your competitors.

Analyzing the Competition

At the end of your initial meeting with ABC, Gilmore asked which other consulting firms were likely to bid on the project. Norm Williams named three competitors. One is a firm similar to your own, with similar capabilities, against whom Paramount has competed numerous times. The other two are local companies specializing in facilities planning, plant layout, materials handling, and productivity improvement. In fact, ABC had used one of those consultants several years ago to help solve a materials handling problem.

Your task is threefold: first, to understand these competitors' strengths and weaknesses relative to those of Paramount's; second, to determine Paramount's strengths and weaknesses relative to the competition's; and finally, to determine how you can leverage your own strengths and exploit each competitor's weaknesses. Of course you also want to put yourself in your competitors' shoes and think about how they might exploit your weaknesses. To help you complete this task, you prepare a Competition Worksheet, and these are some of your thoughts as you do so:

Gilmore knows the capabilities of your major competitor all too well. Paramount has competed against them with lackluster results. Once they won, three times they lost, and on one occasion Paramount and the competitor both lost to a third firm. Because this competitor's capabilities are every bit as diverse and strong as Paramount's, you believe it's important to have much more intelligence about them than you now have. On the engagement Paramount won, for example, did the client make available this competitor's proposal? If so, what did the proposal contain, and what can you learn from it? On the studies he lost, was he able to find out not only why he lost but also why this competitor won? In all these situations,

Potential Client Evaluation Criteria	"What criteria will the buying committee use, collectively or individually?"	
Evaluation Criteria		**Relative Weighting**
1		
2		
3		
4		
5	None Identified to Date	
6		
7		
		100%

Exhibit 6.6. Evaluation Criteria Worksheet.

did the proposal evaluation committees use evaluation sheets or circulate memos or otherwise keep records of their deliberations, and if so, did Gilmore request access to those documents? If he did not get insight at the time, can he get it now? Have there been other instances when your firm (but not Gilmore specifically) bid against this competitor on similar kinds of studies, and if so, what lessons were learned?

At this point, you wonder if your firm even *has* a "lessons learned" process, an established procedure for answering questions like the preceding and a computerized database containing the answers. You decide to discuss this issue with Gilmore, along with the matter about the evaluation criteria.

This competitor's weaknesses? Perhaps because of their success rate against Paramount and because of their excellent reputation, your competitor might be somewhat complacent in addressing ABC's needs. Or perhaps the ABC project may not be important enough for them to mount a major proposal effort. But all this, you realize, is pure speculation, and dangerous speculation at that. You're wooing *yourself* into complacency (and making yourself feel less anxious) by surmising that this fierce competitor, this firm that has beaten Paramount all too often, will suddenly become complacent (and just at the right time, too—when *you* are writing this proposal). Nevertheless, you record these supposed weaknesses in the designated place on your worksheet, making a mental note that you're not very satisfied with your analysis.

You have just as much difficulty assessing the two local competitors, but for different reasons: You're not familiar with them and you haven't found any details listed in your research of consulting firms. However, you suspect that they have strong capabilities in specific functional areas to be addressed during the proposed study. And you know, of course, that one of those companies has a major strength: It has already worked successfully with ABC. An equally important strength will be their cost. Since their proposed fees could be tens of thousands of dollars less than yours, how will you be able to communicate value for your higher cost service?

Since they aren't full-service firms, these competitors have definite weaknesses, you believe, because they don't have expertise in all of the functional areas to be addressed during the study, including (among others) customer service and network analysis, nor have they sufficient experience and knowledge to properly evaluate the critical qualitative factors. In addition, their staffs may be too small to enable them to initiate and complete the study quickly, which is a major concern (hopefully, a hot button) to key ABC management.

Your proposal strategy will have to stress the comprehensive nature of the project, which will demand a wide range of business skills probably beyond the more functional capabilities of these two firms. But you must also stress your considerable strength in the specialized skills of these smaller firms while convincing ABC that they need more than such skills. You can counter the one firm's successful experience with ABC by stressing Paramount's successful completion of similar studies for comparable companies. Above all, you will have to stress the added-value provided by your full-service firm and perhaps the risks to ABC of choosing a consulting firm whose more narrow focus could result in a study less comprehensive and thorough.

In these situations, there's always one other possible competitor: in this case, ABC itself, the potential client. Morrison admitted to Gilmore that he had volunteered to do the study in house. For all you know, Morrison might be working behind the scenes even now to sell this approach. Or, during the selection process, he could take one or another of the consultant's methodologies and try to convince Armstrong that Morrison's team could use it. You consider these possibilities unlikely, however. Besides, you will undoubtedly have good themes to counter this in-house competition.

Because, you decide that in-house competition is unlikely, you don't complete that portion on your Competition Worksheet, which looks like Exhibit 6.7.

Determining and Developing the Themes

The themes you selected are in the worksheet in Exhibit 6.8, the worksheet that will supply your proposal and presentation with the majority of its persuasion. In the first column of each row, you record a theme; for example:

Well-defined and agreed-upon evaluation criteria

In the second column (SITUATION), you state ABC's *needs* related to that theme:

Because of the many and varied proposed expansion alternatives, ABC needs well-defined and agreed-upon criteria for evaluating these alternatives.

In the third column (METHODS), you explain how your study will address that need:

Early in the study, we will conduct strategy sessions with all relevant interest areas within ABC to establish and gain consensus on the proper criteria.

Competition

"Based upon the evaluation criteria, how do we counter competitors' strengths?"

Known or Likely Competitors (Including Those In House)	Considering the Evaluation Criteria for This Opportunity..Competitors'	
	Strengths	**Weaknesses**
■ A Major Competitor	■ Strong, diversified consulting skills	■ May not be sufficiently experienced or creative to identify full range of expansion alternatives
■ Local "A" & Local "B"	■ Capabilities equal to those of Paramount's	■ Probably lack marketing abilities needed to assess forecasts
	■ Specialized capabilities in some functional areas relevant to proposed study	■ Probably don't have adequate logistics analysis abilities
	■ Has performed satisfactory work for ABC (Local "B")	■ May lack financial analysis abilities to convincingly evaluate alternatives
		■ May not have sufficient staff to initiate and complete study quickly
		■ May not be sufficiently knowledgeable to evaluate qualitative factors

■ **"How might we counter competitor strengths or exploit their weaknesses?"**

	Our Strengths	Our Weaknesses
■ Demonstrate strong desire to work with ABC by being responsive and by proposing a joint team		
■ Focus on track record of working successfully with ABC-"niche" companies		
■ Emphasize establishing comprehensive nature of project that will require wide range of functional skills to convincingly identify and evaluate alternatives		
■ Without understating need for facility planning, plant layout, and material handling skills (which Paramount can demonstrate), show that needed skills go beyond these capabilities		
■ Counter Local "B's" previous experience by discussing successful projects for similar companies		

	Our Strengths	Our Weaknesses
■ Us	[need to talk to Gilmore]	[need to talk to Gilmore]

■ **"How might competition counter our strengths or exploit our weaknesses?"**
[need to talk to Gilmore]

Exhibit 6.7. Competition Worksheet.

In the fourth column (QUALIFICATIONS), you explain your qualifications for addressing the need for well-defined and agreed-upon evaluation criteria:

> *Our staff understands the range of quantitative and qualitative criteria that might be important to use and is adept at facilitating discussions to secure group consensus.*

In the last column (BENEFITS), you state the benefits of meeting the need:

> *Because the final decision will be based on agreed-upon criteria, the selected alternative will be best accepted by persons with diverse agendas, both within ABC and Consolidated.*

As you complete subsequent rows for your additional themes, you try to stay alert to the interrelationships among the themes, the lines of force that connect them. For example, your *broad business perspective,* a counter to some of the competitors, will help ensure the study's *comprehensiveness,* a hot button. So in writing or rewriting the row for one of these themes, you try to include language that intersects with the another. Your completed Themes Development Worksheet will look like Exhibit 6.8.

You now have your web of persuasion, spun out among the proposal's various slots: SITUATION, METHODS, QUALIFICATIONS, and BENEFITS. In subsequent work sessions, you will place that persuasion strategically, throughout your written proposal (and throughout your discussions and your proposal presentation as well).

Theme	Situation	Methods	Qualifications	Benefits
☐ Urgency	Because forecasted demand will outstrip capacity in near future and because adding new capacity will require long lead time, study must be started and completed and decision must be made quickly.	We will have frequent progress reviews so that you are aware of preliminary conclusions and direction quickly. We will involve you in writing final report, which as we've discussed, will actually be your proposal to Consolidated, thus eliminating one step in the approval process.	We will commit capable staff immediately and complete the study quickly.	By our beginning and completing the study quickly we will help expedite the decision-making process.
☐ Comprehensiveness ☐ Thoroughness ☐ Complexity	Adundance of expansion alternatives, undefined criteria, and need for Consolidated's approval require a comprehensive, thorough study.	We will carefully define and evaluate all viable alternatives, using quantitative and qualitative evaluation criteria. We will make use, when appropriate, of the in-house distribution model developed by Paul Morrison.	Our strong manufacturing, financial, and strategy development capabilities will enable us to define the full range of expansion alternatives and evaluate them thoroughly.	ABC will have basis for making sound expansion decision and convincing Consolidated of its correctness and desirability.

Exhibit 6.8. Themes Development Worksheet.

119

Theme	Situation	Methods	Qualifications	Benefits
☐ Teaching ☐ Training	ABC has the opportunity to train a cadre of its management to analyze and plan for future manufacturing capacity.	We will form a joint ABC/Paramount study team, with ABC managers playing an integral part.	Our people are experts transferring knowledge, building teams, and managing and implementing change.	ABC managers will have the ability to periodically update study and assess capacity needs as business conditions change, with minimal outside support.
☐ Well-defined and agreed-upon evaluation criteria	Because of the many and varied proposed expansion alternatives, ABC needs well-defined and agreed-upon criteria for evaluating those alternatives.	Early in the study, we will conduct strategy sessions with all relevant interest areas within ABC to gain consensus on and establish the proper evaluation criteria.	Our staff understands the range of criteria that might be important to use and is adept at leading discussions to secure group consensus.	Because the final decision will be based on agreed-upon criteria, the selected alternative will be best accepted by persons with diverse agendas.
☐ Broad, business perspective ☐ Extensive functional skills	In selecting the best alternative, ABC must consider each alternative's multiple impacts on their business. [Note: relate to "complexity" theme.]	Our methodology will be designed to draw upon the expertise of our multi-disciplined team with skills in marketing, manufacturing strategy, facilities planning, logistics financial analysis, and human resources.	keting, manufacturing strategy, facilities planning, logistics financial analysis, and human resources.	Given our broad business perspective, ABC can be assured of the right alternative for meeting its needs related to cost and customer service.

Exhibit 6.8. Themes Development Worksheet (*Continued*).

Part 3

Proposal Preparation

If you've done all the work in Parts One and Two, your proposal or presentation is almost ready to write itself, slot by slot: SITUATION, OBJECTIVES, METHODS, QUALIFICATIONS, and BENEFITS. Up to this point, I've shown you how to generate the filling for these slots; now, it's simply a matter of strategically organizing that material by dropping it into the right places. While there are no rules, there is a framework for using all the information you've developed, and a way to use it both logically and psychologically. You'll see how all the work you've done to this point will save you considerable time in preparing the actual document or presentation.

But time, of course, isn't the only issue. I wrote this book not just to help you become more efficient, but also to help you become more effective so that you can gain the additional points you need to win. By the time you finish Part 3, you'll understand not only how to incorporate the information from the worksheets into the various parts of your proposal but also how to construct and organize these parts so they result in a seamless, compelling, and persuasive argument.

7

Writing the Situation and Objectives Slots

In Chap. 1, I emphasized that proposals that win for me aren't a collection of separate sections or chapters or slots but rather a coherent argument woven throughout the document or presentation. For this reason, it's difficult for me to claim that one proposal slot is more important than another. In some situations, cost could be crucial; in others, your or your firm's reputation or qualifications; in still others, the methodology, especially when the tasks are numerous and the project's management will be complex.

But let's limit the variables and try to keep this relatively simple. Let's assume a competitive situation with multiple bidders whose objectives, methods, qualifications, and costs are all similar. Everything else being equal, your competitive edge could lie in the situation slot, which is often formed into a section called "Background" or "Business Issues" or "Our Understanding of Your Situation."

SITUATION is usually my first significant contact with your proposal and, in some cases, with you. It may be my first significant opportunity to sense who you are, what you believe, how strongly you believe it, how knowledgeable and competent you are regarding my problem or opportunity, and how qualified you are to solve or realize it. Later, you'll likely discuss your firm's qualifications. But from the first word in SITUATION, you're already displaying (or not displaying) your abilities, and projecting (or not projecting) a desirable image of you and your firm. You're already demonstrating (or not demonstrating) that you know my industry, organization, and culture and that you can come into my organization, deal with a wide variety of people, sift through masses of often conflicting information, and achieve our objectives. If you do demonstrate all that, by the way, you'll be displaying your qualifications much more persuasively than most qualifications sections can.

The situation slot contains four components: story/S_1, questions, needs, and closing/S_2. As you'll see, each of these components offers you a significant opportunity to convince me that you understand my problem or opportunity and know what it takes to solve or realize it.

The Story/S_1 Component

To describe your understanding of my current situation, your story/S_1 component should tell me a story by narrating a sequence of events. Why tell a story? Because I and my colleagues like stories and become involved in them. History is a story. So are biographies, plays, movies, novels, newspaper articles, soap operas, and even jokes. I like, read, and need stories so much that even when I sleep I can't help but tell stories to and about myself: I dream. Stories are inherently interesting—I've never met anyone who didn't like them. And inherently interesting to me and everyone else on the buying committee is a story about our organization and current situation. That situation has a history—a past that led to and a present that is affected by the problem or opportunity, and, implicitly, a future that will result in our problem or opportunity being solved or realized.

You be the judge. Here are two sentences that began the situation slots in proposals I received when working in the health care industry. Which has more power, more force, more reader-interest?

- Mercy is a 300-bed hospital located in Chicago, Illinois.
- As Mercy grew to 300 beds, its business objectives began to change.

The first sentence contains unnecessary (and redundant) information: I already know that Mercy is a hospital located in Chicago, since the proposal is addressed to Mercy in the first place and I went to work there most every day. The sentence also portrays all the research abilities and problem-solving skills of a fourth grader: it demonstrates only that you can find information from an annual report or a company brochure; it doesn't offer you a good opportunity to begin demonstrating your understanding of my, the reader's, situation.

But even all that doesn't get to the heart of the matter. The plain truth is that the first sentence is dead. Lifeless. Uninteresting. Boring. Why? Because there's no *time* in it, no sequence of causes and effects, actions and reactions. It's static. It doesn't *move*. It's more like a rock, changeless, than an organization that, like my organization and yours, is a living, breathing, organism that constantly changes and whose change needs to be managed, which is *your* job, in this proposed project.

The first sentence, then, is static; the second, dynamic. The first is inanimate, outside of time—like death—and it has about as much interest. The second is animate; it moves because it contains time and the passage of time—like life. The first contains only facts (facts I already know); the second subordinates the facts to the story. As the beginning of a story, the sentence compels my interest because I want to know what will happen next. I want to know the rest of the plot. Your strategy, then, should be to include in your story/S_1 component the necessary information, the facts, about my organization, but to subordinate that information to your story about my problem or opportunity.

Too often, situation slots are written with the goal of feeding back information to me so that I will know that you have listened. But I want you to do more than just listen. I want you to demonstrate that you have not only listened but that you have *understood*—that you can take the information I have given you and analyze it, synthesize it, place it in some context, and even educate me in the process. To demonstrate to me that your project won't be a data dump of undigested information, there are four questions in Exhibit 7.1 germane to the story/S_1 component that you can answer.

Answering the first question, about the causes, the history, of the situation, allows you to begin your story, as you narrate the events that caused the problem or opportunity. These causes can be internal (new company initiatives, changes in management) or external (aggressive moves by competitors, advances in technology, changes in the economic environment). By discussing the internal factors, you can demonstrate your understanding of my company, people, and cultural issues. By analyzing the external factors, you can demonstrate your knowledge of my industry, market, and competition. When possible and appropriate, you want to educate me about my organization, my market, and my perspectives on the situation.

- *Causes:* What is the history, the external and internal factors, that gave rise to our problem or opportunity?

- *Problem/opportunity:* What is the problem or opportunity?

- *Effects:* What are its effects on me and my organization? (The actual ones of not solving the problem; the potential ones of not realizing the opportunity.)

- *Attempted Solutions:* What, if anything, has been done to solve the problem or realize the opportunity, and what resulted?

Exhibit 7.1. The story/S_1 component.

In answering the first question, as well as the second and third, you must keep in mind that *my* perception of our current situation, S_1, and its causes and effects might be different from the perceptions of others on the buying committee. Your goal is to weave a coherent story that incorporates all buyers' individual stories. That is, your story/S_1 component needs to narrate the individual perceptions of S_1, and their causes and effects. This isn't an easy task, especially if our individual stories differ significantly. The danger is that the buying committee's lack of agreement could result in your story component's lack of coherence or consistency.

Frequently, however, you can turn our lack of agreement to your advantage, since lack of agreement on the buyers' part underscores the problematic nature of our situation and reinforces our need to reconcile disagreement to achieve our desired result, S_2, that will remove each buyer's pain or uncertainty. That is, lack of agreement on the buyers' part can reinforce our need for an objective third party sensitive to differing perceptions and desires.

The fourth question, on attempted solutions, applies only if we have previously attempted to move from S_1 to S_2, either through internal efforts or those of consultants. Given that you are being considered for the project, our attempt, quite likely, was unsuccessful. In this part of the story/S_1 component, you can demonstrate your understanding of what went wrong and, implicitly, what pitfalls therefore need to be avoided.

The following paragraphs contain a sample story/S_1 component. Note how the writer discusses the external factors that have caused a transition to a deregulated banking environment as well as the opportunities this transition affords. Should she also have discussed the effects? By understanding that the story/S_1 component can contain causes, problem/opportunity, effects, and attempted solutions, you know what you can write into the component, and you can check what you might have unintentionally omitted.

Background

As international standards for capital requirements force liberalization of financial regulations, your organization is challenged by the tremendous transition currently occurring in the Japanese banking industry. Deregulation is leading to heightened competition for domestic banks, and small community and regional banks are threatened by larger, more capital-rich financial institutions. These institutions have already started to increase market share through mergers and acquisitions.

To remain competitive, regional banks now face new challenges to obtain new retail customer accounts and to maintain the loyalty of their existing customer base. Through your organization, these regional banks seek innovative ways to differentiate themselves and cope with deregulation to compete profitably against the super-regional Japanese banks.

With this transition to a deregulated banking environment, your community bank consortium has the opportunity to become more innovative and differentiated among the competition in providing products and services not formerly available in the regulated atmosphere.

The Questions Component

The story/S_1 component grabs my interest by involving me in a narrative about my organization and about how we got to where we are today. It also demonstrates your problem-solving skills by presenting your analysis of my organization's problem or opportunity. Now, by asking questions, the questions component (Exhibit 7.2) helps to maintain my interest and continue to demonstrate your analytical skills.

> - What key questions must be answered to solve the problem or realize the opportunity?

Exhibit 7.2. The questions component.

Questions encourage my interest because they help you create a dialogue with me; they invite my participation. A spoken statement like "It's cloudy today" leaves little room for my response, but a question like "Is it cloudy today?" invites a response and some judgment. A statement is convergent; it closes things off. A question is divergent; it creates an invitational pause, allowing me to respond and participate in the dialogue. Because reading or listening is a participatory rather than a passive activity, questions encourage involvement and help me move more thoughtfully through your document or presentation.

One of the most important qualities of a good problem solver (that's one of the characteristics I want you to possess) is the ability to ask the right questions. As long as scientists believed malaria was caused by bad air (in Italian, that's what the word means), they were asking the wrong questions and couldn't determine the cause of the disease. When, however, they asked, "Is it caused by a microorganism?" they could begin to identify a specific organism and the process of transmission. By identifying the salient issues of our situation and by phrasing them as questions, you demonstrate to me that you can identify those issues and formulate those questions whose answers will help direct us to ensure a successful project.

Questions can provide yet another strategic advantage: they allow you to address a buyer's issue without your having to take a position on that issue. Consider the situation at ABC. Metzger wants to expand at the current site. Of course, you don't know at the proposal stage if expanding there is ABC's best option, but you can let Metzger know that you're sensitive to that option, that you have heard him, if you use a question like this: "How much expansion potential exists at the current facility?"

Collins and Morrison, on the other hand, are more concerned about service levels and distribution costs, which would quite likely improve if ABC built a new facility closer to the company's growing markets. You can let Collins and Morrison know that you're sensitive to their concerns, that you have also heard them, if you use questions like these: "Even if resources can be provided at the present location, does it make economic sense to add them there or to make the investment elsewhere? For example, will service levels increase and transportation costs decrease at a new geographic location?" Through these questions, you haven't come down on Metzger's side or on Collins' or Morrison's. You haven't alienated any of them by taking a position. In fact, you have probably satisfied all of them by demonstrating that you've listened.

Where do you get the questions for your questions component? The component raises the key questions that must be answered to solve the problem or realize the opportunity. How you will do so is explained in your methodology. Therefore, that's where you want to look.

More specifically, you can go to your pyramid. Consider the pyramids for the proposal to XYZ in Chap. 4:

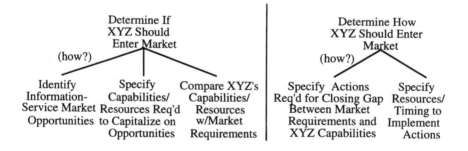

The second line implies that you would answer five key questions to achieve the project's objectives:

- What opportunities exist for XYZ in the information service market?

- What capabilities and resources are required to capitalize on these opportunities?

- What gaps exist between these required capabilities and resources and XYZ's?

- What actions are required to close these gaps?

- What resources and how much time are necessary to close the gaps?

Note the strategy here. A questions component like this not only provides evidence for your problem-solving ability; it also prepares me for your methodology. If I buy the questions in your situation slot, you have presold your methodology.

Of course this component could and should include other questions. If you believe that I desire additional detail, you could list subquestions beneath the five main questions. These subquestions would be taken from lower levels on the pyramid. You might also want to use questions that respond to hot buttons, evaluation criteria, and counters to the competition. Even if you don't, you could phrase the questions derived from your pyramid so that they address hot buttons and other thematic material. For example, if urgency were a theme, the fourth question could be phrased like this: "What actions are required to close these gaps *within the tight time frame required?*"

The following passage, which continues the "Background" section we've been discussing about the Japanese banking industry, contains a questions component:

> However, the transition necessary to change from traditional marketing protocols to new ways of marketing bank services will require a structured investigation that answers the following questions:
>
> - What are the essential customer needs and requirements that will attract new business opportunities for retail banks?
> - What product, pricing, and promotional tools are necessary to implement and support effective marketing plans, new product development, and delivery systems?
> - What type of technology and systems support are necessary to administer new products, services, and marketing efforts?
> - What marketing strategies have successful regional banks in the United States used since deregulation, and what performance resulted from implementing these strategies?

Before I can make the transition from S_1 to S_2, your project will have to answer important questions. Articulating them in the questions component suggests to me that you will be able to do so. Framing these questions also forces you to think hard about the project issues, assumptions, and hypotheses.

- What are the key issues that must be resolved?
- Which issues are crucial and which tangential?
- Given the crucial issues, how will your approach and methodology be designed to resolve them?
- In resolving them, what benefits will accrue to my organization and what value will be added?

The last two questions suggest an important function of the questions component: it helps SITUATION speak to other proposal slots, in this case to METHODS and BENEFITS. In fact, as I'll show you later in this chapter, the questions component is so intimately related to OBJECTIVES that it is sometimes strategic to place your project's objectives and the questions component in a separate section.

The Needs Component

Persuasion, I have said, occurs at the intersection of my needs and your abilities and capabilities. The needs component (Exhibit 7.3) allows you to articulate these needs of mine that you are qualified to meet.

> ■ What is needed (related to hot buttons, evaluation criteria, and counters to the competition) to answer these questions?

Exhibit 7.3. The needs component.

Because the needs component focuses on my hot buttons, my evaluation criteria, and counters to your competition, it should be heavily laden with themes.* In the following sample, a continuation of the proposal we've been discussing, note the several themes (italicized):

> The new methods for marketing bank services will require a measurable *change* in the way small banks provide and market their retail business. This in turn will require a commitment on management's part to *change* from traditional customer service and response methods to new strategies, and to do so *as quickly as possible.* As a result, your organization needs *experienced and innovative professionals* cognizant of the large magnitude of *changes* already and potentially occurring from deregulation. These professionals must be *sensitive to the Japanese cultural and business environment* and aware of how *quickly change* can occur.
>
> The investigation will require reliable data, *organized team players,* and *quick results* to implement these *changes* in a most *critically timely manner;* you need a *"jump start"* on the competition.

You might have noticed that much of the content of this needs component is expressed "objectively." Nowhere in the paragraphs does the writer explicitly state that she is an experienced and innovative professional, an

---

*In fact, as you'll see in this chapter's worksession, your needs component can come almost entirely from your completed Themes Development Worksheet.

organized team player, or sensitive to the Japanese culture and environment. Instead, she defines these qualities as properties that the buyer needs. As early as the next paragraph, in the closing/S_2 component, she will begin to suggest that the qualities the buyer needs are the qualities that she and her firm in fact have. And the remainder of the proposal will weave in and reinforce these points.

The needs component, then, doesn't state your qualifications directly. It's much too early and inappropriate for that. At this point you want only to identify the qualifications worth stating—those you have and will later address in detail. Thus, by framing my needs in terms of the qualities you will bring to the project, you begin early in the proposal to tilt the playing field to your advantage.

The Closing/S_2 Component

The function of the closing/S_2 component (Exhibit 7.4) is to provide smooth transitions from the text above it and to the text below it, to state the project's objective(s), and to conclude the situation slot with a closing oriented toward me, your potential client.

- Backward transition from needs component

- Forward transition to METHODS

- Project objective(s) (the expression of S_2)

- Briefly stated benefits, if not immediately apparent in the objectives

Exhibit 7.4. The closing/S_2 component.

The closing can include briefly stated themes related to hot buttons, evaluation criteria, and counters to the competition. These themes could emphasize your experience, expertise, past performance, or previous relationship with me or others in my organization or industry. Or they could sell certain aspects of your methodology or workplan. Depending on the overall length of the proposal, the closing/S_2 component might be two or more paragraphs or a single sentence such as the one below that completes the sample background section we have been considering:

> To meet these needs, we have designed an approach for developing a plan that, after implementation, will enable the community retail bank consortium to achieve the benefits of increased competitiveness in the deregulated market.

The Questions
Component Is Modular

You probably noticed that the background section I used as an illustration contained both S_1 and S_2, both a discussion of the current situation's problem/opportunity and the objective that expressed the desired result. This strategy allows you, within the document's very first section, to begin by explaining your understanding of where I am now, before the project starts, and to end by describing where I want to be, after the project is completed. All I've done is combine two slots, SITUATION and OBJECTIVES, into one section. The next section, on methods, will then discuss how your proposed approach will get me from one place to the other—that is, from my current situation, S_1, to my desired result, S_2.

Other strategies, however, are possible. (Other strategies are always possible!) For example, you could combine OBJECTIVES and METHODS in one section, which could be called "Objectives and Methods," or just plain "Methods," or any number of things. This strategy also makes sense. In one section, you would begin with the ends, the objectives, and then, in the bulk of the section, go on to describe the means to achieve them.

Another strategy, of course, would be to discuss the objectives in a single section. This strategy, however, can cause aesthetic problems because nestled between two long sections (for example, "Background" and "Methods") would be a very short section on objectives. You can lengthen that section by including the questions component there.

The questions in that component are intimately related both to SITUATION and to the project's objective(s). Therefore, if your project has two or three overall objectives, you can generate salient questions related to each. And you can indicate the logical relationship between each objective and the relevant questions by grouping them.

Exhibit 7.5 provides an example. Note that the exhibit contains a three-paragraph story/S_1 component (discussing the problem, causes, and effects) and a one-paragraph needs component. The questions component is in the objectives section.

This exhibit also demonstrates yet another option: the questions cannot only be moved from "Objectives" to "Background," they can also be distributed among the needs. In this case, you don't have separate questions and needs components but a combined questions and needs component.

I don't mean to overwhelm you with options; I only want to suggest that you have them—and that there aren't any hard and fast rules. You have an entire repertoire of strategic moves, and the more strategies you consider, the better chance you have of choosing the one most appropriate for my situation. What's appropriate will always depend on the situation and how you assess me and my colleagues on the buying committee. Let me summarize some of the options for you:

- The objectives can be stated at the end of the background section, at the beginning of the methods section, or in a separate section in between.

- The questions can exist as a component within the background section, distributed within the needs component, or distributed among the objectives within an objectives section.

Background

Although a great deal of research on writing has occurred in the last 20 years, very little study has been done on the discourse community that, along with government, probably produces more writing than any other: the business environment...

Until recently (and even now, rarely) writing researchers have not studies organizations and "lived" within them long enough to examine how writing is produced. Rarely have they had access to the written products of business writers, and rarer still the opportunity to examine all the drafts such writers use in composing their documents....

Consequently, next to nothing is known about how business writers compose and revise their proposals and reports or about how writers' composing processes are affected by their organizations' traditions and practices. As a result, university teachers need more knowledge about how best to prepare students to write for the world of work.

Gaining that knowledge is possible if at least three needs are met. First is the need to analyze and understand how business communicators write. Second is the need to examine how the writers' organizations influence and perhaps even determine their writing strategies and practices. Third is the need to develop new pedagogies and curricula to enhance the quality of writing instruction in the schools, so that students can be prepared to write effectively for the world of work.

Objectives

To meet these needs, the proposed project will:

- **Determine the composing and revising processes of business writers**

How do they go about defining their writing tasks and intended audience? To what extent are their documents composed collaboratively? What are the methods of collaboration? What processes of composition are used from the time the writing task is assigned to when the document is completed?

- **Describe how documents are produced in the business environment**

What organizational traditions and practices influence the way documents are written? How does the document move through the organization as it is being produced?

- **Determine the requirements for effective undergraduate and graduate curricula in business and professional communication**

What kinds of documents are the most important for students to learn to write? What courses should be offered to better train students to write effectively on the job? What methods and materials would be relevant for such courses? How should those courses be integrated into an intelligent curriculum?

Exhibit 7.5. "Questions" as a modular component.

The Situation Slot and Competitive Advantage

The story/S_1, questions, and needs components allow you to present, not only an interesting story, but more importantly, a logical and persuasive argument. They can help you project an image of yourself as competent, organized, logical, analytical, knowledgeable, thorough, relevant, coherent, insightful, and creative. These are generic attributes of a good problem solver, characteristics that can be presented to me long before a logically written METHODS validates them and a relevant QUALIFICATIONS reinforces them. You are showing me, not telling me, your capabilities within the context of my situation.

Moreover, after considering these components in proposal after proposal, you'll find that you can compose the situation slot more easily and quickly because you will have developed a schema, an internal formula or "script," just as you have probably developed a script for proposals in general. Proposal writers have difficulty writing SITUATION because they haven't developed a formula for what to consider in this slot. The preceding structure supplies you with that formula. While not a rule, it provides a guideline regarding what kind of information to consider and where in the slot to place it.

The components also help you make SITUATION speak to other slots in the proposal. The questions and needs you present relate directly to your stated objectives and your approach to achieve them. Their presentation will provide implied but convincing evidence regarding your qualifications as a problem solver.

Finally, like an overture in a symphony, SITUATION contains the themes developed later, in subsequent slots of the proposal. As a result, your situation slot gets you and your proposal off to a good start, as you begin at the beginning to convince me of one of your proposal's major claims: you know my industry, you know me, you know my organization and its challenges, problems, and opportunities, and you can solve or realize them, maybe not as inexpensively as someone else—but better.

⇨ Chapter 7 Review: Writing the Situation and Objectives Slots

1. The situation slot has four components that help to answer the following questions:

Story/S$_1$

- *Causes:* What is the history, the external and internal factors that gave rise to the problem or opportunity?
- *Problem/opportunity:* What is the problem or opportunity?
- *Effects:* What are the effects on individual buyers and their organization? (The actual ones of not solving the problem; the potential ones of not realizing the opportunity.)
- *Attempted solutions:* What, if anything, has been done to solve the problem or realize the opportunity, and what resulted?

Questions

- What key questions must be answered to solve the problem or realize the opportunity?

Needs

- What is needed (related to hot buttons, evaluation criteria, and counters to the competition) to answer these questions?

Closing/S$_2$

- Backward transition from needs component
- Forward transition to METHODS
- Project objective(s) (the expression of S_2)
- Briefly stated benefits, if not immediately apparent in the objectives

2. The objectives do not have to be stated at the end of the background section. They can begin the methods section or exist as a separate section.

3. The questions component is modular. It can exist as a stand-alone component within the background section, it can be distributed within the needs component, or it can be distributed among the objectives within an objectives section. Questions are derived from the methodology's key actions (pyramid) and activities, especially if these activities are related to themes. Questions can also be used to address differing buyers' perceptions without your having to take a position on them, without having to come down on one side or another of a potentially controversial issue. (See Exhibit 7.6.)

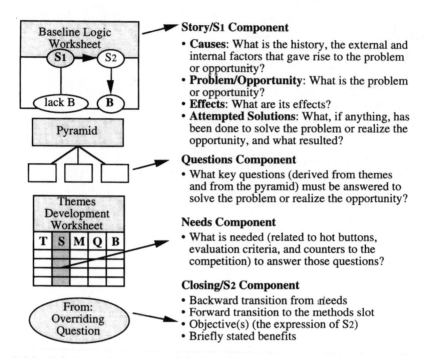

Story/S1 Component

- **Causes**: What is the history, the external and internal factors that gave rise to the problem or opportunity?
- **Problem/Opportunity**: What is the problem or opportunity?
- **Effects**: What are its effects?
- **Attempted Solutions**: What, if anything, has been done to solve the problem or realize the opportunity, and what resulted?

Questions Component

- What key questions (derived from themes and from the pyramid) must be answered to solve the problem or realize the opportunity?

Needs Component

- What is needed (related to hot buttons, evaluation criteria, and counters to the competition) to answer those questions?

Closing/S2 Component

- Backward transition from needs
- Forward transition to the methods slot
- Objective(s) (the expression of S2)
- Briefly stated benefits

Exhibit 7.6. Writing the situation and objectives slots.

Work Session 7: Writing the Situation and Objectives Slots for ABC

Writing the Story/S_1 Component

Before beginning to write the story/S_1 component, you review the Baseline Logic Worksheet (that you filled out in Chap. 2). You also consider the large amount of story-component material from your and Gilmore's notes as well as from the extensive in-house research that you've conducted. From these notes and research, you know, for example, that:

- Industry unit sales have been fairly stable and total market forecasts indicate only modest growth.

- Despite stable industry sales, demand for ABC's products has been growing consistently, with associated (though modest) increases in market share, because of high-quality, good customer service, and competitively priced products.

- Projected demand threatens to exceed available capacity.

- Lack of adequate manufacturing capacity could certainly stall ABC's growth.

- Geographic shifts in both population and households have changed patterns of demand and suggest that to maintain or improve customer service some manufacturing capacity should be located closer to high-growth areas.

- Several expansion alternatives have been proposed, though little agreement exists among ABC's management.

- A major area of disagreement could be the issue of control versus risk as it relates to expanding at the major facility only versus increasing capacity at one or another regional facilities or at another location.

- Consensus exists about ABC's needing a plan and soon.

Your task is to paint a picture of the various buyers' combined perceptions of the current situation, as well as their combined perceptions of the related causes and effects.

In doing so, you want to be certain that you address several of the buyers' concerns: Collins' on customer service and its impact on market share; Armstrong's on the relationship with Consolidated; Morrison's on distribution costs and potential use of his model; Williams' on the threat of increased operating costs; and Metzger's on expanding in other than the major facility. You also want to initiate some themes: "urgency" comes to mind, as does "complexity." After several drafts, and in a fairly forceful voice cognizant of the threats to ABC's market share and position within Consolidated, you come up with the following:

The Situation at ABC

Over the past five years, household appliance shipments by ABC and your competitors have been fairly stable, and projections suggest only modest total growth over the next five years in your mature industry.

Despite the relative stability of these shipments industrywide, ABC has managed to increase its share of the household appliance market primarily by producing high-quality products at competitive costs and by being responsive to customers' needs. As a result, ABC has become a leader in the market and one of the premier divisions within Consolidated Industries.

Your consistent record of success, however, may be threatened. Although your own market forecasts indicate that ABC can continue to increase market share, even the conservative forecast clearly shows that projected product demand will exceed your available manufacturing capacity in less than three years. Without adequate capacity, your competitive position will certainly suffer as a result of declining delivery performance, deteriorating product quality, and increasing operating costs.

Complicating the picture is that demographic shifts and potential foreign exports are moving demand farther away from your existing midwest production facilities. Population and household growth in three geographic regions remote from these facilities has far exceeded that of the Midwest, as well as the nation as a whole.

Undoubtedly, these geographic shifts have contributed to ABC's increased distribution costs, a major factor in the total landed cost of household appliances. In jeopardy are not only ABC's operating objectives but your status as a premier division within Consolidated.

Recognizing these threats, your management group has suggested several options for increasing capacity, but little agreement exists about how that capacity should be deployed, and no agreement exists about the amount of capacity required. Consensus does exist, however, in two areas: additional capacity *will* be needed and the time when it will be needed is fast approaching.

Writing the Questions Component

The questions component, you know, provides you with the opportunity to demonstrate your qualifications as a problem solver, as someone who can demonstrate the ability to ask the right questions (the better to supply the correct answers). It also provides the opportunity to address key questions that you believe are on the minds of the various buyers.

These questions, by the way, allow you to indicate to each buyer that their desires or concerns have been heard, without your having to take a position one way or another. For example, consider the question "How much expansion potential exists at the current facility?" In posing that question, you would address Metzger's desire to expand at the current facility, without having to indicate at this point whether or not such a strategy is desirable. Equally important, the questions component "speaks" to and prepares the way for your methodology because this component presents key questions related to the important actions in your pyramid and, if necessary, important activities necessary for planning and communicating throughout the project. You begin with a transition that continues the themes of "complexity" and "urgency" and that initiates the themes of "thoroughness" and "comprehensiveness":

Complicating the need to move quickly is the need to carefully develop a thorough, convincing, and comprehensive plan that is accepted by both ABC's and Consolidated's management. This plan should answer questions like these:

- Based upon the long-term forecast, how much total factory space, equipment, and manpower are required and when?
- What opportunities exist to better utilize current equipment, space, and new technology?
- What manufacturing factory configuration options will best provide the required space? For example, how much expansion potential exists at the current facility, and what, if any, make/buy scenarios as well as changes in factory roles and locations can provide additional space?
- Even if resources can be added at the present location, does it make more economic sense to add them there or to make the investment elsewhere? For example, will service levels increase and transportation costs decrease at a new geographic location closer to growth markets?
- Which option is most appropriate considering the following qualitative and quantitative evaluation factors?

Writing the Needs Component

In preparing to write this component, you keep two things in mind: first, much of the information will come from the "situation" column of the Themes Development Worksheet; second, that information should be expressed "objectively." That is, you don't want to claim *here* that Paramount can meet ABC's needs; instead, you express those needs as "criteria" by which you would like your proposal to be judged. For example, rather than claiming that you have a multidisciplined consulting team (to counter the competition from the local engineering firm), you state objectively that given ABC's situation, such a team is necessary for a successful study and, implicitly, any other proposal not proposing such a team should be disadvantaged.

Similarly, you decide to focus in this component on the magnitude of the proposed project and the kinds of consulting skills therefore required. In short, you're implying evaluation criteria that will be advantageous to you, and you're setting the stage for later sections of the proposal. Certainly in QUALIFICATIONS and in METHODS, you will clearly demonstrate how your study will satisfy the "criteria" that here you strategically but subtly define. Of course, many of those criteria are themes related to hot buttons and counters to the competition. You begin with a transition from the questions component:

To answer questions like these, ABC needs a study methodology that will enable management to select the most effective plan to increase capacity and persuade Consolidated to approve the necessary funds. This plan must consider quantitative factors like ROI, investment incentives, taxes, and costs related to labor, service levels, distribution, construction, and utilities. The plan must also consider qualitative factors such as labor supply, union climate, work force characteristics, productivity, environmental permitting and regulations, vocational training capabilities, manufacturing support services, risk, controllability, ability to develop and promote employees, and flexibility to react to unanticipated changes.

Consequently, ABC needs a senior, multifaceted consulting team with a broad range of business capabilities. These capabilities should include skills in marketing, manufacturing strategy, facilities planning, logistics, financial analysis, and human resources. These capabilities are necessary to ensure that all relevant options are surfaced and evaluated in a practical manner, that the most desirable options and their attributes are clearly identified and defined, and that ABC's management not only has the ability to make the right decision but that Consolidated is convinced of its appropriateness.

Moreover, to ensure that all likely issues are addressed in this complex engagement, the study's methodology should encourage a close working relationship between ABC and the consulting team. This relationship will expedite the retrieval, development, and analysis of relevant information, thus reducing the time for analysis. It will also enhance the capabilities of ABC's staff, producing a more capable internal team with a better appreciation of business trade-offs and a broader knowledge of company operations. This broader perspective will prove helpful as business conditions change in unpredictable ways in the future.

Writing the Closing/S2 Component

The closing/S_2 component is rather simple: a short and reader-oriented paragraph that moves you gracefully out of the section by way of a smooth transition from the needs component; then, a forward-looking transition that anticipates METHODS and, for strategic closure, some briefly stated benefits:

> After carefully considering ABC's needs, I and my colleagues at Paramount Consulting have designed a methodology that will not only develop a manufacturing strategy to provide the capacity necessary for meeting forecasted demand, but also a concrete plan for implementing that strategy to improve your competitive position.

In rereading all the components together, you're reasonably satisfied. You've supplied good transitions to bridge the junctures between components. You've not only initiated the themes, but by doing so, you also have addressed various buyers' hot buttons, while attempting to counter the competition. In general, you believe you've been responsive to ABC's needs. You've not only told a good story; you've told *their* story. And, you hope, they will begin to see you as part of it.

8
Writing the Methods Slot

In Chap. 4 you saw that your methodology comprises two kinds of tasks: *actions* that must be performed to achieve the objective of the project and *activities* important for planning and communicating during the project. (See Exhibit 8.1.) Note that both kinds of tasks tell me the *how*—how you will achieve the objective and how you will plan and communicate with me while doing so. I might also want to know the *why*. Why, out of a universe of possible approaches, have you proposed the one you have? If you are phasing your project, why are you doing so? If you're not phasing the project, why haven't you? Why have you chosen to conduct progress reviews, and why that many, and why at that point in time? Why are you interviewing that number of people instead of a different number? Why are you interviewing those people instead of others? Why is the project going to take five months instead of four or six? Just why is this particular action necessary?

When you add to your methodology the good reasons for your performing it (the *why* that explains the *how*) then you have written METHODS. (See Exhibit 8.2.) The good reasons go into what I call P-slots, which are part of a simple but powerful technique called PIP, which stands for Persuasion–Information–Persuasion.

PIP

Persuasion primarily involves logical or emotional appeals intended to change belief or produce conviction. Information primarily involves facts. The power of the PIP technique rests on these commonsense assumptions:

- Proposals contain both information and persuasion.
- Proposals (and their sections and subsections) have beginning, middle, and ending slots.

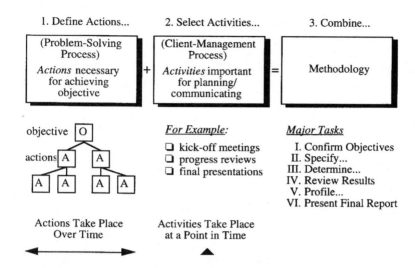

1. Define Actions... 2. Select Activities... 3. Combine...

Exhibit 8.1. Methodology = actions + activities.

■ Because people tend to perceive what is said first or last as being most important, they are likely to remember what they read or hear first and last. Therefore, the first and last slots are the more important.

To sense the importance of the first and last slots, consider a sequence of three proposal presentations. If you were one of three bidders, you'd want to arrange to be first or last. As first presenter, you'd have the opportunity to set the tone and create the standard by which later presenters would be judged. As last presenter, you'd have the opportunity to make the last (and, you'd hope, a lasting) impression. The middle presenter risks getting lost in the shuffle, especially in a very close competition.

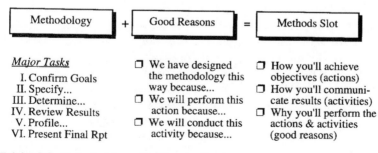

Exhibit 8.2. Methods slot = methodology + rationale.

I call the beginning and ending slots, where you place your proposal's persuasive content, "persuasion slots" (P-slots). The beginning P-slot explains why something should be done, and the ending P-slot explains what will result (for example, the end-product or deliverable) from the doing. Persuasion slots always frame or "sandwich" an information (or "in between") slot, an I-slot. I-slots explain "how." (See Exhibit 8.3.)

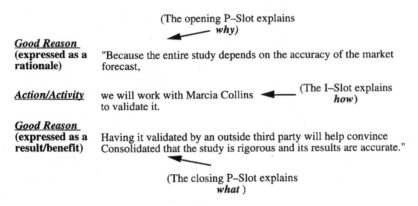

(The opening P–Slot explains
why)

**Good Reason
(expressed as a
rationale)**   "Because the entire study depends on the accuracy of the market
                      forecast,

Action/Activity   we will work with Marcia Collins   ◄—— (The I–Slot explains
                      to validate it.   *how*)

**Good Reason
(expressed as a
result/benefit)**   Having it validated by an outside third party will help convince
                      Consolidated that the study is rigorous and its results are accurate."

(The closing P–Slot explains
what)

Exhibit 8.3. Persuasion-information-persuasion (PIP).

PIP at the Task Level

To see how PIP works in a proposal, let's start small. Assume your document or presentation has a methodology consisting of several tasks. Each task can be organized according to PIP. (See Exhibit 8.4.)

The informational part (the middle, I-slot) is the action or activity itself. It explains *how* the action will be performed, in this case through reviews, interviews, and comparisons. If you sense that I might want to know *why* you are performing an action or activity, you might decide to provide some good reason, in the form of a rationale, for its performance; therefore, you'd fill the opening P-slot by providing that rationale. If you have a good rationale for conducting the task, it's because the task will produce some definable end product, or benefit, some understanding or knowledge or framework or decision point. If that end product is worth mentioning, you can fill the closing P-slot by explaining *what* the task will accomplish or what benefits or value will accrue from its accomplishment.

Can you imagine the difference in persuasion between a series of tasks that are PIP-ed and a series that omits all the P-slots? It's like night and day. The latter would contain only information related to how each of the tasks would be performed. The PIP-ed series would also explain to me why you were doing what you propose to do and what benefit or value I would receive from your doing it.

"Why" P-slot	■ Task 1: Confirm Business Direction A clear understanding of your company's business, mission, and current and future direction is key to the success of this project. This understanding establishes the context within which all further assessments are made and recommendations are developed.
"How" I-slot	Therefore, we will review all relevant materials concerning your company's mission and basic strategy. We will interview members of the board and senior management, and compare Acme's basic mission and strategies with those of similar entities elsewhere...
"What" P-slot	As a result of completing this task, the project team will clearly understand your business direction and underlying strategies, senior management issues and perspectives, and major areas of focus for the balance of the project. We will document the results of the task in a summary presentation and review it with you to ensure a common base of understanding.

Exhibit 8.4. PIP at the task level.

PIP at the Methods Slot Level

The entire methods slot can also be organized according to PIP. In this case, the entire methodology becomes an I-slot, an in-between slot sandwiched between good reasons. (See Exhibit 8.5.)

Slot	Position	Argument
P	Introductory ¶(s)	Considering your hot buttons and evaluation criteria, and our counters to the competition, these are the reasons why, out of a universe of possible approaches, we have chosen this approach.
I	Methodology	These are the tasks we will perform to solve your problem or realize your opportunity.
P	Concluding ¶(s)	As a result of our accomplishing these tasks, you will receive these deliverables; as a result of our approach, you will realize this value-added.

Exhibit 8.5. PIP at the methods slot level.

When you write the introduction to your methods slot, ask yourself if you have filled the P-slot. For example, does your introduction "recommend a three-phase approach" and pretty much leave me with only that *information*? Or should it go on to explain *persuasively* that such an approach will be employed because the phases will, for example:

- Allow me to achieve short-term results to make subsequent phases "pay as you go"

- Allow me to address broader strategic issues early on before focusing on more tactical questions

- Continuously build on each other so that decisions reached in earlier phases influence and screen options in later ones, thus leading to economies because I can choose to limit further evaluation in later phases based on analyses performed in earlier ones

Does your introduction recommend a team approach and pretty much leave me with that information only? Or should it go on to explain that the study is strategically planned to meet my specific needs by employing a team approach that will, for example:

- Generate enthusiasm and commitment for the project

- Keep me informed at every major step of the project

- Result in jointly developed and better accepted recommendations and action plans

- Efficiently resolve newly surfacing issues

- Keep the lines of communication open

- Efficiently transfer to your team my organization's intimate knowledge of our firm

- Most efficiently transfer to my people your team's knowledge, technology, and/or skills

Your introduction to METHODS provides a great opportunity to sell your methodology, to explain persuasively to me and others on the buying committee exactly how your methodology contains elements that will lead us to a more successful and valuable project.

If you have completed a Themes Development Worksheet (see Exhibit 8.7 in the summary to this chapter), then you will already have generated much of the persuasive content for the opening P-slot of METHODS. The "Methods" column of that worksheet provides the opening P-slot material, the rationale for your constructing your approach as you have. These reasons will be persuasive because they are related to my hot buttons and evaluation criteria and to your counters to the competition related to those criteria.

The conclusion to METHODS also contains a P-slot. Rather than ending with a discussion of the tenth task of the third phase, you can persuasively conclude METHODS by itemizing the expected deliverables (if they haven't been identified within the tasks), by summarizing the most important deliverables (if they have been included in the tasks), or by explaining to me the value your approach will add during the project.

Exhibit 8.6 summarizes this discussion of P-slots in METHODS by showing where the P-slots are, what they do, and what content they contain. The exhibit uses the methodology that I revised in Chap. 4. That methodology, you'll recall, included both phases and tasks:

Phase I: Determine If XYZ Should Enter the Market

- Confirm Phase I objectives in a kickoff meeting.
- Identify information–service market opportunities.
  - Identify motor carriers' information needs.
  - Identify customers' needs.
  - Identify competitors' capabilities.
- Specify capabilities and resources required to capitalize on market opportunity.
- Compare XYZ's capabilities and resources with market requirements.
- Report Phase I results, and if necessary, confirm Phase II objectives.

Phase II: Determine How XYZ Should Enter the Market

- Specify actions required for closing the gap between market requirements and XYZ capabilities.
- Specify resources and timing to implement actions.
- Report Phase II results.

A methods section containing this methodology will include P-slots at the task, phase, and section levels. Given just these phases and tasks, 14 opening P-slots exist: one that explains why you have designed the entire approach as you have; two that explain why each phase should be conducted; and 11 that provide a rationale for doing each of the tasks. Fourteen closing P-slots also exist, and by filling them you have the opportunity to explain the value, deliverables, and/or benefits that will accrue from the whole approach and from each of the phases and tasks.

(1st-level heading) Opening P-slot, section-level. Explains *why* this approach has been designed. Probably includes themes. Ends with a forecasting statement of the two phases.	<u>Approach</u> "Out of a universe of possible approaches, this is why we have designed our approach this way, considering this situation. Our approach is divided into the following three phases": ■ ■ ■
(2nd-level heading) Opening P-slot, phase-level. Explains *why* this phase should be performed. Ends with a forecasting statement of the Phase 1 tasks.	*Phase I: Determine If XYZ Should Enter the Market* "This is why this phase should be performed. Phase I includes the following three tasks": ■ ■ ■
(3rd-level heading) Opening P-slot, task-level. Explains *why* this task should be performed.	■ *Task 1: define information–service market opportunities* "This is why this task should be performed."
I-slot, task-level. Explains *how* this task will be performed.	"This is how we will perform the task."
Closing P-slot, task-level. Explains *what* value and/or deliverables will occur from performing this task.	"This is the value/deliverable from performing the task."

————————–Ditto for subsequent tasks, Phase I————

Exhibit 8.6. P–slots at the section, phase, and task levels.

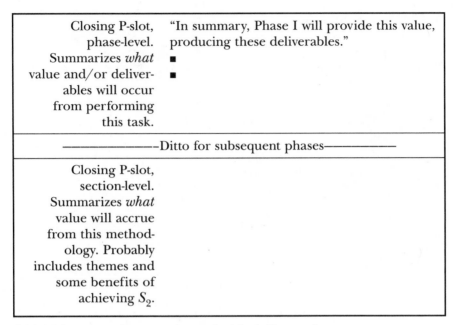

Closing P-slot, phase-level. Summarizes *what* value and/or deliverables will occur from performing this task.	"In summary, Phase I will provide this value, producing these deliverables." ■ ■
————————–Ditto for subsequent phases————	
Closing P-slot, section-level. Summarizes *what* value will accrue from this methodology. Probably includes themes and some benefits of achieving S_2.	

Exhibit 8.6. P–slots at the section, phase, and task levels *(Continued).*

At this point, I'm certain you're asking an important question: "Do all the P-slots have to be filled?" The simple answer, as this chapter's work session and the following chapter's discussion make clear, is "No." And by this point, you should know why: *it all depends on the situation.* It all depends on your judgment regarding the amount of persuasiveness necessary for your proposal to win.

⇨ Chapter 8 Review:
Writing the Methods Slot

1. The methods slot consists of your methodology plus your good reasons for performing it.

2. These good reasons take two forms: first, a rationale for why you will do what you say you will; second, the results or benefits that will accrue from your doing it.

3. The good reasons can go into persuasion slots (P-slots) that precede and follow information or in-between slots (I-slots).

4. The opening P-slot explains why you will do something. The I-slot explains how you will do it. The closing P-slot explains what will happen from your doing it. Hence: PIP.

5. PIP can be used to organize the methods section on several levels: task, phase, and section.

6. How many P-slots should be filled depends on the situation.

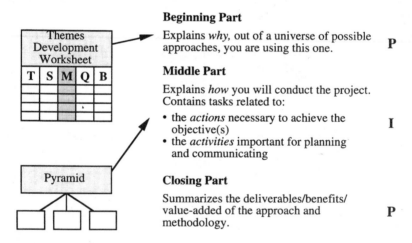

Beginning Part

Explains *why*, out of a universe of possible approaches, you are using this one.   **P**

Middle Part

Explains *how* you will conduct the project. Contains tasks related to:

- the *actions* necessary to achieve the objective(s)   **I**
- the *activities* important for planning and communicating

Closing Part

Summarizes the deliverables/benefits/value-added of the approach and methodology.   **P**

Exhibit 8.7. Writing the methods slot.

Work Session 8: Writing the Methods Slot for ABC

Composing the Opening P-slot for the Methods Section

In your estimation, the individuals on the ABC buying team are a rather diverse lot with solid but rather narrow functional capabilities. In evaluating your proposal, some will look for a technically precise methodology that also addresses their individual, varied concerns and needs—that is, one that responds to their different perceptions of ABC's current situation as well as their sometimes similar but often different hot buttons. Your Themes Development Worksheet addresses these hot buttons as well as some of the competitions' exploitable weaknesses. In fact, the "methods" column of that worksheet provides (as it always does) most of the persuasive material that you can use in the opening P-slot to that section. That column contains the following claims:

- We will have frequent progress reviews so that you are aware of preliminary conclusions and direction quickly. We will involve you in writing the final report, which as we've discussed, will actually be your proposal to Consolidated, thus eliminating one step in the approval process.
- We will carefully define and evaluate all viable alternatives, using quantitative and qualitative evaluation criteria. We will make use, when appropriate, of the in-house distribution model developed by Paul Morrison.
- We will form a joint ABC/Paramount study team, with ABC managers playing an integral part.
- Early in the study, we will conduct strategy sessions with all relevant interest areas within ABC to gain consensus on and establish the proper evaluation criteria.
- Our methodology will be designed to draw on the expertise of our multidisciplined team with skills in marketing, manufacturing strategy, facilities planning, logistics, financial analysis, and human resources.

You use these claims, integrate them within a restatement of the project's objective, and end the P-slot with a statement that forecasts the five major tasks. Your draft of the opening P-slot to the methods section looks like this:

To ensure that ABC's managers have an integral and significant role in this engagement, we will form a joint ABC/Paramount team. Team members from Paramount will have multidisciplined skills in marketing, manufacturing strategy, facilities planning, logistics, financial analysis, and human resources. Working with ABC executives with some of these same functional skills, we will make considerable use of ABC's own market forecast, distribution model, and other in-house analyses.

Early in the engagement we will solicit and obtain agreement on quantitative and qualitative criteria for evaluating the various options, and throughout the engagement the team will conduct meetings to review progress and agree on future direction and emphasis. As a result of these frequent progress reviews, ABC's management will be fully informed of the engagement's ongoing findings and conclusions. The progress reviews will play a key role in expediting the conduct of the engagement, enabling management to keep our efforts focused by providing direction and counsel.

The team's major goal is twofold:

- To provide ABC with a manufacturing capacity plan that is thoroughly documented, cost-effective, and, when fully implemented, capable of enabling the Division to maintain and enhance its competitive position.

- To produce for Consolidated a convincing, comprehensive, and thorough justification for increasing capacity. Ideally, the output of this effort will not only be a report of the recommended expansion plan but an actual proposal to Corporate that justifies the cost of the expansion by articulating the compelling reasons to move forward.

To achieve this goal, we have developed a methodology that consists of the following five major tasks: (note: here, insert a Gantt Chart). Please note that this five-month estimate for completing the study is conservative. Working with your management team, we will make every effort to accelerate the completion of the tasks later discussed in greater detail.

After composing this P-slot, you turn your attention to the five major work tasks that you developed using pyramid logics. Your purpose is to build persuasiveness into the methodology by providing beginning and ending P-slots for each of these major work tasks.

**Composing the P-slots for Task 1:
Confirm ABC's Long-Term
Product Forecast**

The opening P-slot for this task will be particularly important. Without providing a highly persuasive rationale for confirming the forecast, you run the considerable risk of alienating Marcia Collins, who not only developed the forecast but also has confidence in its accuracy. You decide to use two key arguments:

- An accurate forecast is critical for determining the magnitude and timing of additional manufacturing resources (that is, it drives the entire analysis).

- An independent authentication of the forecast will assure Consolidated that ABC's projected growth is real and merits significant capital investment.

Your closing P-slot for this task, where you have the opportunity to explain the results of completing it, will argue that an accurate, authenticated forecast will provide the basis for making a sound first estimate of future resource requirements. Here's your draft of the discussion of Task 1:

> *Task 1: Confirm ABC's Long-Term Product Forecast*
>
> Although ABC already has a forecast of production volume, we believe that the engagement must be conducted with Consolidated constantly in mind. Since Consolidated must release the necessary capital funding, they must be convinced of the engagement's rigor and robustness. For that reason, we believe that the forecast must be confirmed by an independent third party. Therefore, we propose to work with ABC's marketing management to confirm or modify the long-term forecast by:
>
> - Validating ABC's current, overall market forecast
> - Validating ABC's market share and your geographic and product mix projections
>
> The consensus market forecast developed in this task will represent the best thinking of your marketing group and the Paramount team. The forecast, used with various manufacturing data, will enable the engagement team to develop future resource requirements over time.

**Composing the P-slots for Task 2:
Determine Total Factory
Resource Requirements at
Alternate Forecast Levels**

Your initial meeting with ABC's buying team and Gilmore's description of their present operation have given you a high regard for ABC's capabilities. But you also realize that even competent managers can be so close to their operations that they risk taking them for granted, not fully recognizing opportunities for improvement. You also know that ABC hasn't been involved in planning a new facility for years and probably doesn't recognize that facility needs can be either seriously overstated or understated without first establishing a solid base of effective operations from which to project these needs. These are points you develop to formulate an opening P-slot for this task. Importantly, the task will involve identifying opportunities to improve current operations and/or outsource various components to establish a solid base that will be used in conjunction with the forecast to accurately project future requirements.

You know that the output from this task will provide an essential ingredient for developing the overall manufacturing facility strategy. Only when future requirements are known can the study team explore viable options for providing these requirements. You convey this important understanding in the closing P-slot. Your draft of Task 2:

Task 2: Determine Total Factory Space Requirements at Alternate Forecast Levels

An important task of the engagement team will be to use the existing base of production resources (floor space, equipment, and staffing) and modify that base so that it can accommodate the additional future production demands over time indicated by the confirmed market forecast. First, however, the team will carefully evaluate that base to identify improvements or eliminate inefficiencies that might exist today. We don't want ABC to risk adding too much or too little capacity. This risk can be avoided by first establishing a proper base, a "current-improved" base, from which to project future resource requirements. All this will be critical, because determining future needs involves far more than an arithmetic extrapolation of today's activities.

We were very much impressed during our walk-through of your main manufacturing facility. You should know, however, that in nearly every similar engagement we have been able to recommend methods for better utilizing currently available space, thereby increasing manufacturing capacity without actually increasing space. To provide additional capacity and/or space without first determining such improvement opportunities could result in unnecessary capital investment.

We will ensure that ABC is making the most effective use of existing manufacturing resources. Specifically, we will:

- Specify current equipment and space utilization
- Determine opportunities to better utilize current equipment and space and to improve material flow
- Determine opportunities for utilizing new equipment technology
- Specify which products or components, if any, should be made in house versus bought from suppliers

The modified, effective base of production resources coupled with the confirmed market forecast will enable the engagement team to develop an accurate and credible projection of future resource requirements. At this point the joint ABC/Paramount engagement team will have a sound basis for identifying, evaluating, and selecting the most viable options to provide these requirements.

Composing the P-slots for Task 3:
Define Manufacturing Facility Options
to Provide Required Resources

Many different facility configurations could provide ABC's needed additional resources. ABC's buying team understands this as well: Metzger felt that the existing facility should be expanded, Williams thought the same for the satellite facilities, and Collins argued for a "greenfield" site closer to expanding markets.

You try several times to write P-slots for this task, but each of them sounds forced and dry. Eventually, you realize why: The fundamental purpose and result of this task are so fundamental, and so obvious, that opening and closing P-slots are unnecessary. So you introduce this task with nothing more than a transition from Task 2 and end the task's discussion with a transition to Task 4. Your draft of Task 3 looks as follows:

> *Task 3: Define Manufacturing Facility Options to Provide*
> *Required Resources*
>
> Once we know how much additional space and equipment are required, we need to specify the possible manufacturing options that will provide these additional resources. Accordingly, we will develop and analyze various options and determine which configuration of facilities best meets your objectives. Specifically, we will:
>
> - Determine expansion potential at the current facility
> - Specify potential factory roles and locations for increasing capacity
>
> As a result of completing this task, we will have narrowed the field from the possible to the probable, the better to be able to scrutinize the remaining options and to choose the most appropriate.

In re-reading your draft, you realize that the second bullet probably should have some discussion under it.

Composing the P-slots for Task 4:
Select the Most Appropriate Option

This task will help eliminate the uncertainty that must be disconcerting to the ABC buying team. It will reveal whether Metzger's, Collins', or Williams' biases are valid. But in the process you know that a number of "pet" ideas are going to be "shot down." Only considerable agreement among the buying team on the criteria to be used to evaluate the multiple options will avoid hard feelings and assure acceptance of the selected facility option. These thoughts, which also focus on the theme of consensus, help you to formulate an opening P-slot.

For the closing P-slot:

> The proposal team designed this task to define the precise configuration of ABC's future manufacturing facilities that will enable the Division to maintain its competitive status and effectively meet customer demand during the forecast period.

You use this idea in a closing P-slot to the draft of Task 4, which reads like this:

Task 4: Select the Most Appropriate Option

Using ABC's distribution model and Paramount's proprietary models for assessing expansion options, the joint engagement team will evaluate thoroughly each potential expansion option and then select the one most appropriate. Although the range of options will have been narrowed, those remaining will quite likely be diverse. Therefore, we will work with ABC management to develop both quantitative and qualitative criteria that will differentiate carefully among the various options, and will obtain management's agreement on the one most suitable. Specifically, to select the most appropriate option, the engagement team will:

- Define quantitative and qualitative criteria important to ABC and Consolidated
- Evaluate each option against quantitative criteria such as ROI, landed cost, quality, and customer service
- Evaluate each option against qualitative criteria such as flexibility and risk versus control

When this task is completed, you will know precisely how to configure your manufacturing facilities over time so that you can meet customer demand throughout the forecasted period cost-effectively and responsively.

Composing the P-slots for Task 5:
Develop a Plan to Implement the
Selected Option

Merely defining the best facility option for ABC won't be enough. They will need to know precisely how to implement the selected strategy and they will look to Paramount to provide that direction. Since space, equipment, and people will likely be added in stages during the forecast period, ABC will want to know just when and how much new capital and additional planning resources will be needed over that time period. You feel confident that carefully worded statements based on this need will provide an impressive opening P-slot.

Your closing P-slot will stress that completing this task is most important to ABC. It will provide them with an accurate, carefully defined "road map" showing precisely how to implement the facility strategy in a timely, efficient, and cost-effective manner. The draft of the final task looks like this:

Task 5: Develop a Plan to Implement the Selected Option

Because the additional manufacturing resources required will likely be brought on-stream at various times throughout the forecast period, ABC will need a carefully prepared plan to monitor progress during implementation. To that end, we will prepare a plan to ensure that additional manufacturing resources and facilities are in place when and where they are needed to meet forecasted demand. The various steps in our implementation plan will be time-phased so that management will know precisely when additional capacity is required and when other managerial decisions and actions are needed. Specifically, we will:

- Define the tasks necessary to implement the selected option
- Define the resources and responsibilities necessary to complete those tasks
- Develop a critical path to estimate the time required to complete all tasks

As a result of this task, management will know all the tasks required to provide the additional manufacturing resources, when each task should be initiated and completed, and the skills required to complete each task. The implementation plan will provide you with a critical mechanism to monitor overall progress, to efficiently invest required capital and other resources when they are needed, and to take corrective actions if actual market demand differs significantly from that projected.

After completing this task, we will work with you to immediately prepare a capital appropriations request that can be submitted directly to Consolidated for their timely consideration.

Because the closing P-slot to Task 5 discusses some of the project's major outcomes (an implementation plan and a capital appropriations request), you decide to use it as well for the closing P-slot of the entire section.

9

Interlude: Focusing on Persuasion

I want to begin this chapter by telling you a little more about the concept PIP, which as you know stands for Persuasion–Information–Persuasion. The concept itself is fairly easy to understand. What's a little more difficult is conceptualizing how PIP works on various levels of your proposal. Think of these levels as a set of Russian dolls, one of which sits inside another, which sits inside another, which sits inside yet another. (See Exhibit 9.1.)

On the task level (the smallest doll in Exhibit 9.1), each action or activity can be organized according to PIP, as you explain why you're performing the task, how you'll perform it, and what deliverable, value, or benefits will accrue from its performance. On the phase level (the next larger doll), all the related tasks can become an I-slot (an "in-between" slot). That I-slot is also framed or sandwiched between two P-slots. The first discusses the reasons why you're performing that phase, and the second discusses the deliverables, value, or benefits that will accrue from your performing the phase. Of course, the same sort of thing happens on the even higher methods level (the largest doll). All the phases together form the middle of the methods section, which you can begin by providing a rationale for your entire approach and end by discussing its value or benefits and/or by summarizing the deliverables.

But yet another level exists, an even larger Russian doll. The methods section doesn't usually begin or end the proposal; it sits in the middle. Preceding the methods section is an opening P-slot called SITUATION that provides a rationale for why the project should be performed in the first

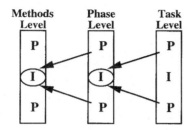

Exhibit 9.1. PIP at the methods, phase, and task levels.

place. After the methods section is a closing P-slot called BENEFITS that discusses the value of performing the project. So at the level of the entire proposal, the argument looks like Exhibit 9.2. In short, much of the entire proposal develops by way of PIP. Your proposal contains a set of four Russian dolls. (See Exhibit 9.3.) By completely implementing the concept of PIP, you can frame many of the levels of your document or presentation with, on the one hand, your reason, purpose, or rationale for doing something, and on the other, with the value-added or benefit of having it done. Consequently, by filling the P–slots you will provide me, on many levels, with good reasons for your doing something and desirable results from the action. Needless to say, this strategy helps to make me more understanding and accepting rather than objecting or rejecting.

P-slot: SITUATION*	This is *why* the project should be conducted, to solve your problem or realize your opportunity.
I-slot: METHODS	This is *how* we will solve your problem or realize your opportunity.
P-slot: BENEFITS	This is *what* you will receive, the benefits of the project itself and of our working with you.

Exhibit 9.2. PIP at the proposal level.

*You should note that SITUATION and BENEFITS are not developed by PIP. SITUATION is an opening P-slot only; it answers the question, "Why should this project be performed?" BENEFITS is a closing P-slot only; it answers the question, "What value will the potential client receive from the project's execution?"

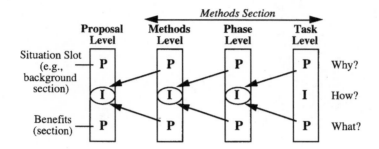

Exhibit 9.3. PIP at all levels.

Determining the Level of Persuasiveness

Because P-slots exist at the beginning and ending of things, they're easy to find. Once you find them, however, you have to decide whether they should be filled. Your decision will depend on your sense of the situation, which will be different every time, as a friend remarked recalling a proposal opportunity some years ago when he was a fairly inexperienced consultant:

> I wrote a proposal that I thought was going to be exactly like another proposal I wrote for another company. Both companies competed in the same industry and manufactured the same products in almost the exact same geographic area. I pulled out that other proposal in order to boilerplate from it. I thought this would be a cakewalk. But by the time I was done, the only thing the other proposal did was to supply some neat ideas for me.

The former proposal was written to a company for which the consultant had done ten previous projects. He knew the president very well (the president's son was also a client), and the company was extraordinarily successful. But the current proposal "was for a company where I had never met anybody; the company was in trouble; there was no warm feeling; there was no ten years of experience; there were no previous assignments." The former proposal ...

> was sort of a "Hey, Stan, this sort of confirms what we will do together, and we will do our best and if we blow it we will change in midstream, and it has been great seeing you." But the current proposal is, "number one you don't know me, number two I have to establish my credentials and my firm's credentials, number three we are sorry we took so long to respond, because we lost your letter (which is really number four); of all the firms you talked to, however, we are the only

one with the exact right qualifications—here they are," and now, suddenly, we have a totally different proposal.*

Obviously, the second proposal had to be much more substantial and persuasive than the first, and therefore more of the P-slots had to be filled. But how do you decide just how persuasive your proposal needs to be? I can think of at least three factors you should consider: your relationship with the buyers, the competition, and your sales objective. (See Exhibit 9.4.)

The first two categories, "Relationship with buyers" and "Competition," are fairly obvious. Assume, for example, that the quality of your relationship with me is excellent, that you've done many studies for me and my organization, and that I'm not talking to any of your competitors. No one else is competing for my attention and, in the past, when *you* have worked for me, you've done so very successfully. Your credibility is a given; you don't have to acquire it. I've asked you to meet with me to discuss a problem that needs to be solved, and you have convinced me, in our two-hour meeting, that you understand the problem and have the right people and approach for solving it. We've also discussed costs, and I've agreed to them. In short, you've sold the job, and I've asked you for nothing more than a confirming letter. As a result, you'd need to do very little with the P-slots. There may be no need whatsoever to itemize your tasks (and explain the purpose of each), discuss the reasons for your specific approach, provide a rationale for why the study should be done, and argue the benefits that will accrue from its doing.

Conversely, if five firms are competing and some of them have capabilities equal to yours and if they, not you, have successfully worked with me, then your proposal will have to be very persuasive indeed. Many of the P-slots will have to be filled, and filled well. At each crucial point, you may

Relationship with buyers	Competition	Sales objective
■ Quality of your relationship with me, the potential client	■ Amount	■ To prequalify for the next opportunity
■ Previous studies done for us	■ Kind	■ To get to the next level
■ Previous studies done for others known by us		■ To win

Exhibit 9.4. Factors influencing level of necessary persuasiveness.

*Glenn J Broadhead and Richard C. Freed. *The Variables of Composition.* Carbondale, IL: Southern Illinois University Press (1986), p. 58.

have to explain why a task is important to perform—and the results of its performance; why you have designed your approach precisely as you have—and the value of your conducting it; and why, from your point of view, the study should be performed—and the benefits to be gained from your performing it.

In this second case, however, you should seriously consider not writing a proposal at all, especially if my issue doesn't play to your strengths or if I'm not one of your target clients or in one of your target industries. Instead, save your resources for some other battle you have a better chance to win.

The third category, "Sales objective," is important because too many proposal writers view the written proposal as having only one sales objective: to close the deal. A good example of this proposal-as-last-effort viewpoint is the requirement at some consulting firms (sometimes by fiat, sometimes by institutional practice) that letter proposals contain signature blocks at the end of the document, prefaced by a sentence like: "If you agree with the terms as set forth in this proposal, please sign in the appropriate space and forward one copy to..." Required even in competitive situations, this procedure views the proposal as a final product rather than as a negotiating tool—one more possible stage in the proposal process to help you get closer to what then could be your best and final offer to me.

Now, of course, in many situations the proposal *is* your best and final offer because I and the other buyers won't allow you any other. But in other situations, the proposal-as-final-offer strategy can be most unstrategic, because your document's sales objective is not always to win but to get you one step closer to what can become a "done deal."

That is, sometimes your immediate sales objective is to get to the next stage, the better to sell to the next level or the better to continue to try to sell at the same level. For example, assume that you don't have access to the economic buyer. In that situation, the strategy could be to write a document whose sales objective is not to close the deal but to get buy-in from the technical and user buyers, who then in effect become part of your team. At that point, they can coach you to meet the new sales objective, which would be to work together to sell to the economic buyer. The new document or presentation could then be specifically tailored to meet the new sales objective.

Even if you have access to all the buyers, you can profitably choose to view the written proposal or oral presentation as a discussion document. Indeed, many experienced consultants try not to include their cost in their written proposal. They label it a "discussion document" so that they can meet with me and my team to hammer out the methodology, workplan, and our level of involvement; agree on the deliverables; and, of course, establish the trust and chemistry necessary for us to say "Yes" with confidence. If by the end of that meeting they haven't yet sold the work, they've at least gotten closer, and they know even more about me, my team, and my organization's problem or opportunity. Their proposal and our relationship will be better because of it.

On some (certainly less frequent) occasions, the objective isn't to sell on any level at all, but simply to get into the game so that you can play next time. A friend of mine, an environmental consultant, decided to play on these terms. He did not originally receive an RFP from a Canadian governmental agency because the agency wasn't aware that his firm did environmental consulting. After finding out about the opportunity through the grapevine, however, he asked for and received permission to bid, and did so, even though a dozen other competitors were involved and the job was probably wired to begin with. His sales objective was not to win but to prequalify for future work. His document functioned less like a proposal and more like a response to an RFQ (Request for Qualifications).

P-slots and Themes

Much of my argument in Part Two of this book goes something like this:

- You want to prepare a persuasive proposal.
- Persuasion is the intersection of my (the buyer's) needs and your (the seller's) qualities. That is, no matter the breadth or depth of the abilities and capabilities you bring to the party, they are only relevant in so far as they can be brought to bear to meet my specific needs in this situation.
- My needs are addressed by your articulated results/benefits and hot buttons.
- Your qualities (that is, the selling points you will use) are derived from the results/benefits you propose to deliver, your responsiveness to our individual hot buttons, the degree to which you can meet evaluation criteria, and the demonstrable difference between you and your competition.
- These selling points are the persuasive content of your proposal.
- Your persuasive content goes into the proposal's P-slots.
- When P-slots are filled with similar ideas, this repetition makes these ideas thematic.
- Because themes are related to the qualities of the seller as they intersect with the needs of the buyer, they inherently make the proposal persuasive.

The relationship is depicted in Exhibit 9.5.

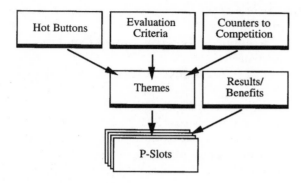

Exhibit 9.5. What fills the P-slots.

Hot buttons, evaluation criteria, and counters to the competition repeated as themes, along with results and benefits to me and my organization, are the filling of the P-slots.

Themes, however, should be subtle things, food for thought rather than fodder for the digestive tract. They are what helps make me say "Yes! These people understand," even though I might not be able to articulate why. Themes are a delicate psychological complement to the logical presentation of your information. They need to taste smooth to the palate, not gritty or overbearing. Don't overuse them or use too many.

⇨ Chapter 9 Review: Focusing on Persuasion

1. P-slots and I-slots exist on at least four levels:

Level	Opening P-slot	I-slot	Closing P-slot
Proposal	This study should be performed because ...	These are our METHODS.	These are the expected benefits of the project.
Methods section	We propose this methodology because ...	This is how we will perform the tasks.	These are the expected results of our methods.
Phase	This phase should be performed because ...	This is how we will perform the phase.	These are the expected results of this phase.
Task	This task should be performed because ...	This is how we will perform the task.	These are the expected results of this task.

2. Whether or not and how much P-slots are filled depends on how persuasive the document or presentation needs to be. The level of necessary persuasiveness is conditioned by your strategic evaluation of the situation as you consider:

- Your relationship with the buyers
- The amount and kind of competition
- Your sales objective (e.g., to prequalify for the next opportunity, to get to the next level, or to win).

10
Writing the Qualifications Slot

Now, back to preparing specific proposal slots: in this chapter, QUALIFICA-TIONS. I've probably seen more boilerplate in qualifications sections than in a furnace factory, especially from the larger consulting firms, the ones with big research/information departments. These firms' proposals list everything they can about what they've done and whom they've done it to. Give me a break! There's a better way, and I'll tell you what it is.

The situation and methods slots allow you to demonstrate your qualifications implicitly. In SITUATION, for example, you can display your abilities as a problem solver by demonstrating your understanding of our problem's causes and effects and by indicating your awareness of the important questions that must be answered before this problem can be solved. Your understanding of these matters can be crucial to the successful conduct of the project, and your clear and accurate presentation can be evidence of your experience, expertise, perspicacity, ingenuity, insight, and whatever other characteristics you wish to convey. In SITUATION and METHODS, you're *showing* your qualifications, implicitly. In QUALIFICATIONS, you're *telling* them, explicitly. You're explicitly attempting to answer the question: "Why are you best qualified for *this* project?"

The answer to that question should focus on abilities and capabilities *related to my specific situation.* Abilities are qualities of people, like experience, kind and level of expertise, and personal characteristics. Capabilities are qualities of things, like your firm or proprietary intellectual capital like methodologies or models. In a great many proposals, abilities are discussed in resumes (often attached in an appendix) and in "staffing" sections or subsections that often include brief biographies as well as the roles and responsibilities of those who will play a part in the project. These abilities are certainly part of the qualifications slot, even though they might not be in a section called "Qualifications."

If you are a consultant, you have computer files filled with descriptions of abilities and capabilities: resumes of your professional staff; a record of the studies your firm has done, in various industries, in achieving various objectives; a history of the firm itself and how it's grown and developed; prepackaged statements about the firm's commitment to quality or effective implementation and so on. All that boilerplate is important. And everyone else, including your competitors, has it too.

So you and they keep using it, especially in qualifications sections. I've read proposals that didn't once mention my organization's name in the qualifications section because the section contained nothing but generic fluff lifted whole cloth from a computer file. I've read other proposals that did contain the name of a firm, but not my own, because the section was lifted whole cloth from another proposal. And I've read still other documents that contained place holders for where my organization's name should have gone—for example: <insert client's name>. Computers are wonderful things; but they're not a remedy for laziness, carelessness, lack of strategy, or logical thinking about why you are, in fact, the best firm to meet my needs.

Remember what I said in the last chapter and elsewhere: persuasion occurs at the *intersection* of your abilities and your firm's capabilities with my potential client needs. By that definition a qualifications section that focuses only on abilities and capabilities isn't persuasive, or at least not as persuasive as it could be. It must focus on those abilities and capabilities *as they relate to my needs.*

Many qualifications sections don't address those needs because they are written by someone who doesn't know them, much less understand them. Consider, for example, the not untypical situation at a large consulting firm I'm familiar with. Our hypothetical firm has four people working on a particular proposal, and they represent the four levels in the firm's professional ranks: partner, manager, consultant, and researcher.

Although the partner is the only one who has met with the potential client, she will write little if any of the proposal. She will, however, review it, though her review will focus primarily on staffing and costs, since she will get the proposal only 15 minutes before it has to go out the door. The manager will manage the proposal writing effort, composing some of the document's parts and assigning others to the consultant. Partner, manager, and consultant will have discussed the situation at the potential client's firm and the strategy for preparing the document. The researcher rarely if ever writes proposals because he spends almost all of his time doing research on the projects themselves; he is not involved in selling work. He has neither met with the potential client nor been apprised of the situation or the study's objectives or possible methodology. Can you guess who is assigned to write the qualifications section?

The researcher finds several previous proposals written to similar clients, perhaps for similar studies. The qualifications sections in these proposals were written by others like him. The sections aren't directed to specific readers in specific situations, with specific needs, problems, or opportunities. They are directed to what I call "Generic World." They contain discussions of abilities and capabilities that could be read by most any reader in most any situation. They don't focus on the intersection of your abilities and capabilities and my needs or evaluation criteria, and neither will the new qualifications section that the researcher will write—or copy from the old ones. In this chapter I'll show you how to write a qualifications section that focuses on that intersection.

Your Qualifications Section Needs to Be an Argument

In Chap. 4 I showed you how to construct a pyramid to develop the actions in your methodology. That pyramid structured an argument to address the key question I wanted your methodology to answer: "*How* will you achieve the project's objective?" Your qualifications section also is an argument, and it also can be developed with a pyramid. Now, however, my key question is not "how?" but "why?": "*Why* are you the best qualified firm to conduct this project?" (See Exhibit 10.1.)

The principles in building this "why" pyramid are similar to those used to build the "how" pyramid in the methodology. Each box in one row of the pyramid stakes out a claim you must substantiate, and each group of boxes below it argues why that claim is true.

Exhibit 10.1. The pyramid for the qualifications slot.

Typical Qualifications Sections
Don't Present an Argument

Qualifications sections written to Generic World can't present an argument whose claim is "We are the best qualified firm," because "best" implies "in *this* situation." Such sections tend to be organized by easy-to-boilerplate categories, rather than as specific claims that answer the question "why?":

If I ask you, "Why are you the best qualified firm?" I doubt that you would answer, "Description of the firm, industry experience, and oh yes, consulting philosophy." You wouldn't be answering my question. You'd be answering something like, "What categories will you use in organizing your qualifications section?" I don't care about that question. I want to know why you believe you're the best qualified firm so I can judge for myself.

These categories, you see, focus inwardly only on *your* abilities and capabilities, not outwardly on their intersection with *my* needs. Consider the subsection "Description of the Firm." (Yes, this qualifications section was written by the same researcher I previously discussed, and yes, it was part of a proposal sent to me.) The subsection contained information on the history of the consulting firm, the number of employees, and the number and location of offices. Terrific!

All this information could be relevant and persuasive in our situation. For example, assume the proposed project would take several years, require vast consulting resources and expertise, and affect my organization's facilities throughout the world. In this case, I might want to engage a stable firm that's been around a long time, with vast resources and diverse expertise, and offices and capabilities around the world. On the other hand, my proposed project could require only specialized expertise, and affect only one of our operations. Of course, that was the case. But the consulting firm's qualifications section was written by someone with scant knowledge of my organization and my organization's current situation, S_1, and our desired result, S_2. It didn't matter to the writer that *I* was reading the section. The section wasn't written to me and my world but to Generic World.

The subsection "Proprietary Methodologies" began this way: "The general operating practice of QRS Consulting is to develop frameworks and approaches to client-specific problems—not cookbooks that are simply transferred from client to client..We tailor each approach for each client to ensure a unique and competitive solution to that client's specific problem." Would you trust someone who uses boilerplate to assure you that you and your organization are unique? This passage is worse than insincere. It borders on the hypocritical.

Don't think I can't sense boilerplate. Don't think I'm stupid. You are the one who comes off, not necessarily stupid, but insincere, untrustworthy, unthinking, uncreative, uncaring.

Use Your Themes Development Worksheet to Structure Your Argument

Themes, I remarked in Chap. 6, are related to the qualities of the seller as they intersect with my needs as the buyer. So if you want to focus on your qualifications as they intersect with me, you need to look to your themes. Specifically, you need to capture the information in the "Qualifications" column of your Themes Development Worksheet. Why are you best qualified? Because, as that column will reveal, you can respond to my hot buttons. Because your abilities and capabilities are in line with my evaluation criteria. Because you can counter the competition against these criteria.

Let me be more specific. Assume that I and my organization want from our consultants personal service when and where we demand it and that you are a small firm bidding against two much larger ones. Why are you the best qualified? Because your small size avoids levels of bureaucracy. You can move quickly if I need you quickly. You're lean and fast, and therefore attentive. So if I ask you why you're the best qualified firm, you can give me, not a category, but a good reason:

Now you can discuss how big your firm is, not in a subsection called "Description of the Firm," but in this one. That is, you will discuss the size of your firm *because it is relevant,* in this case to your ability to provide close personal service, which is relevant to this project, because it's relevant to me. It's an instance of your qualifications intersecting with my needs. You are describing your firm not simply to describe your firm but to provide evidence for your claim: ".We are the best qualified firm, in part because our relatively small size..." Now you can also discuss your consulting philosophy, but again, only as it relates to close personal service, only as it provides evidence for your claim.

And so on down (and across) the pyramid. A fully fleshed out pyramid, like the one you'll see in the work session, will have many filled boxes, and every one is there for a reason, because it supplies a good reason that answers my question: "Why should I select *you?*"

⇨ **Chapter 10 Review:**
Writing the QUALIFICATIONS Slot

1. The qualifications *slot* explicitly discusses abilities and capabilities as they intersect with the buyers' needs.
   - Abilities are qualities of people, like experience, kind and level of expertise, and personal characteristics.
   - Capabilities are qualities of things, like your firm or proprietary methodologies or models.
   - Abilities and capabilities are often discussed in resumes, staffing sections or subsections (which might be in a section other than Qualifications), and in qualifications sections themselves.

2. The qualifications *section* is an argument that provides evidence for the claim, "We are the best qualified firm."
   - That claim forms the top box in a pyramid that can be used to organize the section.
   - A "how" pyramid organizes the actions in the methodology; a "why" pyramid organizes the qualifications section to demonstrate why yours is the best-qualified firm for this situation.

3. The content for your argument can be gathered from the Qualifications column of your Themes Development Worksheet.
   - The Themes Development Worksheet expresses your qualifications as they are related to hot buttons, evaluation criteria, and counters to the competition based on these criteria.
   - Therefore, that content phrases your abilities and capabilities as they intersect with the buyers' needs. (See Exhibit 10.2.)

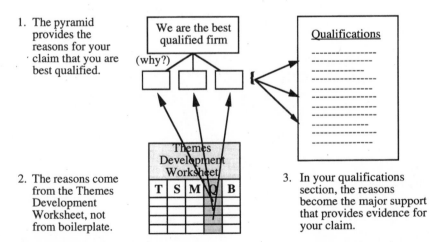

1. The pyramid provides the reasons for your claim that you are best qualified.

2. The reasons come from the Themes Development Worksheet, not from boilerplate.

3. In your qualifications section, the reasons become the major support that provides evidence for your claim.

Exhibit 10.2. Writing the qualifications slot.

Work Session 9: Writing the QUALIFICATIONS Slot for ABC

You know very well that a proposal's qualification section can be a key factor in convincing a potential client to select your firm instead of a competitor's. Your qualifications section will have to incorporate and reinforce the themes developed and played out in preceding sections of the proposal and also demonstrate clearly and conclusively that Paramount is superior to its competitors in having the resources and the ability to conduct the proposed methodology expeditiously, to produce a more comprehensive and effective plan, and if necessary to help ABC implement the selected alternative in a timely manner.

You feel that your own time pressures are building and you're hopeful that you can draw on materials from previous proposals that responded to similar situations. But when you get into the proposal file, you find that the same situation exists that you had encountered during your last proposal effort and thought had been corrected by now: The proposals are not filed by industry or even by type of engagement. This frustrates you because you know you're going to waste precious time finding relevant proposals. You decide to bring this problem to Gilmore's attention.

After fishing through a large stack of previously submitted proposals, you find a few that look like they might be helpful, but you're disappointed again—though not really surprised. All the qualifications sections appear interchangeable, and in fact, you conclude, they pretty much are. They contain some useful and well-written paragraphs on Paramount's history and on its experience within ABC's industry. But they are generic: they use too much boilerplate and never read as if they are written to real readers in specific situations with specific problems. The paragraphs aren't formed into an argument. They won't sufficiently differentiate you from the competition and convince ABC that Paramount is the firm that should be engaged for the study.

When you and Gilmore began developing a strategy for the proposal to ABC, you and he spent considerable time preparing a Themes Development Worksheet. You now want to take advantage of the thought that went into this effort, so you review the worksheet's column labeled "Qualifications." Here, basically, is the content in that column:

- We'll commit capable staff quickly.

- Our strong manufacturing and financial capabilities will enable us to define the full range of expansion alternatives and evaluate them thoroughly.

- Our people are experts in transferring knowledge, building teams, and managing and implementing change.

- Our staff understands the range of criteria that might be important to use and is adept at leading discussions to secure group consensus.

- Our multidisciplined team will have expertise in manufacturing strategy, facilities planing, marketing, logistics analysis, human resources, etc.

Using that content, you construct the following argument:

These five claims address most of the themes on the Themes Development Worksheet, and the claims will each head a subsection in the body of the qualifications section. The last claim, you realize, provides you an opportunity to look ahead to what you hope will be another project at ABC—implementing the plan developed during this planning project.

One group of themes not addressed in your pyramid is that related to comprehensiveness, thoroughness, and complexity. This theme you decide to include in the introduction to the section by stressing that ABC's problem is complex, that the right solution will not come easily, and that they don't have much time left to conduct a comprehensive study. The results of your efforts are shown in the following:

Qualifications of Paramount Consulting

ABC is faced with a most formidable challenge as it begins the task of providing additional manufacturing capacity to avert the shortfall expected in the next few years. This capacity shortfall should be considered imminent as you examine the numerous tasks that must be completed effectively within the narrow available time frame.

Time will be required for sufficient interchange between ABC and Consolidated to agree on the decision to commit scarce financial, planning, managerial, and other resources needed to implement the selected option. Then, substantially more time will be needed to put in place additional resources and to provide the necessary training for an effective start-up.

As described in the following paragraphs, Paramount has the diverse capabilities to help you complete this challenging engagement successfully and expeditiously. Specifically, we have:

- The resources to begin this engagement immediately and to complete our study in 4 to 5 months
- Substantial manufacturing, financial, and strategy-development experience within the household appliance industry
- The ability to address the wide range of issues related to this engagement
- The ability to develop a sound joint ABC/Paramount team
- Proven experience in planning and controlling implementation of the strategy we will develop with you

Paramount Has the Resources to Begin and Complete This Study Quickly

Of the nearly 100 consultants in our nearby Midwest office, we have already identified several individuals with the skills and experience needed to help develop a sound plan for increasing capacity. Each of these professionals has worked on similar engagements, is substantially "down the learning curve," and will therefore be able to function effectively at the very beginning of the engagement. In fact, several of them have participated in developing this proposal.

Our proposed engagement team of four consultants will entirely comprise individuals from this group. As discussed, we would like to introduce this team to you so that you feel as comfortable with them as we do. We will use no subcontractors, and we will be able to begin the engagement immediately after your approval to proceed.

We Have Substantial Manufacturing, Financial, and Strategy-Development Experience Within Your Industry

For almost 40 years, Paramount has served clients with a high level of satisfaction. In fact, 80 percent of our consulting engagements come from previous clients. Paramount originated with a strong manufacturing and strategy capability that has grown significantly over the years; this strength will enable us to address all of the diverse issues that must be resolved during the proposed engagement.

In the past five years we have conducted over 200 manufacturing strategy engagements of which nearly 25 were conducted for companies within the appliance industry. Furthermore, approximately 60 of those studies specifically involved our developing a broad range of manufacturing capacity plans. Many of them were designed to answer questions similar to yours: "How can we provide additional manufacturing capacity most effectively?"

We Are Able to Address the Wide Range of Issues Related to This Study

The team proposed for this engagement will have expertise in all aspects of this study. We understand the marketing and manufacturing issues from a business perspective so that we can develop various capacity expansion options; evaluate them with your management team, considering each of the team members' individual (and often differing) perspectives; select the most appropriate option; prepare for Consolidated a comprehensive appropriation request; and plan for its successful implementation within your tight time frame.

We Have the Ability to Build a Sound ABC/Paramount Team

Because the staff to be assigned will have considerable expertise in conducting similar studies, building consensus, and transferring their knowledge, skills, and expertise, we have been able to carefully structure our approach so that ABC management will participate actively and become an integral part of the engagement team. Thus, on completion of the engagement, ABC will possess a base of residual knowledge that will be invaluable in addressing future capacity and other strategic manufacturing questions. For example, we believe that ABC members of the engagement team will be able, even more effectively than at present, to monitor sales forecasts, plant productivity, and capacity utilization to project accurately when additional capacity might be needed in the more distant future.

We Have the Ability to Plan and Control Implementation

Once the most appropriate capacity expansion option has been selected, it will be extremely important to implement the plan without delay. Although an implementation phase lies outside the scope of this proposed engagement, you should be aware that our significant experience in successfully implementing comprehensive plans for increasing capacity could be invaluable to ABC. Our engagement teams that work on such implementation projects routinely use a variety of sophisticated project-control software packages. These programs are necessary for properly allocating resources; monitoring task completions and costs, thereby assuring adherence to budget; identifying potential problems or delays; and reallocating resources to maintain schedules and achieve time and cost objectives. These control techniques will ensure that implementation of the selected option will proceed smoothly and will be completed on time and within budget.

Even if we are not actively involved in implementation, we will have developed the new manufacturing plan considering ABC's resources and capabilities. Our goal is not just to produce a plan for increasing capacity, but to bring that capacity on line as soon as possible. That is, we are not in the business of just developing plans. We want to see those plans implemented whether or not you decide to engage us to help you do so.

11

Writing the
Benefits Section

Let's consider the last major part of a typical proposal, perhaps one of yours written or delivered orally to me and my organization. Your proposal begins informally and maintains a friendly and informal "we can work together" tone. It conveys the right chemistry; it's responsive to my needs and contains benefits; and, yes, it even includes a few themes. But in your last section, Timing and Cost, the tone changes dramatically and becomes abrupt. Although the proposal began in a friendly way, now it seems distant. Although it began informally, even addressing me by my first name, now it seems official and formal, with phrases like: "Invoices are payable upon receipt" and "We are also reimbursed for expenses" and "It is our policy to..."

Now, of course, you can and you should try to change the tone so that your costs slot is more aligned with what has preceded. But information in that slot will always seem relatively distant and official, and sometimes it will have to be. So except for one or two perfunctory closing statements ("Thanks for the opportunity, please call to clarify, blah, blah, blah"), I am left at the end of your proposal with the distant, the formal, and the official. Your proposal not only ends with straight information (on costs and terms of payment), it concludes with the most distasteful information (unless, of course, you happen to be the low bidder).

The solution is not to end with timing and costs, by telling me how many pounds of flesh you will extract, but by explaining the benefits, the value I am going to get for the money you're asking me to spend. That is, your proposal's last major element can be much more persuasive by discussing the expected benefits of your efforts and, as I will show you, much more.

The Kinds of Benefits

You have already done most if not all of the groundwork necessary to think about benefits and value. We've discussed and you've completed in the work sessions four worksheets:

- Baseline Logic Worksheet (discussed in Chap. 2)
- Benefits Worksheet (Chap. 5)
- Hot Buttons Worksheet (Chap. 6)
- Themes Development Worksheet (Chap. 6)

You are now in a position to reap what you have sown, to summarize for me in a compelling, persuasive finale the benefits from using your services. These benefits fall into two categories: product benefits, which focus on *what* you will deliver; and process benefits, which focus on *how* you will deliver it.

Product benefits accrue from my objective(s) being achieved. We first discussed these in Chap. 4. There, I showed you how each action in your pyramid needs to express a result, a deliverable, because each group of actions on one level produces a result on a higher level. That result and others at its level are also actions that produce a result on the next level higher. At the very top of the pyramid is a project objective, resulting from the actions below. That objective expresses an action related to providing insight, developing a plan, or implementing a plan. In fact, that objective produces still other "results"; these are product benefits. (See Exhibit 11.1.)

In the simplest possible terms, product benefits accrue because (a) my current situation, S_1, is less satisfactory than my desired result, S_2; (b) your methodology will move me and my organization from one state to another, better one; and (c) that movement, by definition, will be beneficial. If my current situation is such that I lack insight and if your objective is to provide that insight, I will certainly benefit if you achieve that objective.

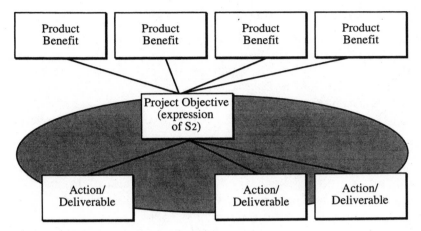

Exhibit 11.1. Benefits are the result of achieving an objective.

Those are the simplest possible terms: when your efforts will move us one step along the continuum, for example from lacking insight to having insight. If your project will move us two steps (for example, from lacking insight to having a plan) then your study will have two objectives. Once you achieve these objectives, we will benefit from the insight you deliver *and* from the plan you develop. Product benefits accrue from your achieving *each* project objective.

You've already listed product benefits on your Baseline Logic Worksheet and on your Benefits Worksheet. The former worksheet focuses on general benefits to the overall organization. The latter focuses more specifically on benefits germane to each person on the buying committee. Both worksheets contain benefits that will accrue once you deliver what you propose to deliver: insight, a plan, and/or an implemented plan.

Unlike product benefits, *process benefits* accrue, not from the objectives being achieved, but from your process of achieving them. Assume, for example, that I want to be intimately involved in reviewing the progress of your project, providing guidance and counsel all along the way. You would no doubt see my desire for involvement as a hot button. And if you address it by designing your methodology so that I can participate at the level I desire, I will perceive a benefit. Because hot buttons are concerns that must be addressed *during* the project, during the process of conducting the project, some of the benefits on your Hot Buttons Worksheet will be process benefits. These tend to be related to how you will conduct your methodology. Additionally, because one or more of your themes could be derived from hot buttons, some of the benefits on your Themes Development Worksheet may also be process benefits.

The Function of the BENEFITS Slot

If you're smart and strategic, you'll discuss benefits throughout the proposal. I've already shown you how the closing component of SITUATION can end with briefly stated benefits. That statement provides a logical and persuasive movement from a discussion of the current situation, a state of pain or uncertainty or opportunity, to a discussion, however brief, of another result, one that is more pleasurable or certain or that has capitalized on the opportunity.

You can integrate benefits into other slots as well by considering, for example, the benefits of your methods and of the deliverables accruing from them, and the benefits of your staff's abilities and your firm's capabilities. Your Themes Development Worksheet can help you here. If, for example, one of my hot buttons is "urgency," your approach will be beneficial if it will deliver results quickly, and your QUALIFICATIONS slot will be persuasive if it argues that you're capable of and experienced in doing so.

But you might not want to leave all the separate strands of benefits scattered throughout the document or presentation, especially since they can make a powerful conclusion to your proposal if you bring them together, in one final section or series of summary paragraphs. Then, the overall movement of your proposal will be like this: It will begin by discussing my organization's current situation; and it will end by describing how we will benefit from your achieving our desired result and by summarizing how and why your methods and your qualifications for performing them will best achieve that result.

Therefore, you should consider this part of your proposal, whether it's a separate section or not, a persuasive summary—a strategically presented conclusion of your proposal's major selling points. It will be a persuasive *summary,* if you summarize the most important elements to us in some of the preceding generic structure slots (e.g., METHODS and QUALIFICATIONS). It will be a *persuasive* summary, if you summarize the benefits you have articulated throughout.

The Content of the Benefits
Section (Work Session 10)

To show you how to compose a persuasive summary of your written or oral proposal, I've decided to complete the last work session of this book myself. (Who said potential clients can't be helpful and accommodating?) Although the process illustrated will result in a benefits section for the planning project for ABC, you can use the same process for other kinds of proposed projects as well. Using a Benefits Section Worksheet like the blank one in Appendix B, you can generate a persuasive summary. That worksheet contains three columns:

Inputs: Process benefits	Outputs: Product benefits of having the plan	Outputs: Product benefits of implementing the plan
From *Themes Development Worksheet* ("methods" and "qualifications" columns)	From *Baseline Logic Worksheet* (deliverables and plan benefits), *Benefits Worksheet, Hot Buttons Worksheet,* and *Themes Development Worksheet* ("benefits" column)	From *Baseline Logic Worksheet* (implemented plan benefits) and *Benefits Worksheet*

Inputs: Process benefits relate to what you will do to move me and my organization from S_1 to S_2. These inputs exist because my and my organization's desired result will be reached because of your methods as they are performed by your staff and supported by your firm's resources. To fill out the "Inputs" column, look to the "methods" and "qualifications" columns of your Themes Development Worksheet (i.e., to your firm's inputs into the process). I've already shown you how to use content within the methods column to generate the opening P-slot to your methods section; now you can use some of that content again in your persuasive summary, your benefits section. Similarly for the content in the qualifications column. That has already been used to help organize your entire qualifications section; now, you want to recapture that important persuasion at the end of your proposal.

Outputs: Product benefits of having the plan relate to outcomes of your project, either in the form of achieved objectives or realized deliverables. To fill out column 2, you need to look to your Baseline Logic Worksheet. That worksheet contains the deliverables that you incorporated from your pyramid, as well as plan benefits. Plan benefits also exist on your Benefits Worksheet, and they might also exist on the Hot Buttons and Themes Development Worksheets.

Outputs: Product benefits of implementing the plan are also found on the Baseline Logic and Benefits Worksheets. By articulating these benefits, you can look past the current project, which will develop a plan, to that point in time when the plan is implemented. This "future perspective" incorporates into your proposal the measurable results orientation we discussed in Chap. 3.

Exhibit 11.2 contains a completed Benefits Section Worksheet that incorporates persuasive content from your other worksheets.

The three columns in your Benefits Section Worksheet will help you structure the entire benefits section, because they are related to three crucial propositions. I'll state these propositions as if you were talking to me, your potential client:

Benefits Section Worksheet

Inputs: Process Benefits From Themes Development Worksheet "Methods" and "Qualifications" Columns	Outputs: Product Benefits of Having the Plan From Worksheets: Baseline Logic (deliverables and plan benefits), Benefits, Hot Buttons, and Theme Development ("Benefits" Column)	Outputs: Product Benefits of Implementing the Plan From Worksheets: Baseline Logic (implemented plan benefits) and Benefits (implemented plan benefits)
(From Themes Worksheet: "Methods") ■ We will have frequent progress reviews so that you're aware of preliminary conclusions and direction quickly. ■ We will involve you in writing the final report, which will actually be your proposal to Consolidated, thus eliminating one step in the approval process. ■ We will carefully define and evaluate all viable alternatives, using qualitative and quantitative evaluation criteria. We will make use, when necessary, of the in-house distribution model. ■ We will form a joint ABC/Paramount study team, as members of which ABC managers will play an integral part. Early in the study, we will conduct strategy sessions with all relevant interest areas within ABC to gain consensus on and establish the proper criteria. ■ Our methodology will be designed to draw upon the expertise of our multi-disciplined team.	**(From Baseline Logic: Plan Benefits)** ■ The right "road map" for providing the Division with additional, needed capacity to ensure the meeting of objectives related to cost, quality, and service. **(From Baseline Logic: Deliverables)** ■ Validated market forecast ■ Validated market share and product mix projections ■ Specified current equipment and space utilization ■ Specified opportunities to better utilize current equipment and space ■ Specified opportunities for utilizing new equipment technology ■ Specified make vs. buy options ■ Specified potential factory roles and locations for increasing capacity ■ An implementation plan specifying required resources and timing	**(From Baseline Logic: Implemented Plan Benefits)** ■ Cost-effective operations ■ Improved product quality ■ Improved service levels ■ Maintained/increased market share ■ Continued good reputations of ABC at Consolidated ■ Continued autonomy vis à vis Consolidated ■ Increased productivity ■ Protected compensation levels ■ Support for business and marketing strategies ■ Better flexibility in implementing business and marketing strategies ■ Decreased relative maintenance costs ■ Higher morale and better retention rates ■ Decreased costs for training

Exhibit 11.2. Completed benefits section worksheet.

Benefits Section Worksheet (cont.)

Inputs: Process Benefits	Outputs: Product Benefits of Having the Plan	Outputs: Product Benefits of Implementing the Plan
(From Themes Worksheet: "Quals") ■ We'll commit capable staff quickly. ■ Our strong manufacturing and financial capabilities will enable us to define the full range of expansion alternatives and evaluate them thoroughly. ■ Our people are experts in transferring knowledge, building teams, and managing and implementing change. ■ Our staff understands the range of criteria that might be important to use and is adept at leading discussions to secure group consensus. ■ We have skills in manufacturing strategy, facilities planning, logistics analysis, human resources, etc.	**(From Hot Buttons Worksheet)** ■ Report will be thorough and comprehensive and well-documented; and because directed to Consolidated, it will respond to urgency and therefore improve ability to compete for capital funding. ■ The beginnings of a sound internal team w/an appreciation of different functional disciplines and broad knowledge of company operations, encouraging diversity and different perspectives. **(From Themes Worksheet: "Benefits")** ■ ABC will have basis for making sound expansion decision and convincing Consolidated of its correctness and desirability. ■ ABC managers will have the ability to periodically update study and assess capacity needs with minimal outside help. ■ Because the financial decision will be based on agreed-upon criteria, the selected alternative will be best accepted by persons with diverse agendas. ■ Given our broad business perspective, ABC can be assured of the right alternative for meeting its needs related to cost and customer service.	

Exhibit 11.2. Completed benefits section worksheet *(Continued)*.

183

- *Column 1:* These (process benefits) are the most important aspects of our methods and our qualifications that will move you from your current situation to your desired result.

- *Column 2:* Because of those inputs, these are the (product) benefits you will receive and the value you will be provided once you have achieved your desired result.

- *Column 3:* These are the (product) benefits you will receive and the value you will be provided once that plan is implemented.

With these three propositions in mind and the completed Benefits Section Worksheet, I spent less than 30 minutes writing the following draft of a benefits section for the proposal to ABC. The writing was quick and relatively easy because I had organized my thoughts logically and completely. Note how each subsection takes content from columns 1 through 3 respectively. I hope you'll agree that the section provides a powerful conclusion, a powerful persuasive summary, to the proposal. The section begins by addressing Norm Williams, ABC's VP of Operations, to whom Gilmore directed the proposal.

Benefits

I would like to summarize for you, Norm, some of the most important points we've made in our previous discussions and in this proposal. Then, I will describe the benefits we believe you will receive from our developing a plan for meeting ABC's forecasted demand and from that plan's subsequent implementation by ABC (possibly with our support, if appropriate).

The Benefits of Leveraging Our Efforts

By forming a joint ABC/Paramount team, with ABC managers playing an integral part, we will be able to leverage the substantial knowledge, expertise, and tools both ABC and Paramount will bring to this project and to develop, sell, and implement the plan as quickly as possible.

This team will hold frequent progress reviews so that various constituencies within the Division (as well as, if appropriate, within Consolidated) will be aware of preliminary conclusions and direction quickly. We plan for these reviews to include strategy sessions, during which we can gain consensus on answers to the wide variety of questions posed in this project and get agreement across various interest areas on the appropriate criteria to be used to select the most effective expansion option. Finally, we will involve the team in preparing the final report, which we would like to be, in fact, a proposal and capital expenditure request to Consolidated. This strategy would eliminate an entire and possibly time-consuming step in the approval process.

This teaming strategy will work exceptionally well because Paramount's professionals have extensive expertise in building effective client/consultant teams, transferring knowledge, and managing and implementing change. We also understand the range of criteria important in this analysis, and are adept at facilitating discussions to gain consensus on these criteria. We will commit our broad-based team quickly to begin the project immediately after your approval to proceed. Using our exceptional expertise in marketing, manufacturing strategy, facilities planning, logistics, financial analysis, and human resources, we will provide ABC with the right "road map" for increasing capacity.

Your Benefits at the End of This Study

Our report/proposal to you and to Consolidated will be thorough, comprehensive, and well documented, providing ABC with the basis for making a sound expansion decision that considers and balances all the quantitative and qualitative factors. And because that decision will be based on agreed-to criteria, it will be well accepted by ABC management with divergent agendas. Just as important, the report will convince Consolidated of the expansion decision's correctness and desirability, and answer their "what-if" questions.

In addition to our recommended expansion option, the report will contain:

- A confirmed market forecast, and market share and product mix projections
- Specified current equipment and space utilization, and opportunities to better utilize current equipment and space, as well as new technology
- Specified make versus buy options as well as potential factory roles and locations for increasing capacity
- An implementation plan

Our implementation plan will specify the tasks, resources, requirements, and timing necessary to bring additional capacity on line over time in a controlled yet expeditious manner.

Your Benefits Beyond This Study

We are confident that, once implemented, our jointly developed plan will significantly improve ABC's processes; lead to more cost-effective operations, improved service levels, and product quality; and maintain if not enhance your market share. Your productivity should increase, your compensation levels should be protected, and you should realize greater flexibility in implementing your business and marketing strategies. Most importantly, after subsequent implementation you should improve your competitive position and maintain your excellent reputation with Consolidated.

*   *   *

Quite obviously, Norm, we believe that Paramount is the right consulting firm for conducting this engagement. We have a comprehensive understanding of your situation and a logical and robust methodology for capitalizing on what we consider a substantial opportunity to continue your growth in the marketplace and solidify your position within Consolidated Industries. Just as soon as possible, we would like to discuss that methodology and how we can best work together with you, President Armstrong, and others so that we can all agree on the proper magnitude of effort, the specific roles ABC and Paramount personnel should play, and the exact cost of the engagement. This is a critically important study for ABC, and we look forward to supporting you as you develop the base for continued competitive success.

I, as a potential client, want to achieve a result and the benefits associated with that result. Because benefits, real or imagined, imply value, they are one of the most important factors in my decision-making process. And one of the biggest deficiencies I find in your proposals is the lack of in-depth discussion about how I, my colleagues, and my organization will benefit from using your services, both during and after your proposed project. Never again should you be unable to provide that in-depth discussion. I've given you four tools—four worksheets (see Exhibit 11.3)—that help you to generate persuasive content, and a fifth tool—the Benefits Worksheet—that helps you to organize that content for your benefits section.

Now you know that you can distribute benefits throughout the proposal, and you can gather them in a persuasive summary that ends your document or presentation by focusing, not on your qualifications or your fees, but on the value I will receive. This orientation toward value should certainly get you a portion of the additional 2 to 5 points you need to win. If you sweep me off my feet with persuasive benefits from using your services, I'll be less inclined to go with the lowest bidder, unless of course they demonstrate that they can provide similar benefits.

What a delightful situation this would be for me: comparing bidders based on their perception of benefits to my organization. How different from my usual experience: reading or listening to a battle of wits between two unarmed opponents. By generating, incorporating, and elaborating on benefits, you will have the arms to win many more battles and to set clearer expectations after your victory.

⇨ Chapter 11 Review: Writing the Benefits Section

1. As illustrated in Exhibit 11.3, you can generate persuasive content using four worksheets and then gather that content in a fifth worksheet that helps you structure your benefits section.

2. Your proposal should have two kinds of benefits: product and process.
   - Product benefits are those that accrue from the objectives being achieved.
   - Process benefits accrue from the process of achieving these objectives.

3. Benefits can exist throughout the proposal (for example, in the closing component of SITUATION, in the closing P-slots of METHODS, and in QUALIFICATIONS).

4. Although they can exist throughout the proposal, benefits can be gathered at the end to form a persuasive summary, a value-laden conclusion, to your document or presentation.

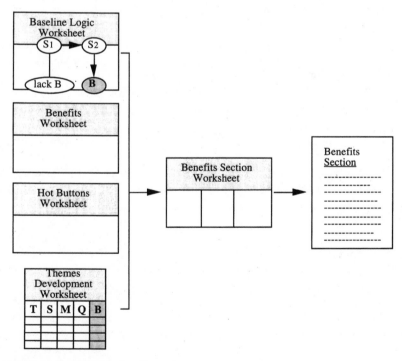

Exhibit 11.3. Writing the benefits section.

12

Summary—
The Proposal
Development Process

This is the last chapter in *Writing Winning Business Proposals.* You've come a long way in helping yourself get the 2 to 5 points that make the difference between winning and coming in a close second. Very few people know what you have learned. Although you have gained considerable insight by reading this book, and although you now have a plan for increasing your percentage of winning proposals, you know that insights and plans aren't much good unless they are implemented. So I encourage you to *use* the insights you've gained and the plan you now have. Use them consciously and often. I've brought you out of the forest and to the water; now you have to drink.

This chapter summarizes the plan I've presented to you in this book, which has helped you understand how to use proposal logics and psychologics to prepare your documents and presentations. The summary provides you with a snapshot of the proposal development process I've discussed with you as well as a road map you can use as you develop future proposals.

After that summary, you will find a Rating Guide for Proposals (Exhibit 12.6). You can use the guide to evaluate your own proposals, since the guide reflects many of the concepts and principles I've been helping you to learn. Although the guide is based upon a 100-point scale, I've arbitrarily assigned points to its six major sections. The sections related to benefits and methods, for example, are worth 20 points each, while those related to the situation and to qualifications are allotted 15. Obviously, you should adjust the allotments, based on your proposal situation. In a given situation, for example, qualifications and costs might need to be weighted more heavily than benefits and methods.

You also might be able to use the rating guide to help me, your potential client, to establish evaluation criteria, if I haven't already done so, or to revise these criteria, if it's in your interest to do so. That is, you might find it opportune and helpful to discuss the guide with me. As a result, you might have a clearer idea of what I expect and therefore of what you need to deliver.

In the introduction to this book, I challenged you to work hard to understand the concepts and principles that I would present. None of these concepts and principles is particularly difficult to understand. But using them intelligently and well takes effort and practice. Now I challenge you to work hard to practice, to implement. Practice never makes perfect, because perfect doesn't exist. But practice does lead to continuous improvement. You've already improved; continue to do so.

The Proposal Development Process

(Proposal Logics)

1. *Use the Baseline Logic Worksheet to create and test the baseline logic* $(S_1 \rightarrow S_2 \rightarrow B)$.

   - Specify the current situation (S_1), which includes the potential client's problem or opportunity as well as lack of benefits.
   - Given that current situation, specify the desired result or results (S_2) that your proposed project will achieve. S_2 can be one or a combination of three kinds: insight, a plan, or an implemented plan.
   - Given that desired result, specify the benefits (B) likely to accrue from achieving S_2.
   - If the desired result is insight or a plan, use a measurable results orientation to estimate the benefits that would likely accrue after subsequent implementation.
   - Test the alignment of the elements within the baseline logic to be certain that:
     - The project objectives are aligned with S_2.
     - The benefits are aligned with both S_2 and the project's objectives.
     - S_1 and B are aligned.

2. *Construct the methodology to define how to achieve the objective.*

   - Clearly identify the objective (or objectives), based on the buyers' overriding question (or questions). If the project will move the buyer one step on the continuum (for example, from lacking insight to having insight), there will be only one overriding question and objective. If the project will move the buyer two or more steps on the continuum (for example, from lacking insight to having a plan), there will be two or more overriding questions and therefore two or more objectives.

- Place the objective atop a pyramid that organizes the actions necessary to achieve it. (Be certain each action specifically expresses a result.) Build one pyramid for each objective.
- Once the pyramid is constructed, list the action–results in sequence.
- Within that sequence, integrate the activities important for planning and communicating.
- Identify the deliverables within the pyramid, and include them on the Baseline Logic Worksheet. If possible, generate additional benefits that will accrue from achieving these deliverables.

(Proposal Psychologics)

3. *Identify the role or roles played by each buyer on the selection committee, and specify the individual benefits that will accrue to each buyer from achieving the desired result.*

- Classify all of the members of the buying team according to the following role or roles each will play in making the decision: economic buyer, user buyer, technical buyer, coach, ratifier.
- Identify for each buyer the likely individual benefits that will accrue from achieving S_2, remembering that these benefits will be conditioned by the buyer's role and position in the organization.
- If at all possible, develop at least one coach.

4. *Identify, select, and develop themes* (see Exhibit 12.1).

A. Identify possible themes by considering:

- *Hot buttons*—the emotional needs and desires of *individual* buyers that will have an effect on the project and must be addressed during the project. After identifying hot buttons, be certain to generate on the Hot Buttons Worksheet at least one benefit that will accrue from addressing each hot button.
- *Evaluation criteria*—the technical needs and desires of the *collective* buyers often contained in RFPs and other documents.
- *Counters to the competition*—your strengths relative to the competition, especially as these differences apply to the evaluation criteria.

B. Select the themes by considering:

- *Breadth*—the degree to which the theme is or could be relevant to most of the buyers.
- *Weight*—the degree to which the theme is or could be important to one or more of the buyers.

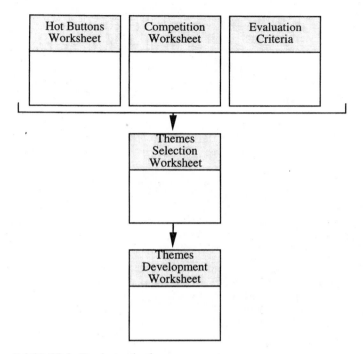

Exhibit 12.1. Developing the themes.

- *Leverage*—the degree to which the theme intersects with or "speaks" to other themes.

   C. Develop the themes on the Themes Development Worksheet.

5. *Use the Benefits Worksheet to derive the benefits to each buyer of having insight or a plan, or having the plan implemented.*

(Proposal Preparation)

6. *Write a situation and an objectives slot that discusses* (see Exhibit 12.2):
   - The current situation and its causes and effects (use the Baseline Logic Worksheet);
   - The key questions that must be answered to eliminate the problem or capitalize on the opportunity (use the second and subsequent lines of the pyramid of the methodology to generate some of these questions); and
   - The buyer's needs, as they intersect with your themes (use the "Situation" column of the Themes Development Worksheet).

7. *Write a methods section that, when necessary and appropriate* (see Exhibit 12.3):

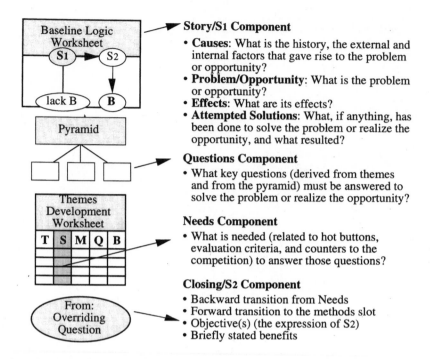

Story/S1 Component

- **Causes**: What is the history, the external and internal factors that gave rise to the problem or opportunity?
- **Problem/Opportunity**: What is the problem or opportunity?
- **Effects**: What are its effects?
- **Attempted Solutions**: What, if anything, has been done to solve the problem or realize the opportunity, and what resulted?

Questions Component

- What key questions (derived from themes and from the pyramid) must be answered to solve the problem or realize the opportunity?

Needs Component

- What is needed (related to hot buttons, evaluation criteria, and counters to the competition) to answer those questions?

Closing/S2 Component

- Backward transition from Needs
- Forward transition to the methods slot
- Objective(s) (the expression of S2)
- Briefly stated benefits

Exhibit 12.2. Writing the situation and objectives slots.

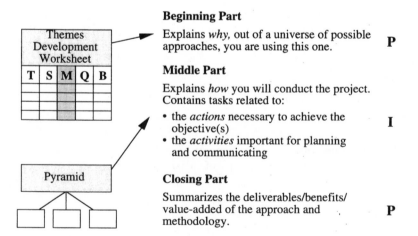

Beginning Part

Explains *why,* out of a universe of possible approaches, you are using this one. **P**

Middle Part

Explains *how* you will conduct the project. Contains tasks related to:

- the *actions* necessary to achieve the objective(s) **I**
- the *activities* important for planning and communicating

Closing Part

Summarizes the deliverables/benefits/ value-added of the approach and methodology. **P**

Exhibit 12.3. Writing the methods slot.

- Fills opening P-slots by providing a rationale for tasks, phases, and the entire approach (for the introduction to the methods section, use the "Methods" column of the Themes Development Worksheet); and
- Fills closing P-slots by discussing the outcomes of tasks, phases, and the entire approach.

8. *Write a qualifications section that* (see Exhibit 12.4):

- Explicitly discusses abilities and capabilities as they intersect with the buyers' needs; and
- Uses a pyramid to develop the claim, "We are the best qualified firm." (Use the "Qualifications" column of the Themes Development Worksheet to develop this pyramid.)

9. *Write a benefits section (use the Benefits Worksheet) that summarizes the proposal's major selling points and that includes, when necessary and appropriate* (see Exhibit 12.5):

- Benefits related to themes
- Benefits from having insight or a plan
- Benefits from having an implemented plan
- Benefits from having hot buttons addressed.

10. Evaluate the proposal using the Rating Guide, making certain to weight the various factors based on the situation (Exhibit 12.6).

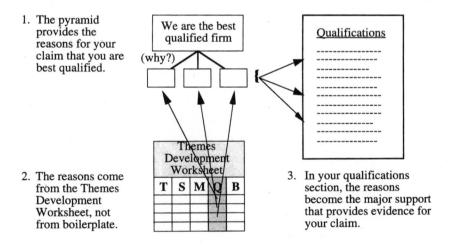

1. The pyramid provides the reasons for your claim that you are best qualified.

2. The reasons come from the Themes Development Worksheet, not from boilerplate.

We are the best qualified firm

(why?)

Themes Development Worksheet

T	S	M	Q	B

Qualifications

3. In your qualifications section, the reasons become the major support that provides evidence for your claim.

Exhibit 12.4. Writing the qualifications slot.

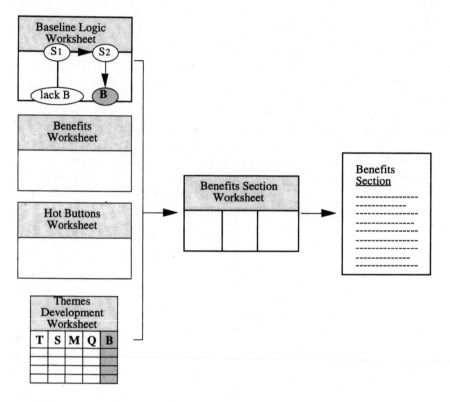

Exhibit 12.5. Writing the benefits section.

Evaluation Criteria	Points Possible	Your Proposal
The proposers have established the foundation for a good *working relationship*. ■ The proposers understand my firm's internal sensitivities ■ These individuals can work with my people. ■ I believe that they can and will do what they say they will. ■ They have been responsible, reliable, and responsive. ■ They've tailored this proposal to my situation; they've avoided boilerplate.	15	☐
The proposers understand our *situation*. ■ The proposers clearly understand our problem or opportunity. ■ They know how this situation developed and how it affects us. ■ They understand the key questions we need to answer. ■ They understand our issues within a larger business/industry context.	15	☐
The proposers clearly understand the project's overall *objective(s)*. ■ The objective(s) expresses our desired result (e.g., insight; a developed plan; and/or an implemented plan) at the end of this project. ■ I understand how that objective(s) related to our problem or opportunity and to the benefits we will receive from achieving that objective(s).	15	☐

Exhibit 12.6. Rating guide for proposals.

Evaluation Criteria	Points Possible	Your Proposal
The proposers have a logical ***methodology*** for achieving that objective. ■ I understand the relationship between the overall objective(s) and the tasks that will be performed to achieve it. ■ The proposers provide a clear rationale for their proposed methods in *this* project; I don't sense that theirs is a canned methodology.	20	☐
They have clearly communicated the ***qualifications*** that I feel are critical for achieving this project's overall objective. ■ Given our situation, I understand how the propersers' qualifications relate to the objective(s) and to the methods necessary to achieve them.	15	☐
I believe that the *cost* of the project is justified by the ***bemefots*** articulated. ■ I understand the benefits likely to be realized *during* the project, as a result of how the proposers will work with my people. ■ I also understand the benefits likely to be realized *after* the project, as a result of the project's objectives being achieved. ■ If possible, and within reasonable ranges, the proposers have quantified the tangible benefits likely to accrue.	20	☐
Total Points:	100	☐

Exhibit 12.6. Rating guide for proposals *(Continued).*

Paramount Consulting's Proposal Opportunity at the ABC Company: A Case Study

Dramatis Personae:

Stan Gilmore, a partner in Paramount Consulting; also, your boss

Ray Armstrong, President of ABC Co.

Norm Williams, ABC's Vice President of Operations

Marcia Collins, ABC's Vice President of Marketing

Paul Morrison, ABC's Chief Industrial Engineer

Frank Metzger, ABC's Plant Manager

Wednesday, February 1:
The First Contact

Stan Gilmore, a partner in Paramount Consulting responsible for his firm's manufacturing practice, just received a letter from a Norm Williams, Vice President of Operations for the ABC Company, a division of Consolidated Industries. The letter states that ABC manufactures and markets a line of major household and commercial appliances, has annual sales of several hundred million dollars, and has enjoyed a consistent record of growth. Future growth, however, might be curtailed by available manufacturing capacity. ABC, the letter continues, wants to engage a consulting firm to help it answer its manufacturing capacity questions. Paramount has been recommended to them, and if Paramount is interested in pursuing a possible relationship, it should contact Williams.

Gilmore is anxious to pursue this opportunity because he recognizes ABC's brand name as having an outstanding reputation for product quality and delivery performance, and knows that it holds a significant share of its market. Furthermore, Consolidated Industries is well known for acquiring and developing companies that hold dominant positions in their respective markets. Gilmore is confident that Paramount can help.

Gilmore calls Williams to affirm that Paramount can, indeed, provide the needed consulting assistance and welcomes the opportunity to do so. According to Williams, ABC plans to meet separately with representatives from each of the four consulting companies that survived their initial screening. During those meetings, ABC will discuss the need for the study and provide the basic information necessary for the consultants to prepare their proposals. Gilmore asks who will represent ABC at the meeting, and Williams says that he and the following will attend:

- Marcia Collins, Vice President of Marketing
- Frank Metzger, Plant Manager
- Paul Morrison, Chief Industrial Engineer

They conclude their conversation by agreeing to meet the following week at ABC's division office in a large Midwestern city.

Thursday, February 2: Research

Gilmore calls in one of his group's research associates and tells her he needs background data that will give him a better understanding of ABC's operations. She immediately embarks on a Lexis search, a review of Consolidated's annual and 10K reports, a study of S&P's industry reports, and a review of an industry report from the research department of a local brokerage firm.

As they analyze the results of the research, Gilmore can see that Consolidated is indeed a very successful company. Headquartered in New York City, it ranks in the upper quartile of most of the factors used by *Forbes* to measure the success of major industrial companies, and ABC contributes significantly to that success. ABC's products are distributed through a strong national network of distributors and dealers and also to major department store chains that market them under their private labels. Its products enjoy high brand-name recognition and have a well-established reputation for product quality, and the Division is recognized within its industry for providing superior customer service. Industry forecasts indicate that the overall market will grow modestly over the next several years and that little technological product change is expected. The forecasts also show that ABC is expected to retain its share of the market, which is highly competitive. Just four major producers accounted for 86 percent of total shipments last year. Because of the favorable characteristics of its product line and its high service levels, ABC has consistently increased its market share and participated fully in a modestly growing overall market driven by replacement demand, residential and commercial construction, and general economic conditions.

One of the concerns of the industry is the increasing cost of distributing its products. Apparently, the configuration of the product and its weight yields a bulk/weight ratio that makes distribution costs a major component of total operating costs. Furthermore, geographic demand for the product is following demographic shifts to the South, Southeast, and Southwest. Industry reports also show that most of ABC's production takes place in one Midwestern city, but that manufacture of some special-purpose units in the product line occurs in two smaller satellite facilities located in relatively small Midwestern cities.

With this basic understanding, Gilmore looks forward to the meeting to learn more about ABC's manufacturing capacity situation. He has already decided that he will take along one of his associates, you.

Thursday, February 9:
Meeting with Williams, Collins,
Metzger, and Morrison

At the meeting, Williams introduces the attendees identified in the previous conversation. He explains that the four of them will serve as ABC's consultant selection committee along with the division president who is away that day at Consolidated's headquarters in New York.

Williams introduces Marcia Collins, the Vice President of Marketing, who sets the stage for the meeting. Collins joined ABC two years ago after spending four years as director of marketing for a large, national grocery products company. Prior to that, she received an undergraduate degree from Northwestern and an MBA from its Kellogg School. Collins' basic discussion document is a graph that shows two market forecasts for ABC, one labeled optimistic and the other conservative. (See Exhibit A.1.)

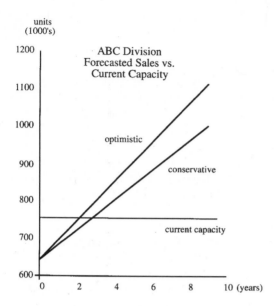

Exhibit A.1. ABC's market forecast.

Obvious from the graphs is that ABC's forecasts assume its ability to continue to increase market share. This is confirmed in a subsequent chart that shows ABC modestly increasing its market share in each year of the forecast. (See Exhibit A.2.)

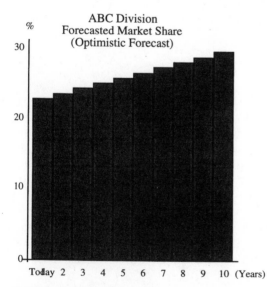

Exhibit A.2. ABC's market share.

Most revealing is a line on the forecast graph that represents the capacity of the existing production facility. It shows that in fewer than three years existing capacity will be exceeded even in the conservative forecast—beyond that point, the shortfall in production capacity will become progressively worse.

Williams next introduces Frank Metzger, the Plant Manager, explaining that he has been with ABC his entire working career. Metzger worked as an hourly employee in both the press and maintenance departments before becoming press department foreman. Williams stresses that Metzger was highly successful in the press department and succeeded him as plant manager three years ago when he was promoted to vice president. Williams asks Metzger to describe the current situation related to utilizing production capacity.

According to Metzger, the plant is meeting its current production schedules by working two full shifts of operation, with some overloaded work centers working a third shift. Most scheduled equipment maintenance is also performed on the third shift so that little overtime premium is incurred because of weekend work. While showing the group a site drawing of the current facility, Metzger describes how the site is well utilized with manufacturing and office space, truck docks, and parking areas.

"Let me point out," says Williams, referring to the drawing, "that the site can't be expanded because it's bounded by railroad tracks in one direction, a major thoroughfare in another, and by residential areas in the other two directions."

"But," Metzger counters, "there's still some space available within the current site into which the present manufacturing facility could expand. Most of ABC's additional capacity requirements could be met by expanding the current facility into the space remaining." He suggests, however, that to meet the projected forecasts they would probably have to operate a full third shift.

"Are there any downside risks to operating a three-shift schedule?" Gilmore asks.

"It would be a challenge," Metzger admits, "because maintenance work would have to be done on the weekends, in which case we'd have to incur additional overtime costs."

Gilmore pursues the issue: "Could productivity and quality on the third shift be expected to attain the level of the other two shifts?"

They would undoubtedly experience additional absenteeism and turnover, according to Metzger, and might even have some difficulty in recruiting for that shift. But even if operating costs are higher, ABC's capital investment would be considerably lower by expanding the existing facility. "It's also possible that we could hold expansion space to a minimum by using outside storage for raw materials and finished goods, if necessary."

Williams introduces Paul Morrison, ABC's Chief Industrial Engineer, to apprise the group of the manufacturing capacity situation. Morrison has an undergraduate degree in Industrial Engineering from Michigan and an MS in that discipline from Georgia Tech where, as a graduate assistant, he taught undergraduate courses in quantitative methods. He joined ABC three years ago, and one of his projects was to develop a computer model to enable the Division to improve its distribution methods and to track and control those costs, which are an important part of their total operating costs.

According to Morrison, he and his department have not studied the capacity situation to any great extent because they have been occupied in helping the production departments to maintain productivity levels so that they could meet increasing schedule demands. However, after examining current work center loads to judge the amount of new equipment that will be required and in estimating the amount of additional storage space that will be needed for higher production levels, he questions whether the space available on the existing site is adequate: "Even though investment costs might be lower, I would be hesitant to put all of ABC's eggs in one basket, giving us no protection against natural catastrophes or labor difficulties. Furthermore, ABC's markets are growing faster outside of the Midwest." He suggests that even if the projected forecasts could be satisfied at the present site, if they were able to increase market share further, or if the overall market grew more rapidly than expected, they would be facing the same dilemma again in the near future. "In my view the consultants must carefully define what ABC needs in terms of additional manufacturing capacity, develop logical alternatives to meet these needs, and then quantitatively and qualitatively evaluate those alternatives."

Williams thanks everyone for their input and remarks that one of Morrison's points is especially important—that virtually all of ABC's production occurs at this facility, which makes them somewhat vulnerable. He also expresses some surprise that no one has mentioned another possible expansion option: "What about our two satellite manufacturing facilities? Neither one is on a site large enough to accommodate our full expansion requirements, but maybe one of the product lines could be relocated to one of these sites, thereby freeing up space at the existing facility." However, he agrees with Morrison that they will look to the consultants to develop possible alternatives and that those alternatives will have to be analyzed very thoroughly and convincingly because ABC could anticipate a major capital investment.

Williams asks Gilmore what else they can provide that will help him prepare the proposal. Gilmore requests copies of the site plan; the market forecast data; samples of various productivity, work center loading, and scheduling reports; equipment lists; and manning tables. He also asks Williams to identify the other three consultants who will bid on the project. Gilmore recognizes one of Paramount's competitors, which has strong, diversified consulting capabilities. Not recognizing the other two, he wonders if Williams will tell a little about them. According to Williams, they are local companies who specialize in facilities planning, plant layout, materials handling, and productivity improvement. One of them had helped ABC with a materials handling problem in the past. "How satisfied were you with their work?" Gilmore asks. Williams responds briskly, but not curtly: "Satisfied enough to ask them to bid."

The material provides Gilmore with a good understanding of ABC's current situation related to manufacturing capacity. To make certain that Paramount's proposal will be entirely responsive, Gilmore remarks, he would like to meet with each of the people present to understand their problems better and to probe the advantages and disadvantages of the alternatives they had discussed as well as some others that might be worth considering. At that time, it would also be important for him to make an extensive tour of the manufacturing operations. Williams is pleased with Gilmore's willingness to take the additional time to do this and, after polling his group, suggests that the following week would be convenient. He also mentions that Ray Armstrong, the Division President, will be back in the office then and Gilmore could probably meet with him. Gilmore says he will call each person to schedule a specific time. He spends the balance of the meeting telling the group about Paramount's overall capabilities, history and reputation, its specific expertise in the areas relevant to the proposed study, and the capabilities of its staff, and then describes some consulting assignments in which Paramount had been successful in helping clients with similar problems.

The two of you leave the meeting feeling that you have a good understanding of ABC's capacity situation and that you have established a reasonable rapport with the group. However, you recognize that you need to know much more about ABC's operation to scope the proposal properly. This, you both feel, can be accomplished through Gilmore's interviews. You also agree, however, that a major objective of the interview process should be to better understand the people on the selection team, including their interests and perceived study objectives, and how the results of the study could affect them. Then you can make the proposal responsive to each member of the team.

Tuesday, February 14: Individual Meetings with the Major Players

"I believe that your market forecasts will play a major role in the proposed study." Gilmore is talking to Marcia Collins, the Vice President of Marketing. "So I would like to understand better how they were developed."

"Most of my data," she says, "come from reports published regularly by the industry trade group, the Association of Home Appliance Manufacturers, in which ABC participates. These data were supplemented by others from *Appliance* and *Appliance Manufacturer* magazines surveys, Standard & Poor's industry surveys, and ABC's own historical data." Because there is a good deal of consistency among the data from the different sources, Collins is confident that her conclusions on the overall industry forecasts are valid. "However," she points out, "my development of optimistic and conservative forecasts is based on my interpretation of ABC's position in the market." She explains that the Division's steady increases in market share are due to its ability to control costs, to maintain quality, and to provide a high level of service to its customers: "The optimistic forecast assumes that ABC will be successful in maintaining those positions; the conservative forecast assumes some slippage."

According to Collins, maintaining or increasing market share is important to ABC's success: "Not only does it affect our operating results; it is also a performance measurement in our bonus plan. Furthermore, it affects the level of autonomy we enjoy as well as the ease with which we can obtain capital funds from Consolidated."

Gilmore asks Collins to assess the various possibilities for expanding capacity that were discussed last week. Collins isn't really knowledgeable about manufacturing operations, she says, and has little sense of just how many additional resources would be required. However, she is concerned about adding the total expansion capability at the existing site: "High service levels are important in increasing market share, and ABC's current service levels could be jeopardized if all manufacturing were in one location." Her reasoning appears sound: First, as she says, their major markets are shifting away from the Midwest, resulting in increased delivery times; second, if there should be a fire or other catastrophe, their reputation for good service would certainly deteriorate. "I feel so strongly about maintaining or improving current service levels that I think service levels should be a criterion for evaluating the various alternatives for expanding capacity."

Metzger's office is centrally located in the manufacturing area of the facility. After Gilmore enters, Metzger immediately apologizes: He has to delay their meeting for at least an hour to meet with his maintenance, press, and assembly department foremen. One of the major fabrication lines has broken down and they have to find a way to complete a production run because the customer's trailers are waiting at the shipping dock. In the meantime, he asks his assistant to give Gilmore a tour of the plant.

Gilmore is immediately impressed with the excellent housekeeping in the plant. Aisles are clear and well-marked, storage areas are orderly with good use of clear height, individual work areas are clean and well-organized, and there are many examples of point-of-use storage where materials are stored close and easily available to the production operators. The assistant explains that each operator is responsible for his own workplace—that housekeeping personnel are used only to maintain major travel aisles. Gilmore is also impressed with the production equipment, which appears reasonably state of the art. The assistant remarks that the industrial engineering group has an aggressive program to continually evaluate and upgrade equipment and that the plant engineering department is adept at designing and installing special-purpose equipment.

When Metzger returns, he again apologizes profusely and explains that they were able to make some equipment substitutions that will minimize the downtime on the assembly line as well as increase the rate of delivery of the finished product to the customer's trailers. Gilmore compliments Metzger on the general appearance of the manufacturing facility and comments that it could be a model for many of his clients' plants. He asks Metzger to expand a bit on his background as portrayed last week at the initial meeting.

Metzger augmented his high school education with numerous in-house courses offered by ABC. He broadened himself beyond those offerings by taking courses in human relations, shop supervision, quality control, and advanced shop math at the local community college. These efforts served him well because he was promoted to a maintenance group leader and then succeeded the press department foreman when that individual became ill. As he explained last week, he was fortunate in replacing Williams as plant manager when Williams was promoted.

Gilmore would like to hear more about Metzger's concept of increasing capacity at the existing site. Metzger replies that, although he doesn't know just how much additional capacity would be needed, there is quite a bit of land available on the present site for expanding the manufacturing building. Although some of that space is now used for employee parking, he thinks this could be overcome by double-decking the remaining parking area. If the present facility were expanded, he would have the opportunity to promote some well-deserving first-line supervisors into positions of greater responsibility. The capital requirements for that option would probably be less, and he heard that Consolidated was becoming less generous in releasing funds to the competing divisions.

At Chief Industrial Engineer Morrison's office, located in the same area, Gilmore remarks that the caliber of the equipment he saw on his plant tour was evidence of his group's successful program to continually monitor and upgrade major production equipment. Morrison thanks him and shows him a stack of reports that Gilmore had requested at last week's meeting. They discuss the reports in some detail and Morrison suggests that the documents could be very useful in determining ABC's capacity requirements. Gilmore readily agrees.

Gilmore compliments Morrison about some of the latter's comments last week: Several of the factors that would have to be considered in the proposed study were, in his experience, right on the mark. But Gilmore wonders about a factor not discussed: "What about distribution costs?" he asks. "Distribution costs are a major component of total operating costs throughout the industry."

"These are very important to the Division," Morrison says, "and you're right—they weren't sufficiently discussed last week. Because of the weight and configuration of our product, these costs are virtually the same as those for fabricating and assembling our product. They are such a concern," he adds, "that a few years ago my group worked with the information systems and distribution managers to develop a computer model. This model enabled us to analyze different logistics strategies, select the best, and then monitor the costs of distributing product to our nearly 150 demand points on an ongoing basis."

Morrison explains that this model had been properly validated and could be used to determine distribution costs for different manufacturing capacity alternatives. The model had been developed because Division President Armstrong was concerned about escalating distribution costs and their negative impact on profits. Learning that Armstrong planned to engage a consultant to develop the model, Morrison discussed with the systems and distribution managers the possibility of developing such a model in house. They agreed that it could be done if Morrison, because of his academic background, would lead the project. They subsequently met with Armstrong and convinced him that the in-house project was feasible and cost-effective. Armstrong also saw that the project would provide a beneficial learning experience, so he gave his approval to proceed. Morrison's team overcame a number of problems (which he had anticipated) and successfully completed the project, although it took them four months longer than expected.

"I should tell you," Morrison confides, "I recommended to Armstrong that ABC also conduct the capacity expansion study in house. But Armstrong believed that I and my group were stretched thin, that additional staff would have to be hired, and that the Division needed answers to its capacity concerns without delay. Armstrong acknowledged that my group had proven capabilities for the study, but he held firm to his decision to use outside consultants. At this point I am only interested in seeing the study done and done right."

He thinks the study will be complicated because there are so many different alternatives, many with their own devotee. And yet these alternatives are being tossed around without the knowledge of just how much additional capacity is needed. "So, let me repeat what I said last week: One of the initial major tasks of the consultants will be to carefully define capacity requirements. Then, alternatives for satisfying those require-ments can be developed and evaluated." The development of sound, agreed-upon evaluation criteria would be very important, too, to over-come any built-in prejudices that people might have in favor of their own ideas. Gilmore tells Morrison he completely shares his ideas.

Gilmore mentions that he is meeting with Division President Armstrong later that afternoon and asks if Morrison can tell him a little about Armstrong's background. Armstrong, it turns out, was recruited from out-side the company and he has a marketing and financial background. Armstrong became vice president of marketing of a large manufacturing company and was recruited away from that position by a search firm to fill a CEO spot at another company. A few years after that, Consolidated recruited him to head ABC. Morrison doesn't really have that much involvement with Armstrong, but thinks him open-minded, analytical, and firm in his decisions once he has heard and thoroughly considered all sides of an issue.

The office of Norm Williams, the vice president of operations, is near the conference room in which they had met last week. Williams receives Gilmore very cordially and asks him about his interviews and plant tour. They were very informative and helpful, Gilmore responds, and he is beginning to get a good "feel" for ABC's operation, its organization, and its manufacturing capacity situation—background that will help Paramount write a good proposal.

Gilmore says it would be helpful if he knows something more about the vice president's background. After graduating in industrial engineering from Purdue, he replies, he joined ABC's I. E. Group. During several years in the group, he worked in many different manufacturing areas including plant layout, process engineering, equipment justification and selection, wage incentives, job evaluation, and others. When the incumbent plant manager announced his retirement, he was offered the position, which he readily accepted. As plant manager, he set several goals for the plant, including meeting the continually increasing production schedules, con-trolling costs by improving manufacturing methods and processes, main-taining and improving product quality levels, and fostering harmonious employee relations. He believes he has been reasonably successful in meet-ing those goals and, apparently, so did top management because after about five years he was promoted into his present position and became part of the president's management team.

Gilmore asks Williams to tell him about ABC's satellite manufacturing operations since he mentioned them last week during their discussion of capacity expansion alternatives. "They are relatively small operations in two rural cities," he says, "producing certain low-volume, special-purpose units in the product line. Both of the facilities are on plant sites large enough to accommodate some building expansion." But the manufacturing work force in both cities is rather small and might not support a major expansion. His supervisory groups there are relatively thin and would have to be "beefed up." But an expansion to accept a limited part of the product line in addition to expansion at the existing facility would probably enable ABC to meet its forecasted demand for several years.

Gilmore finds President Armstrong to be very congenial, with a demeanor that reflects his guidance of a successful key Consolidated division. They spend some time discussing business conditions generally and Consolidated and ABC in particular. Armstrong asks Gilmore to tell him about Paramount, which he is pleased to do since Armstrong hadn't attended the previous week's meeting.

Gilmore then leads the discussion to the proposed study. Armstrong believes a sound, comprehensive study is critical to the future of the Division. Only by providing manufacturing with the resources it needs to operate cost effectively and to maintain and improve product quality and service levels can the Division hope to maintain its reputation, to compete effectively in the marketplace, and to assure success for the company and its employees. He wants to initiate the study quickly because he knows that if, for example, a new facility is required, it will probably be close to two years before it reaches full production. And, he points out, some critical work centers are already operating on the third shift. Gilmore replies that Armstrong's time estimates are realistic and that Paramount can initiate the study quickly.

Armstrong again emphasizes that the study would have to be thorough and convincing. He tells Gilmore that, although he operates ABC with a great deal of autonomy and that although ABC is very successful, it—like other Consolidated divisions—has to compete for funds "at the company trough." "Therefore," as you've probably been told, "the study will have to be well documented and the returns from the investment clearly defined, because an expansion project of this probable magnitude will require capital funding by Consolidated, and our request will receive close scrutiny at corporate headquarters." Others *had* remarked about the study needing to be thorough and convincing; this was an additional reason why.

Gilmore asks Armstrong what deliverables he expects from the study. Armstrong and his management team have given considerable thought to that topic; indeed, the depth and diversity of their discussions convinced him they would need outside assistance. He goes on to say that the team agreed the study would definitely have to answer at least the following questions:

- What will it take in terms of space, equipment, and manpower to meet both the conservative and optimistic forecasts?

- How much of those resources can be provided by expanding the present facility?
- Even if those resources can be added at the present location, does it make economic sense to do that or to make the investment elsewhere?
- Can service levels be increased and transportation costs reduced at a new geographic location to provide greater leverage in selling to mass marketed customers?
- What ROI will result from the substantial new investment?
- Which alternative generates the greatest profit during the forecast period?

Gilmore responds that these are important and realistic expectations and that in judging different alternatives certain qualitative analyses would also have to be made regarding labor supply, union climate, available technical training assistance, and the like. Armstrong acknowledges this and says he wants to leave Gilmore with one additional point before they end their discussion. He explains that even though they are seeing a shift in the market demand away from the Midwest, they have no intention of relocating the existing facility because of its central geographic location and experienced work force, the significant cost involved in relocating many pieces of equipment and numerous personnel, and the large "sunk cost" in land, building, and fixed equipment.

Gilmore says he appreciates that comment because in the back of his mind he had considered these factors. He thanks Armstrong for his time and tells him that he can probably have a proposal to him by the end of the following week. Armstrong says the proposal should be sent to Williams, who is heading the selection committee.

Wednesday, February 15: Next Steps

When he returns to the office the following day, Gilmore meets with you to brief you on his visit to ABC. Gilmore wants you to spearhead the preparation of the proposal, which he will help you with as time is available.

Appendix B
Worksheets

Baseline Logic Worksheet: Page 1

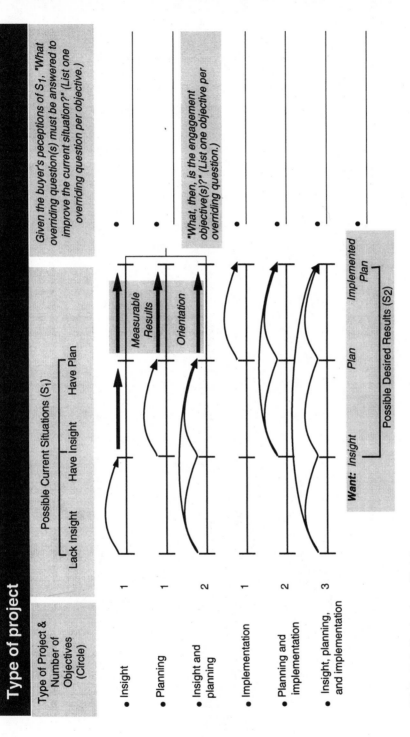

Exhibit B.1. Baseline Logic Worksheet.

211

List

1. In the column "Current Situation," list the relevant **problems.**

2. Within the relevant benefits categories, list as many **benefits** as possible.

Expand

3. **For each problem identified, list the problem's effect and the effects of that effect. Draw arrows that** show the causal relationship between problems and effects and between effects and their effects.

4. **For each benefit identified, try to list a beneficial effect and the effects of that effect. Draw arrows** that show the causal relationship between benefits and effects and between effects and their effects.

Align

5. **Draw a double-headed arrow between each problem** in the column "Current Situation" **and its related benefit** in one of the benefits columns.

6. In the column "Current Situation," locate each problem unconnected to a benefit. In a benefits column, try **to create a benefit related to each unconnected problem. Draw double-headed arrows to** make the connections.

7. In the benefits columns, locate each benefit unconnected to a problem. In the column "Current Situation," try **to create a problem related to each unconnected benefit. Draw double-headed arrows** to make the connections.

8. **Repeat Step 3** for the newly created problems.

9. **Repeat Step 4** for the newly created problems.

Repeat

10. Continue the process **until you reach a point of diminishing returns.**

Exhibit B.1. Baseline Logic Worksheet (*Continued*).

Baseline Logic Worksheet: Page 2

"What is the potential client's current problem/opportunity/critical issue?"

PC's Current Situation

S_1

Exhibit B.1. Baseline Logic Worksheet *(Continued).*

213

Baseline Logic Worksheet: Page 3

Desired Result if _Insight or Plan_

Desired Measurable Result if _Implementation (or Measurable Results Orientation_ if Plan and/or Insight Engagement)*

*Include deliverables ⟱➤ from pyramid

Benefits of a _Plan_

*Include deliverables ⟱➤ from pyramid

Benefits of an _Implemented Plan_

S_2

B

Exhibit B.1. Baseline Logic Worksheet (Continued).

Benefits Worksheet

Benefits

"For each buyer, what are the benefits of achieving the project's objective(s)?"

Buyer/Title	Buyer Role(s)			Benefits From Insight or Plan	Measurable Benefits From Implemented Plan
	E	U	T		
1					
2					
3					
4					
5					

Exhibit B.2. Benefits Worksheet.

215

Hot Buttons Worksheet

Hot Buttons		
Buyer	**Buyer's Hot Buttons**	*"What desires/concerns of each buyer must be addressed during this project?"* **Benefits to Each Buyer From Addressing Their Hot Buttons**

Exhibit B.3. Hot Buttons Worksheet.

Evaluation Criteria Worksheet

Potential Client Evaluation Criteria	"What criteria will the buying committee use, collectively or individually?"
Evaluation Criteria	**Relative Weighting**
1	
2	
3	
4	
5	
6	
7	
	100%

Exhibit B.4. Evaluation Criteria Worksheet.

Competition

"Based upon the evaluation criteria, how do we counter competitors' strengths?"

Known or Likely Competitors (Including Those In-house)	Considering the Evaluation Criteria for This Opportunity, Competitors'	
	Strengths	**Weaknesses**

■ How might we counter competitor strengths or exploit their weaknesses?

Our Strengths	**Our Weaknesses**

■ Us

■ *"How might competition counter our strengths or exploit our weaknesses?"*

Exhibit B.5. Competition Worksheet.

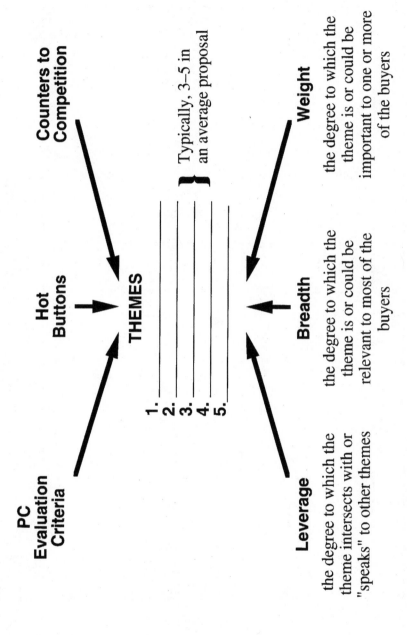

Counters to Competition

Hot Buttons

PC Evaluation Criteria
the degree to which the theme intersects with or "speaks" to other themes

THEMES

1.
2.
3.
4.
5.

} Typically, 3–5 in an average proposal

Weight
the degree to which the theme is or could be important to one or more of the buyers

Breadth
the degree to which the theme is or could be relevant to most of the buyers

Leverage

Exhibit B.6. Themes Selection Worksheet.

Theme	Situation (express as needs)	Methods	Qualifications	Benefits

Exhibit B.7. Themes Development Worksheet.

Benefits Section Worksheet

Inputs: Process Benefits	Outputs: Product Benefits of Having the Plan	Outputs: Product Benefits of Implementing the Plan
From Themes Development Worksheet "Methods" and "Qualifications" Columns	From Worksheets: Baseline Logic (deliverables and plan benefits), Benefits, Hot Buttons, and Theme Development ("Benefits" Column)	From Worksheets: Baseline Logic (implemented plan benefits) and Benefits (implemented plan benefits)

Exhibit B.8. Benefits Section Worksheet.

Appendix **C**

Paramount's Proposal Letter to the ABC Company

February 25, 19XX

Mr. Norm Williams
ABC Company
234 Raintree Road
Midwestern,
Illinois 66666

Paramount Consulting
401 East River Run
Midwestern, Indiana 00000
(000) 000-0000

Dear Norm:

Thank you for the time you and your colleagues have spent with us to describe in detail ABC's urgent need for additional capacity to meet antici-pated market demand. We have given your situa-tion considerable thought, which we have reflected in this proposal to develop a manufacturing strat-egy that will provide the capacity necessary to meet forecasted demand. Our proposal presents our understanding of your situation, our proposed methodology for developing the most appropriate capacity plan for you, our qualifications for sup-porting you, and the benefits we believe you will realize from our participation in this most chal-lenging engagement. As you have requested, we have submitted under separate cover our estimated fees as well as the resumes of our proposed team and references from similar projects

The Situation at ABC

Over the past five years, total household appliance shipments have been fairly stable, and projections suggest only modest total growth over the next five years in your mature industry (Figure 1).

**Figure 1:
Historical and
Forecasted
Industry
Shipments.**
*Industry forecasts
show modest growth
over the next five
years.*
(Source: *Appliance
Magazine*)

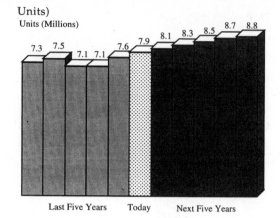

Units)
Units (Millions)

7.3   7.5   7.1   7.1   7.6   7.9   8.1   8.3   8.5   8.7   8.8

Last Five Years   Today   Next Five Years

Despite the relative stability of these shipments industrywide, ABC has managed to increase its share of the household appliance market primarily by producing high-quality products at competitive costs and by being responsive to customers' needs. As a result, you have become a leader in the market and one of the premier divisions within Consolidated Industries.

Your consistent record of success, however, may be threatened. Although your own market forecasts indicate that ABC can continue to increase market share, even the conservative forecast clearly shows that projected product demand will exceed your available manufacturing capacity in fewer than three years. Without adequate capacity, your competitive position will certainly suffer as a result of declining delivery performance, deteriorating product quality, and increasing operating costs.

Complicating the picture is that demographic shifts and potential foreign exports are moving demand farther away from your existing Midwest production facilities (Figure 2). Population and household growth in three geographic regions remote from these facilities has far exceeded that of the Midwest, as well as the nation as a whole.

Undoubtedly, these geographic shifts have contributed to ABC's increased distribution costs, a major factor in the total landed cost of household appliances. In jeopardy are not only ABC's operating objectives but your status as a premier division within Consolidated.

Figure 2: Percent Change by Selected Region in Population and Households (Last 10 Years). *Three geographic regions have household and population growth that exceed the national average and growth in the Midwest.* (Source: *Statistical Abstract,* Table #60)

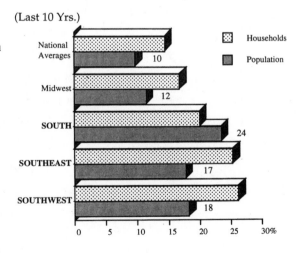

Recognizing these threats, your management group has suggested several options for increasing capacity, but little agreement exists about how that capacity should be deployed, and no agreement exists about the amount of capacity required. Consensus does exist, however, in two areas: additional capacity *will* be needed and the time when it will be needed is fast approaching.

Complicating the need to move quickly is the need to carefully develop a thorough, convincing, and comprehensive plan that is accepted by both ABC's and Consolidated's management. This plan should answer questions like these:

Key questions we will answer in this engagement ...

- Based on the long-term forecast, how much total factory space, equipment, and manpower are required and when?

- What opportunities exist to better utilize current equipment, space, and new technology?

- What manufacturing factory configuration options will best provide the required space? For example, how much expansion potential exists at the current facility, and what, if any, make/buy scenarios as well as changes in factory roles and locations can provide additional space?

- Even if resources can be added at the present location, does it make more economic sense to add them there or to make the investment elsewhere? For example, will service levels increase and transportation costs decrease at a new geographic location closer to growth markets?

- Which option is most appropriate considering the qualitative and quantitative evaluation factors discussed below?

What ABC needs in this engagement ...

To answer questions like these, ABC needs a study methodology that will enable management to select the most effective plan to increase capacity and persuade Consolidated to approve the necessary funds. This plan must consider quantitative factors like ROI, investment incentives, taxes, and costs related to labor, service levels, distribution, construction, and utilities. The plan must also consider qualitative factors such as labor supply, union climate, work force characteristics, productivity, environmental permitting and regulations, vocational training capabilities, manufacturing support services, risk, controllability, ability to develop and promote employees, and flexibility to react to unanticipated changes. Consequently, ABC needs a senior, multifaceted consulting team with a broad range of business capabilities. These capabilities should include skills in marketing, manufacturing strategy, facilities planning, logistics, financial analysis, and human resources. These capabilities are necessary to ensure that all relevant options are surfaced and evaluated in a practical manner, that the most desirable options and their attributes are clearly identified and defined, and that ABC's management not only has the ability to make the right decision but that Consolidated is convinced of its appropriateness.

Moreover, to ensure that all likely issues are addressed in this complex engagement, the study's methodology should encourage a close working relationship between ABC and the consulting team. This relationship will expedite the retrieval, development, and analysis of relevant information, thus reducing the time for analysis. It will also enhance the capabilities of ABC's staff, producing a more capable internal team with a better appreciation of business trade-offs and a broader knowledge of company operations. This broader perspective will prove helpful as business conditions change in unpredictable ways in the future.

After carefully considering ABC's needs, I and my colleagues at Paramount Consulting have designed a methodology that will not only develop a manufacturing strategy to provide the capacity necessary for meeting forecasted demand, but also a concrete plan for implementing that strategy to improve your competitive position.

Our Proposed Methodology

Our methodology promotes strong cooperation and provides a multidisciplined study team ...

To ensure that ABC's managers have an integral and significant role in this engagement, we will form a joint ABC/Paramount team. Team members from Paramount will have multidisciplined skills in marketing, manufacturing strategy, facilities planning, logistics, financial analysis, and human resources. Working with ABC executives with some of these same functional skills, we will make considerable use of ABC's own market forecast, distribution model, and other in-house analyses. Early in the engagement we will solicit and obtain agreement on quantitative and qualitative criteria for evaluating the various options, and throughout the engagement the team will conduct meetings to review progress and agree on future direction and emphasis. As a result of these frequent progress reviews, ABC's management will be fully informed of the engagement's ongoing findings and conclusions. The progress reviews will play a key role in expediting the conduct of the engagement, enabling management to keep our efforts focused by providing direction and counsel.

Our twofold goal ...

The team's major goal is twofold:

- to provide ABC with a manufacturing capacity plan that is thoroughly documented, cost-effective, and, when fully implemented, capable of enabling the Division to maintain and enhance its competitive position
- to produce for Consolidated a convincing, comprehensive, and thorough justification for increasing capacity

Ideally, the output of this effort will not only be a report of the recommended expansion plan but an actual proposal to Corporate that justifies the cost of the expansion by articulating the compelling reasons to move forward quickly.

To achieve this goal, we have developed a methodology that consists of the following five major tasks shown in Figure 3.

Please note that this five-month estimate for completing the study is conservative. Working with your management team, we will make every effort to accelerate the completion of the tasks discussed in greater detail below.

**Figure 3: Proposed
Timing and Major
Tasks.**

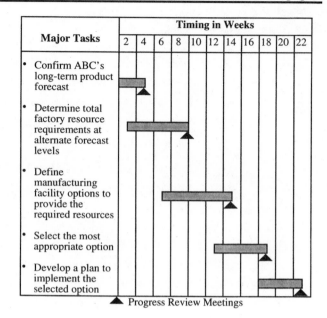

Major Tasks	Timing in Weeks										
	2	4	6	8	10	12	14	16	18	20	22
• Confirm ABC's long-term product forecast											
• Determine total factory resource requirements at alternate forecast levels											
• Define manufacturing facility options to provide the required resources											
• Select the most appropriate option											
• Develop a plan to implement the selected option											

▲ Progress Review Meetings

Task 1 ...

Confirm ABC's Long-Term Product Forecast
Although ABC already has a forecast of production
volume, we believe that the engagement must be
conducted with Consolidated constantly in mind.
Since Consolidated must release the necessary capital funding, they must be convinced of the
engagement's rigor and robustness. For that reason, we believe that the forecast must be confirmed by an independent third party. Therefore,
we propose to work with ABC's marketing management to confirm or modify the long-term forecast by:

■ validating ABC's current, overall market forecast

■ validating ABC's market share and your geographic and product mix projections

The consensus market forecast developed in this task will represent the best thinking of your marketing group and the Paramount team. The forecast, used with various manufacturing data, will enable the engagement team to develop future resource requirements over time.

Task 2 ...

Determine Total Factory Resource Requirements at Alternate Forecast Levels

An important task of the engagement team will be to use the existing base of production resources (floor space, equipment, and staffing) and modify that base so that it can accommodate the additional future production demands over time indicated by the confirmed market forecast. First, however, the team will carefully evaluate that base to identify improvements or eliminate inefficiencies that might exist today. We don't want ABC to risk adding too much or too little capacity. This risk can be avoided by first establishing a proper base, a "current-improved" base, from which to project future resource requirements. All this will be critical, because determining future needs involves far more than an arithmetic extrapolation of today's activities.

We were very much impressed during our walk-through of your main manufacturing facility. You should know, however, that in nearly every similar engagement we have been able to recommend methods for better utilizing existing space and equipment, thereby increasing manufacturing capacity without actually increasing space. To provide additional capacity and/or space without first determining such improvement opportunities could result in unnecessary capital investment.We will ensure that ABC is making the most effective use of existing manufacturing resources. Specifically, we will:

- specify current equipment and space utilization

- determine opportunities to better utilize current equipment and space and to improve material flow

- determine opportunities for utilizing new equipment technology

- specify which products or components, if any, should be made in house versus bought from suppliers

The modified, effective base of production resources coupled with the confirmed market forecast will enable the engagement team to develop an accurate and credible projection of future resource requirements. At this point the joint ABC/Paramount engagement team will have a sound basis for identifying, evaluating, and selecting the most viable options to provide these requirements.

Task 3 ...

Define Manufacturing Facility Options to Provide Required Resources

Once we know how much additional space and equipment are required, we need to specify the possible manufacturing options that will provide these additional resources. Accordingly, we will develop and analyze various options and determine which configuration of facilities best meets your objectives. Specifically, we will:

- determine expansion potential at the current facility
- specify potential factory roles and locations for increasing capacity

As a result of completing this task, we will have narrowed the field from the possible to the probable, the better to be able to scrutinize the remaining options and to choose the most appropriate.

Task 4 ...

Select the Most Appropriate Option

Using ABC's distribution model and Paramount's proprietary models for assessing expansion options, the joint engagement team will evaluate thoroughly each potential expansion option and then select the one most appropriate. Although the range of options will have been narrowed, those remaining will quite likely be diverse. Therefore, we will work with ABC management to develop both quantitative and qualitative criteria that will differentiate carefully among the various options, and we will obtain management's agreement on the one most suitable. Specifically, to select the most appropriate option, the engagement team will:

- define quantitative and qualitative criteria important to ABC and Consolidated
- evaluate each option against quantitative criteria such as ROI, landed cost, quality, and customer service

■ evaluate each option against qualitative criteria such as flexibility and risk versus control

When this task is completed, you will know precisely how to configure your manufacturing facilities over time so that you can meet customer demand throughout the forecasted period cost effectively and responsively.

Task 5 ...

Develop a Plan To Implement the Selected Option
Because the additional manufacturing resources required will likely be brought on-stream at various times throughout the forecast period, ABC will need a carefully prepared plan to monitor progress during implementation. To that end, we will prepare a plan to ensure that additional manufacturing resources and facilities are in place when and where they are needed to meet forecasted demand. The various steps in our implementation plan will be time-phased so that management will know precisely when additional capacity is required and when other managerial decisions and actions are needed. Specifically, we will:

■ define the tasks necessary to implement the selected option

■ define the resources and responsibilities necessary to complete those tasks

■ develop a critical path to estimate the time required to complete all tasks

As a result of this task, management will know all the tasks required to provide the additional manufacturing resources, when each task should be initiated and completed, and the skills required to complete each task. The implementation plan will provide you with a critical mechanism to monitor overall progress, to efficiently invest required capital and other resources when they are needed, and to take corrective actions if actual market demand differs significantly from that projected.

After completing this task, we will work with you to immediately prepare a capital appropriations request that can be submitted directly to Consolidated for their timely consideration.

Qualifications of Paramount Consulting

Timing to provide needed resources is critical ...

ABC is faced with a most formidable challenge as it begins the task of providing additional manufacturing capacity to avert the shortfall expected in the next few years. This capacity shortfall should be considered imminent as you examine the numerous tasks that must be completed effectively within the narrow, available time frame.

Time will be required for sufficient interchange between ABC and Consolidated to agree on the decision to commit scarce financial, planning, managerial, and other resources needed to implement the selected option. Then, substantially more time will be needed to put in place additional resources and to provide the necessary training for an effective start-up. As described in the following paragraphs, Paramount has the diverse capabilities to help you complete this challenging engagement successfully and expeditiously. Specifically, we have:

- the resources to begin this engagement immediately and to complete our study in 4 to 5 months

- substantial manufacturing and strategy-development experience within the household appliance industry

- the ability to address the wide range of issues related to this engagement

- the ability to develop a sound joint ABC/Paramount team

- proven experience in planning and controlling implementation of the strategy we will develop with you

Paramount has the resources to begin and complete this engagement quickly …

Of the nearly 100 consultants in our nearby Midwest office, we have already identified several individuals with the skills and experience needed to help develop a sound plan for increasing capacity. Each of these professionals has worked on similar engagements, is substantially "down the learning curve," and will therefore be able to function effectively at the very beginning of the engagement. In fact several of them have participated in developing this proposal.

Our proposed engagement team of four consultants will entirely comprise individuals from this group. As discussed, we would like to introduce this team to you so that you feel as comfortable with them as we do. We will use no subcontractors, and we will be able to begin the engagement immediately after your approval to proceed.

We have substantial manufacturing experience ...

For almost 40 years, Paramount has served clients with a high level of satisfaction. In fact, 80 percent of our consulting engagements come from previous clients. Paramount originated with a strong manufacturing and strategy capability that has grown significantly over the years; this strength will enable us to address all of the diverse issues that must be resolved during the proposed engagement.

In the past five years we have conducted over 200 manufacturing strategy engagements of which nearly 25 were conducted for companies within the appliance industry. Furthermore, approximately 60 of those studies involved our developing a broad range of manufacturing capacity plans. Many of them were designed to answer questions similar to yours: "How can we provide additional manufacturing capacity most effectively?"

We are able to address the wide range of issues related to this engagement ...

The team proposed for this engagement will have expertise in all aspects of this study. We understand the marketing and manufacturing issues from a business perspective so that we can develop various capacity expansion options; evaluate them with your management team, considering each of the team member's individual (and often differing perspectives); select the most appropriate option; prepare for Consolidated a comprehensive appropriation request; and plan for its successful implementation within your tight time frame.

We have the ability to build a sound ABC/Paramount team ...

Because the staff to be assigned will have considerable expertise in conducting similar studies, building consensus, and transferring their knowledge, skills, and expertise, we have been able to carefully structure our approach so that ABC management will participate actively and become an integral part of the engagement team. Thus, on completion of the engagement, ABC will possess a base of residual knowledge that will be invaluable in addressing future capacity and other strategic manufacturing questions. For example, we believe that ABC members of the engagement team will be able, even more effectively than at present, to monitor sales forecasts, plant productivity, and capacity utilization to project accurately when additional capacity might be needed in the more-distant future.

We have the ability to plan and control implementation ...

Once the most appropriate capacity expansion option has been selected, it will be extremely important to implement the plan without delay. Although an implementation phase lies outside the scope of this proposed engagement, you should be aware that our significant experience in successfully implementing comprehensive plans for increasing capacity could be invaluable to ABC. Our engagement teams that work on such implementation projects routinely use a variety of sophisticated project-control software packages. These programs are necessary for properly allocating resources; monitoring task completions and costs, thereby assuring adherence to budget; identifying potential problems or delays; and reallocating resources to maintain schedules and achieve time and cost objectives.

These control techniques will ensure that implementation of the selected option will proceed smoothly and will be completed on time and within budget.

Even if we are not actively involved in implementation, we will have developed the new manufacturing plan considering ABC's resources and capabilities. Our goal is not just to produce a plan for increasing capacity, but to help you bring that capacity on line as soon as possible. That is, we are not in the business of just developing plans. We want to see those plans implemented whether or not you decide to engage us to help you do so.

We hope you agree that Paramount Consulting has all the critical capabilities needed to help you select the best expansion option and to plan for its expeditious and effective implementation.

Benefits

I would like to summarize for you, Norm, some of the most important points we've made in our previous discussions and in this proposal. Then, I will describe the benefits we believe you will receive from our developing a plan for meeting ABC's forecasted demand and from that plan's subsequent implementation by ABC (possibly with our support, if appropriate).

The benefits of leveraging our efforts ...

By forming a joint ABC/Paramount team, with ABC managers playing an integral part, we will be able to leverage the substantial knowledge, expertise, and tools both ABC and Paramount will bring to this project and to develop, sell, and implement the plan as quickly as possible.

This team will hold frequent progress reviews so that various constituencies within the Division (as well as, if appropriate, within Consolidated) will be aware of preliminary conclusions and direction quickly. We plan for these reviews to include strategy sessions, during which we can gain consensus on answers to the wide variety of questions posed in this project and get agreement across various interest areas on the appropriate criteria to be used to select the most effective expansion option. Finally, we will involve the team in preparing the final report, which we would like to be, in fact, a proposal and capital expenditure request to Consolidated. This strategy would eliminate an entire and possibly time-consuming step in the approval process.

This teaming strategy will work exceptionally well because Paramount's professionals have extensive expertise in building effective client–consultant teams, transferring knowledge, and managing and implementing change. We also understand the range of criteria important in this analysis, and are adept at facilitating discussions to gain consensus on these criteria. We will commit our broad-based team quickly to begin the project immediately after your approval to proceed. Using our exceptional expertise in marketing, manufacturing strategy, facilities planning, logistics, financial analysis, and human resources, we will provide ABC with the right "road map" for increasing capacity.

*Your benefits at
the end of this
engagement ...*

Our report/proposal to you and to Consolidated will be thorough, comprehensive, and well-documented, providing ABC with the basis for making a sound expansion decision that considers and balances all the quantitative and qualitative factors. And because that decision will be based on agreed-to criteria, it will be well accepted by ABC management with divergent agendas. Just as important, the report will convince Consolidated of the expansion decision's correctness and desirability, and answer their "what-if" questions.

In addition to our recommended expansion option, the report will contain:

- a confirmed market forecast, and market share and product mix projections

- specified current equipment and space utilization, and opportunities to better utilize current equipment and space, as well as new technology

- specified make versus buy options as well as potential factory roles and locations for increasing capacity

- an implementation plan

Our implementation plan will specify the tasks, resources, requirements, and timing necessary to bring additional capacity on line over time in a controlled yet expeditious manner.

*Your benefits
beyond this
engagement ...*

We are confident that, once implemented, our jointly developed plan will significantly improve ABC's processes; lead to more cost-effective operations, improved service levels, and product quality; and maintain if not enhance your market share.

Your productivity should increase, your compensation levels should be protected, and you should realize greater flexibility in implementing your business and marketing strategies. Most importantly, after subsequent implementation you should improve your competitive position and maintain your excellent reputation with Consolidated.

*   *   *

Quite obviously, Norm, we believe that Paramount is the right consulting firm for conducting this engagement. We have a comprehensive understanding of your situation and a logical and robust methodology for capitalizing on what we consider a substantial opportunity to continue your growth in the marketplace and solidify your position within Consolidated Industries. Just as soon as possible, we would like to discuss that methodology and how we can best work together with you, President Armstrong, and others so that we can all agree on the proper magnitude of effort, and the specific roles ABC and Paramount personnel should play. This is a critically important study for ABC, and we look forward to supporting you as you develop the base for continued competitive success.

Sincerely yours,

Stan Gilmore, Partner
Paramount Consulting

Internal Proposals (Make Certain They're Not Reports)

Let's consider a situation that might have occurred at the ABC Company, the appliance manufacturer we've discussed throughout the work sessions. Let's assume that Marcia Collins, VP of Marketing, has completed her market forecast and therefore believes that ABC will soon run out of manufacturing capacity. Consequently, she has several meetings with Paul Morrison, the Chief Industrial Engineer, to discuss manufacturing and distribution costs, customer service as it relates to capacity utilization, and various scenarios for increasing capacity. As a result of these discussions, Collins decides to "propose" a different way of utilizing existing capacity. So she meets with Norm Williams, VP of Operations, to discuss her ideas. Very much interested in and intrigued by that discussion, Williams suggests that Collins develop a proposal that the two of them could present to President Armstrong.

Williams suggested a proposal. Will Marcia Collins in fact be preparing one? To answer that question, we need to understand the major difference between proposals and reports. Proposals argue: "This is how we would go about answering your overriding question." Reports (more specifically, final or recommendation reports) argue: "This *is* our answer to the overriding question." Therefore, to determine whether the product of Collins' efforts will be a proposal or a report, we need to know what Armstrong's overriding question is and whether or not Collins' presentation will answer it.

Let's assume that Armstrong's overriding question is similar to the one Paramount Consulting has defined: "How should ABC provide the additional manufacturing capacity needed within the next few years to meet forecasted demand?" Will Collins' presentation answer that question? Because she has already determined "a different way of utilizing existing capacity," the answer is "Yes." Armstrong's question asks "How?" Collins' answer is, "*This* is how." Collins will be preparing a *report,* not a proposal.

Why is all of this important to you? Because proposals and reports are tools that attempt to achieve very different purposes: for proposals, to explain how you will answer a question; for reports, to answer it. You would no less want to write a proposal to answer a reader's overriding question than you'd want to use a chainsaw to pound in a nail. Unfortunately, many confuse these two common genre (or kinds of communications), for at least three reasons.

First, the two genre share several common elements. Proposals and reports both contain SITUATION, OBJECTIVES, METHODS, and BENEFITS slots, though the tense in these slots is different. For example, a proposal presents readers with the writer's understanding of the situation; a report reminds readers what that situation was. A proposal presents the objective to be achieved; a report reminds readers what that objective was. A proposal describes the methods that will be used to achieve the objective; a report describes the methods that were used to achieve it.

People also confuse the two genre for a second reason: the similarities between terms like "propose" and "recommend." You can "propose a solution," and you can "recommend a solution." But to be precise, given the concepts we've been discussing, you can't really "propose a solution," you can only recommend one. If you propose a solution, then you've already found one, and therefore you're not proposing at all; you're reporting. You're recommending, on the basis of some analysis or study that you've already completed, the answer to a question. You're not, as you would in a proposal, proposing a method—before a study—that will derive the answer. Because of the similarities between the terms "propose" and "recommend," many managers ask their subordinates for a proposal even though they are in fact requesting a report. So if you're asked to prepare a proposal, as Williams asked Collins, consider whether your task is to cut down a tree or to sink a nail. Then you can decide whether you need a chainsaw or a hammer.

Third, people confuse the two genre because although they have completed a study and answered an overriding question, they're often not aware of having done so. For example, suppose you work in a small company whose organizational structure is less effective than you believe it could be. In your spare time, you've been thinking about this problem off and on for months—as you daydream at work, when you shower at home, etc.—and over these months you've doodled several possible organizational structures, one of which you believe is better than the current. You decide to write a document to your boss that "proposes" the new structure.

No one told you to do your little study, and you really didn't tell yourself to do it either. You "studied" your current organizational structure by dint of having lived within it. You've observed it, analyzed your observations, and done so probably without realizing that you had. But clearly, you have answered a question: "How can my company better organize itself to achieve our various goals?" If that is also your boss's question and you can support your answer logically and persuasively, you have a good chance of convincing her of your *report's* recommended solution. But you'll be less successful if you try to write a proposal. To take just one example, you'll spend much time trying to figure out how to construct a methodology that will answer the overriding question you've already answered.

In summary, then, reports and proposals are different, because they serve different purposes, but they are also similar enough that people sometimes request one when they really want the other, and writers sometimes try to write one when they ought to be composing the other.

Now that we understand how reports differ from proposals, you probably want to know how to write them better. Unfortunately, that would require another book, something like: *Writing Effective Reports: Your Guide to Convincing the Client or Persuading the Boss.* However, my business responsibilities are such that I don't have time to write that book right now. But I can offer you some tips that build on the concepts I have already presented for logically structuring your proposals.

Organizing the Body of Your Report: The Single Recommendation

You already know the best tool you can use to organize your report: a pyramid. As we discussed in Chap. 4, a "how"-pyramid can be used to organize the actions in your proposal's methodology. As we discussed in Chap. 10, a "why"-pyramid can organize a qualifications section. Reports also use these two kinds of pyramids, but to an even greater degree. Whereas pyramids can be helpful in organizing a proposal's entire qualifications section or a part of the methodology, a single pyramid can help you structure the entire body of a report. The examples in this appendix all use "why"-pyramids. You should be aware, however, that although most recommendation or final reports support their recommendation by answering "why?" at the top level of the pyramid, lower levels can answer other questions like "how?" and "what kind of?"

To better understand how to build a pyramid for a report, let's assume that Collins has decided to recommend that ABC increase capacity at the current site by expanding the current facility (call this "option A"). The entire body of her report would be organized to provide evidence and support for that recommendation. (See Exhibit D.1.)

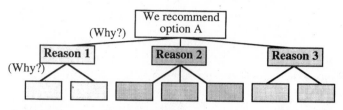

Exhibit D.1. A pyramid for recommendation reports.

The pyramid is designed to answer Armstrong's questions as he engages in the report's dialogue. His first question is the overriding one, related to how best to provide additional capacity. The top box, the report's major recommendation, supplies the answer: "Expand the current facility to increase capacity." This recommendation, however, generates another question: "Why?" The boxes on the next line provide the answer, in the form of three good reasons. The report's major argument, then, comprises the recommendation and the good reasons that justify and support it. Each of these good reasons, however, likely necessitates an additional argument, because each good reason again causes Armstrong to ask, in his dialogue with the report, "why?" and "why?" again for justification. If Armstrong needs no further justification, the pyramid above would suffice. If he does need further justification and desires to search deeper for the underlying rationale, the report should continue building arguments at lower levels. When do the arguments end? When Collins believes that all of Armstrong's questions have been answered.

No matter how far down the pyramid goes, each box on every level contributes to validate the pyramid's major claim: Option A is the best possible recommendation.

Now let's look at a much more traditional and frequently presented structure that I and my potential client organization have received. Note how this reporting structure is much more difficult to understand using writing patterns typically found in most reports:

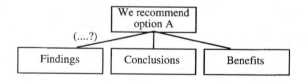

Here, the boxes on the second level don't answer any clear-cut question that could be posed after hearing or reading the recommendation. The body of the report contains separate buckets for findings, conclusions, and benefits. The findings bucket typically will consist of a data dump of facts and figures. The conclusions bucket will contain a large number of conclusions, seemingly unrelated to the previously discussed findings. To make matters worse, in reading some reports I don't even know the recommended answer until I've been overwhelmed with findings and conclusions. Then, I'm subjected to a recommendations bucket and forced to tie together previously presented information to determine whether or not the recommendations are supported.

When you use a pyramid, however, the categories of findings and conclusions are irrelevant. Instead, you just focus on answering at any level my question on the level above:

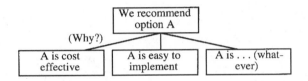

Embedded within the preceding argument may be the notion of "better" or "best." That is, option A may be preferred because it is at least better in some ways than other options, and overall it's the best of all possible options. Therefore, the boxes on the second line might express these comparisons: "A is more cost-effective" or "A is the easiest to implement." Even if your argument is that "A is cost-effective," the implication may remain that option A is more cost-effective than something else. Therefore, you should be certain that the argument supporting the claim "A is cost-effective" considers the relative, not just the absolute, value of the recommended alternative.

Organizing the Body of Your Report: Multiple Recommendations

Let's assume that Collins' answer to Armstrong's overriding question is not to increase capacity at the current facility only. Instead, her recommendation is actually three recommendations: Increase capacity at the current facility, increase capacity at one of the satellite facilities, and outsource certain components from outside suppliers. Faced with this three-part recommendation, Collins' tendency might be to build a pyramid like this:

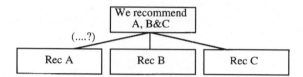

Here, the same problem exists that affected the pyramid organized by findings and conclusions: The pyramid provides Armstrong with no clear-cut answer after he reads or hears the recommendation. This pyramid could prove the validity of Recommendation A, the validity of Recommendation B, and the validity of Recommendation C. However, it does not answer the question, "Why the combination of A, B, *and* C?" That is: "Why this *combination* of actions?" This is the overriding question. The following pyramid does provide an answer:

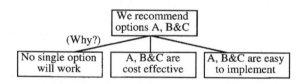

Organizing the Whole Report

As Exhibit D.2 illustrates, every pyramid row after the recommendation organizes the *body* of your report, not the whole document or presentation. The recommendation itself, along with its supporting reasons, ends the introduction. When these reasons are bulleted, they provide a good forecast of the content and organization of the body, which in a longer report would contain sections corresponding to each of the reasons on the second row of the pyramid. Before the recommendation, other slots are typically provided. These slots explain the problem or opportunity necessitating the study, as well as the study's objectives and methodology. The concluding part of the document or presentation can restate the recommendation and summarize the benefits of acting on it.

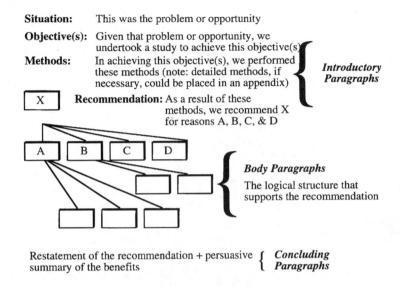

Situation: This was the problem or opportunity

Objective(s): Given that problem or opportunity, we undertook a study to achieve this objective(s)

Methods: In achieving this objective(s), we performed these methods (note: detailed methods, if necessary, could be placed in an appendix) } *Introductory Paragraphs*

X **Recommendation:** As a result of these methods, we recommend X for reasons A, B, C, & D

A B C D } *Body Paragraphs*

The logical structure that supports the recommendation

Restatement of the recommendation + persuasive summary of the benefits { *Concluding Paragraphs*

Exhibit D.2. The organization of recommendation reports.

Many of the techniques and strategies we've discussed relative to proposals are also useful in preparing reports. Generally speaking, a proposal "sells" a future service; a report "sells" the knowledge gained from providing that service. Therefore, you still have buyers, not of your service (because that's been performed) but of your ideas. As in proposal situations, these buyers play different buying roles in evaluating your report, and different benefits will be perceived based in part on their different roles. These buyers will also have hot buttons, and they will use various criteria to evaluate your recommendation. You might even have competition, in the form of alternative initiatives being recommended by others in your organization: These initiatives might be competing for the same funding you are seeking. In short you should find helpful, in preparing your report, the same worksheets that are so useful in completing a proposal. There is no magic in writing effective reports. The key is a logical structure designed to answer my overriding question.

Appendix E
A Few Comments About Writing Effective Sentences (and Paragraphs)

This chapter isn't at all about how to write correct sentences—about avoiding misplaced modifiers, dangling participles, run-on sentences, superfluous commas, or comma splices. And it's far less than comprehensive in discussing effective sentences. So you won't find topics like sentence variety, subordination, and emphasis, just a few reasonably brief comments about strategies you can use and problems you can avoid when writing proposals.

If you want more (either about writing correct sentences or effective ones), consult an English handbook, which most people find as enjoyable as memorizing a telephone directory, though considerably more useful. Buy a good handbook and consider it a business expense. Consider it part of your business to know what a comma splice is and how to fix one or never to write one in the first place. (Please don't tell me that you've never been able to understand a comma splice. If you're reading this book, you're a very smart person. You can understand comma splices.)

If you study the handbook, you won't have to use a computer grammar checker, which can find a comma splice easily enough but hasn't the foggiest notion (despite its fog index) about context. To understand what I mean, type out a stanza or two of Lewis Carroll's "Jabberwocky," a nonsense poem by the author of *Alice Through the Looking-Glass*:

'Twas brillig, and the slithy toves

Did gyre and gimble in the wabe:

All mimsy were the borogoves,

And the mome raths outgrabe.

Your spell checker will go crazy, of course. But you will score very well on the "fog index." The sixth-grade level will suggest that your prose is clear and understandable.

Your grammar checker can't understand context, and context determines whether you should or could write a sentence fragment or use the passive voice. Occasionally, fragments are effective, and sometimes the passive voice is necessary. You know all that because I've been telling you since the introduction to this book. The rest of this chapter will try to reinforce the importance of situational context because, as I provide some guidelines for improving the effectiveness of your sentences, I'll phrase most of the guidelines as questions rather than statements. The guideline "Prefer the Active Voice?" really means, "In this situation, given these readers and your attempt to achieve this purpose, should you consider using the active voice?"

Avoid Abstract Nouns in the Subject Slot?

When you were six years old, you didn't need to know the rules of grammar to be able to speak a perfectly grammatical sentence. Similarly, you don't need to know much about grammar to write well. It is helpful, however, to be able to identify the sentence's subject, predicate, and main clause. If you can, you will know how to fix the problem in the following sentences. Each of these sentences contains examples of the worst, most prevalent, and easiest-to-fix problem that affects your writing style (in certain contexts!)—abstract nouns in the subject slot:

1. A new *approach* to the air flow problem has made ACME a major player in the design and construction of complex commercial buildings.

2. New *regulations* from the state and tighter building *codes* from the city are taking up more and more of the engineers' time.

3. The *shortage* of support staff and the *absence* of proper control systems are causing inefficiencies in your operation.

The italicized words are the grammatical subjects in the sentences, and each word is what I call an abstract noun. Now it's true that given certain contexts some of these words could be considered concrete rather than abstract. For example, if the paragraph or document containing sentence 2 were about regulations, then the word "regulations" would be concrete within that context. Or, for example, if you were writing part of a methods section, the word "methods" would be concrete in that context. Generally speaking, however, concrete nouns are people and places (including organizations like businesses), not things. Each subject in the preceding sentences is a thing. What's wrong with your placing "things" (i.e., abstract nouns) in the subject slot?

Abstract subjects tend to increase the distance between the subject and verb, making the text more difficult to comprehend and remember. When you read, you don't process text letter by letter or word by word. If you did, you'd have considerable difficulty remembering the content even of short sentences. Instead, you process text in chunks like phrases and clauses. Because a clause is a group of words with a subject and a predicate, you can't process the clause until you get to the verb. When a sentence begins with a subject and takes a long time to get to the verb, the reader has to keep a great deal of information in short-term memory until the clause is complete.

Abstract subjects tend to increase the distance between subject and verb because you have to explain the abstraction. Take the abstract noun "shortage" in sentence 3. Because it's an abstraction, you have to concretize it, you have to tell the reader *what kind of* shortage it is, before you can explain what it does. That requires the prepositional phrase "of support staff" that separates noun and verb. Just one prepositional phrase isn't bad. But an abstract subject is often responsible for more difficult-to-read sentences, like this one:

> The urgent *request* for all employees of our company to submit their time sheets at the same time *is being made* so that the Accounting Department can more efficiently do its work.

In this case, the writer's answer to the question "what kind of request?" takes three prepositional phrases and 14 words.

The previous example illustrates another problem with abstract nouns as subjects: they tend to take passive verbs (e.g., "is being made"), because abstractions can't act. The effect is lifeless prose, because the sentence's most important slots (subject and predicate) are filled with a noun that can't take action and a verb that can't express action.

Fixing the Problem.   Eliminating abstract nouns is fairly easy, and once you get the hang of it, you won't write many of them even in an initial draft. Here's what to do:

1. Look carefully at the subject slot to see if it contains, not a person or an organization, but a thing.

2. If you find an abstraction, look elsewhere in the sentence to see if the subject (the topic) you're discussing really is explicitly or implicitly about a person or people or an organization. Sentence 1 is about ACME. Sentence 2 is about engineers. Sentence 3 is about business operations.

3. Place the subject you're discussing into the subject slot of the sentence.

4. See if the sentence is trying to express a causal relationship (the majority of sentences with abstract nouns try to do so).

5. If the sentence is trying to express a causal relationship, use a sentence structure that immediately announces to your reader that such a relationship will be drawn: for example, "Because of X, Y occurs" or "As a result of X, Y occurs."

By following these steps, you can easily revise the three problem sentences:

1. Because of its new approach to the air flow problem, *ACME has become a major player* in designing and constructing complex commercial buildings.

2. Because of new regulations from the state and tighter building codes from the city, *the engineers are less efficient.*

3. Because of the shortage of support staff and the absence of proper control systems, *your business is less efficient.*

I've italicized the main clauses (or parts of the main clauses) to illustrate the effects of these transformed sentences. Notice that the subjects and verbs are closer together and that the main clauses, the groups of words that really contain and emphasize your message, are clear and emphatic. The message in sentence 2 is no longer that "new regulations from the state and tighter building codes from the city are taking up more and more of the engineers' time," but that "the engineers are less efficient." The original sentence focuses on regulations and codes; the revision, on engineers and their problems. The original talks about things; the revision discusses a problem that people have.

The Subject Slot in SITUATION, METHODS, and BENEFITS. The generic structure slots SITUATION, METHODS, and BENEFITS each in their own way call for concrete nouns in the subject slot. In SITUATION, the subject (the topic, the idea you're writing about) is an organization's problem or opportunity. Therefore, a good many of the sentences in SITUATION should take as their grammatical subjects the name of the organization or pronouns that refer to it. Consider these paragraphs from the first draft of a situation slot in the ABC proposal:

> For many years now, *ABC* has grown by increasing its share of the modestly expanding household and appliance market, primarily by producing high-quality products at competitive costs and by being very responsive to the needs of its customers. As a result, ABC has become one of the premier divisions within Consolidated Industries....
>
> Recognizing these threats, ABC's *management group* has suggested several alternatives for increasing capacity, but little *agreement* exists about how that capacity should be developed, and no *agreement* exists about the amount of capacity required. *Consensus* does exist, however, in two areas: Additional capacity will be needed and the time when it will be needed is fast approaching.

Here, the first three subjects (the ABC organization itself or a group within it) are all concrete. The next subject ("agreement") is abstract, but the following two ("agreement" and "consensus") are concrete because of the context established by the first use of "agreement." By using concrete subjects in SITUATION, you focus on *my* question: "What is your understanding of *my* problem?" rather than some anonymous question like "What is the problem?"

In METHODS, similarly, you usually don't want to answer, "What will be done?"; you probably want to answer "What will *you* (or *your firm*) do?" The first question calls for an anonymous answer, with an abstract noun as subject: "In Phase I, the resources that are required will be specified." The second question calls for a concrete noun as subject, "we" or the name of your firm: "In Phase I, we will specify the resources required to..."

In BENEFITS, you should try to place either the benefactor (you) or the beneficiary (me) in the subject slot. That is, the template sentence should be either "We will give this to you" or "You will receive this from us." In either case, the subject slot will contain a concrete noun.

Problems are only problems to people or organizations; they aren't abstractions floating in the air affecting no one or some anonymous others. Too many proposals I've read describe my organization's problems or opportunities as if they weren't mine, as if I weren't affected by them. The situation slots tend to address some situation, but not one that's concretely and recognizably mine. Similarly with benefits. When proposals I've read include benefits they sound like generic blandishments, and bland ones at that, not benefits that I sense can be mine or that are written with me in mind. In almost all cases, the problems described and the benefits articulated seem abstract because the proposal's sentences don't include me and my organization as grammatical subjects.

Change Nouns into Verbs?

The "original" sentence that follows contains an abstract noun in the subject slot; in the "revised" sentence, I've corrected that problem and improved the sentence further by changing nouns into verbs:

original: The *understanding* of design can be helpful in the *construction* of attractive buildings.

revised: By *understanding* design, you can *construct* attractive buildings.

Some words like "understanding" are spelled the same in their noun and verb forms, and the vast majority of words ending in -tion, -sion, and -ment have verb or -ing verb forms. *Construction* can be *construct* or *constructing*. *Dissension* can be *dissent* or *dissenting*. *Development* can be *develop* or *developing*. Note what happened when I changed the nouns to verbs in the preceding sentences: I could delete the article ("the") before the noun as well as the preposition ("of") that follows. "The understanding of" becomes "understanding"; "the construction of" becomes "construct." My revision contains fewer words, and the sentence is less noun heavy, less formal, and more active.

Prefer the Active Voice?

In an active voice sentence, the subject does the acting: "John hit the ball." In a passive voice sentence, the subject is acted upon: "The ball was hit by John." Note that in this instance the passive sentence takes fifty percent more words to express the same basic idea. If conciseness is your overriding objective, you ought to prefer the active voice.

Of course, we can reduce the second sentence by two words if we eliminate "by John." This construction is sometimes called the anonymous passive because nothing in the sentence explains who (or what) acted. If avoiding blame or attribution is your overriding objective, you ought to prefer the anonymous passive. In some situations, that is, you might prefer "A poor decision was made" to "The CEO screwed up."

As with everything else in writing, your decisions ought to be defined by the situation, by your strategy, by your analysis of your intended readers or listeners and their relationship to you.

Combine "There," "It," "That," "Which," or "Who" with "To Be"?

When words like "there" and "it" are combined with a form of the verb "to be," they often signal wordiness. As with the first two sentences, the only revision needed is a simple deletion. The third sentence requires a little more.

- A problem exists with the air conditioning system ~~that was~~ recently purchased.
- When the system crashes, those employees ~~who are~~ working on the system have to reenter their data.
- ~~There are likely to be~~ thousands of people (are likely to be) laid off at the automobile plant.

Avoid "There is ..that" and "It is ..that"?

When the sentence begins with "there" or "it," takes a form of the verb "to be," and contains a following "that" or "which," you can very easily revise by eliminating all of the offending words:

- ~~It is~~ the lack of space, however, ~~that~~ is the problem.
- ~~There is~~ one other disadvantage ~~that~~ makes renovating an unattractive option.

Use Parallelism

Do you like swimming, fishing, and hunting? Or do you like swimming, to fish, and hunting? If you focus not on the activities but on the sentences, I hope you say that you like the first sentence rather than the second. The first places similar ideas (in this case, things you might like to do) within similar grammatical structures (in this case, -ing verbs). The second sentence places similar ideas within unparallel structures. That's why the sentence probably sounded strange to you; and if you had written it, you would sound strange and perhaps stupid to your reader. So one good reason to use parallelism is that you avoid sounding stupid.

Another good reason is that your writing (and speaking) will sound more coherent. Incoherent writing, like incoherent behavior, appears random and disconnected:

> I like swimming. Fishing is another enjoyable activity to me. You know, to go out and hunt really enlivens your senses.

Someone who speaks like that, you might conclude, can't quite get all his thoughts together. Nothing seems to "flow." When you say that a paragraph doesn't flow, you mean that it lacks coherence. Compare the preceding paragraph to this one:

I like swimming because it's invigorating. I like fishing because it's enjoyable. I like hunting because it enlivens my senses.

This paragraph is coherent because it contains three related ideas, and each idea is expressed in the same way: "I like X because..."

In your proposals, I most often see problems with parallelism in lists. By convention, a list is a group of related ideas, and therefore the ideas need to be expressed similarly. Usually, a list is preceded by a string of words that end with a colon. These words are called *determiners* because they determine how the items in the list need to be phrased. If, for example, the determiner were "I like," then your list might go like this:

- Swimming because it's invigorating.
- Fishing because it's enjoyable.
- Hunting because it enlivens my senses.

If, on the other hand, the determiner were "I like to:" then you'd have to change all the -ing words to verbs like "swim."

Even writers who do a good job of using parallelism within a list sometimes have trouble with lists within lists. The following bulleted text, taken from a slide in a presentation, contains not one list but three. The first includes the two items with the hollow bullets. The second and third are separate lists of solid bullets under each larger one.

- □ Costly administrative organization.
  - Three separate and fully equipped companies exist in a fairly small market.
  - Considerable overlap occurs in administrative responsibilities.
- □ Logistics are costly.
  - Long chain of distribution from production to customer.
  - The tonnage is small.
  - Many small customers.
  - Low rate of turnover in stock.

To check for parallelism in text like that, read each list separately to be certain that all items *within* each list are parallel. In that way, you can quickly and clearly determine that the two hollow bullets are out of synch. The first one is a fragment; the second a complete sentence. To correct the parallelism, make both into fragments or both into sentences. Although the smaller bullets in the top group are parallel to each other, the bottom group contains a second item that's not the same as the others. Again, the solution is to make all four items into complete sentences or to make all four into fragments. No problem would exist if the first group of solid bullets contained all sentences and the second group contained all fragments, because each group is a separate list.

I've given you two reasons to use parallelism: you can avoid sounding stupid, and you can ensure that your writing "flows," that it's coherent. There's a third reason: You can increase the stylishness of your sentences. Now most business documents are written in what's called a "plain style" because documents need to be used efficiently. But that doesn't mean that you can't incorporate some flourishes, occasionally and judiciously. Effective parallelism can help avoid monotony by creating interesting rhythms, as Thomas Jefferson knew so well:

> In matters of principle, stand like a rock; in matters of taste, swim with the current.

If Jefferson isn't to your taste, at least in a business context, perhaps the following is:

> Most important, we will ensure that simple things get done correctly: that all workers are doing their jobs, that routine responsibilities aren't falling through the cracks, that simple maintenance and housekeeping are provided, that there are proper controls of raw materials and work in process, that scheduling is done effectively, and that all activities are aimed to flow as smoothly as possible during the transition.

Here we have what I call the persuasive force of style. Perhaps just as important as the content in this long sentence is the long string of clauses that suggest a flurry, a whirlwind, of activity. Whether you're writing or speaking, *how* you express yourself can be just as persuasive as *what* you say. Good parallelism can be the "how" that lets the "what" sing.

Write Coherent Paragraphs

As I said in the last section, when you read a paragraph that "flows," it has "coherence." The ideas move one from the other smoothly, and you don't get lost because you always seem to know, in the flow of ideas, where you've been, where you are, and where you're going. You've seen that parallelism is one technique you can use to achieve coherence. There are at least four others:

- Pronouns
- Forecasting
- Transitions
- Key repetitions

The following paragraphs use these techniques (and parallelism, which I've indicated with underscoring). Read the paragraphs; then we can talk about them.

1   Top Notch Corporation's *goal* is to maintain or enhance its position of
2   market leadership by being the best producer in the industry. To achieve
3   *this goal,* you have adopted *three overall strategies*:
4   ❐ Improve customer service and quality.
5   ❐ Become the low-cost producer.
6   ❐ Increase market share through differentiated positioning.
7   *All three of these strategies* have signigicant implications for Top Notch's
8   distribution strategy.
9   *   *   *
10   Top Notch Corporation has attempted to become more *flexible* by
11   developing *partnerships* with customers, such as the Excel-Mart
12   "electronic-links" relationship, the Superway exclusive provider program,
13   and various hospital contractual *relationships*. However, *these partner*
14   *relationships* still work best when the customers agree to follow *the Top*
15   *Notch system.* Unfortunately, *Top Notch's system* is not *flexible* enough
16   to meet the diverse value-added requirements of individual customers.
17   *This flexibility* will be a prerequisite for future success in this changing
18   market.

Pronouns contribute to coherence because they have antecedents (nouns that come before them). Therefore, a pronoun in one sentence that refers to a noun in a previous sentence helps to "glue" the two sentences together. The pronoun "this" (line 3) refers to "goal" in (line 1). Similarly, "these" (7) looks back to "strategies" (3), and "these" (13) refers to "relationships," which ends the previous sentence. Note how the writer is careful to follow every "this" or "these" that begins a sentence with the word it refers back to. In that way, the reader doesn't have to stop reading to look back at the previous sentence to find the antecedent.

Forecasting tells readers where you're taking them, what you're going to be discussing. The bulleted list (lines 4–6) serves to forecast the next three paragraphs (which I haven't included). Each of these paragraphs discuss in turn one of the three overall strategies.

Unlike forecasting, which lets readers know where they're going, *transitions* provide a bridge from one juncture to another. "However" (line 13) and "unfortunately" (line 15) are good examples. They prepare readers for a change in thought that will be expressed in the sentences that the transitions begin.

Using *key repetitions* is one of the most effective techniques for increasing the coherence of your paragraphs. Like pronouns, key repetitions tend to glue sentences together, especially when a word or phrase at the end of one sentence is picked up at the beginning of the next one. The sentence ending on line 13, for example, concludes with the word "relationships," which is repeated near the beginning of the next sentence. That sentence, in turn, ends with the phrase "Top Notch system" (line 15) and is followed, at the beginning of the next sentence, by "Top Notch's system." The writer also achieves coherence by using "goal" (line 1) and "goal" (line 3); "strategies" (line 3) and "strategies" (line 7); "flexible" (line 10), "flexible" (line 15), and "flexibility" (line 17); and "partnerships" (line 11) and "partner" (line 13). These key repetitions contribute to the paragraphs' "flow."

*   *   *   *

I've tried to present some of the important techniques that you can use to write more effective sentences. Like all things related to writing, these techniques take some practice to master. But once you've mastered them, they don't go away: From then on, you simply write better from first draft to last. Your sentences will be crisper, clearer, cleaner, and livelier. Most important, your more effective sentences will convince a reader that you can analyze problems, formulate methods to solve them, and articulate the benefits that will accrue from their solution. Your sentences will contain many of the characteristics of the previous sentence in this paragraph, which has a concrete noun as a subject, little distance between the subject and verb, an active verb, and coherence created by parallelism, pronouns, and key repetitions.

Glossary

Benefits: The value derived from the manner of achieving and from the achievement of S_2, the desired result. (This value will differ from buyer to buyer depending upon buying role, organizational responsibility, and individual hot buttons.) See also "Process benefits" and "Product benefits."

Buying Roles:

- *Economic buyer:* a single person on the buying committee whose role is to give final approval to buy. This person has direct access to monies, controls the release of the monies, and has discretionary use of them. The economic buyer's focus is on the bottom line and on the overall impact on the organization. This person asks: "What will be the overall performance improvement and return on this investment?"

- *User buyer:* one or more people on the buying committee whose role is to judge the impact of the project on operational performance. User buyers will use or supervise the use of your service and will have to live with the results of your service. The user buyer's focus is on the adequacy and practicality of the proposed solution and on that solution's effects on the potentially affected organizational unit. This person (or people) asks: "How will the project affect my job and those I manage?"

- *Technical buyer:* one or more people on the buying committee whose role is to screen out bidders. Technical buyers judge the proposal by quantifiable, measurable criteria, act as gatekeepers, and make recommendations. They can't say "Yes," but they can and often do say "No." Their focus is on your service per se. This person (or people) asks: "Do the proposed approach and qualifications meet our specifications?"

- *Coach:* one or more people on the buying committee (or not on the buying committee but within the potential client's organization, within your organization, or outside both) whose role is to act as a guide for this proposal opportunity. Coaches provide and interpret information about the situation, other buyers, and how each wins. Their focus is on the success of this sale. This person (or people) asks: "How can we pull this off?"

- *Ratifier:* one or more people, usually higher up in the organization and outside the official buying committee, whose role is to bless the recommendation of the economic buyer. The ratifier's focus is on potential organizational conflicts (for example, with colleagues, constituencies, other programs, and organizational culture). This person (or people) asks: "Will this project and these proposers meet my broader 'political' and/or personal objectives?"

Note: a single person on the buying committee can play more than one role.

Deliverables: The outputs produced during the process of achieving the desired result, S_2.

Generic Structure: The "slots" that make a proposal a proposal.

Generic Structure Slots:

- SITUATION: What is the problem or opportunity?

- OBJECTIVES: Given that problem or opportunity, what are your objectives for solving or realizing it?

- METHODS: Given those objectives, how will you achieve them?

- QUALIFICATIONS: Given those methods, how are you qualified to achieve them?

- COSTS: Given the methods and qualifications, how much will it cost?

- BENEFITS: Given those costs, what benefits/value will accrue?

Hot Buttons: Desires, concerns, etc. of an individual buyer that must be addressed during the project. For example: "urgency," "thoroughness," "complexity." Hot buttons usually have emotional content.

I-Slot: (see PIP)

Measurable Results: Quantifiable, measurable impacts on the client's business process. (Measurable results are realized only upon implementation.)

Measurable Results Orientation: A focus on measurable results, even in projects that by definition cannot achieve such results.

P-Slot: (see PIP)

PIP: Persuasion–Information–Persuasion

- *P-slot:* a persuasion slot, often containing benefits or themes related to hot buttons, qualifications, counters to the competition

- *I-slot:* an information (or "in-between") slot that contains little or no persuasion (and doesn't need to).

Process Benefits: The good effects that occur because of the manner in which you will conduct the project. Benefits derived from addressing hot buttons are often process benefits.

Product Benefits: The good effects of achieved objective(s) or realized deliverables. Most often, the effects of the potential client having insight, having a plan, and/or implementing that plan.

Projects, Kinds:

- *Insight:* (e.g., audits or benchmarking studies)
  Potential client says: "We don't know if we should change."

- *Planning:*
  Potential client says: "We want to change but don't know how."

- *Implementation*
  Potential client says: "We want to change and know how, but we need help to do so."

S_1: The current situation (the current problem or opportunity) as perceived by the buyers.

S_2: The desired result(s): insight, plan, and/or an implemented plan. The end product(s) of the project or of phases of the project agreed on by sellers and buyers. The project objective(s) are the expression of S_2.

Themes: The repeated expression of selling points related to hot buttons, evaluation criteria, and counters to the competition. Often found in major P-slots.

Index

Abstract nouns, using in subject slot, 252-254
Actions:
  ordering, 64-67
  sequencing, 67-68
  specifying, 66
Active voice, use of, 256
Activities, identifying/integrating, 68-70

Baseline logic, 18-48
  assessing alignment of, 22
  Baseline Logic Worksheet, 41, 47-48, 70-72, 211-214
  kinds of current situations/desired results/benefits/objectives, 20-21
  for multiple buyers, 89
  relationship between slots, proposed project and, 36-37
  testing, 28-31
  understanding, 3-4
Baseline Logic Worksheet, 41, 47-48, 70-72, 211-14
Benefits Section Worksheet, 182-183, 216, 221
BENEFITS slot, 13
  Benefits Section Worksheet, 182-183, 216
  content of, 180-86
  function of, 180
  kinds of benefits, 178-179
  subject slot in, 254-256
  writing, 171-187
Buyers:
  analyzing, 81-96
  coach, 85-87
  economic buyer, 83
  individual vs. organizational, 5
  ratifier, 86-88
  roles, 86-88
  technical buyer, 84
  user buyer, 83-84

Closing/S_2 component, *See* S_2 component
Coach, as buying role, 85-87
Coherent paragraphs, 259-261
Competition Worksheet, 116, 117, 218
COSTS slot, 13
Counters to the competition, 104, 108
Current situation:
  aligning with benefits, 31-36
  kinds of, 20-21

Desired results, 36, 37
  aligning with benefits and objectives, 26-28
  kinds of, 20-21

Economic buyer, 83
English handbook, using, 251
Evaluation criteria, 101-104, 108
Evaluation Criteria Worksheet, 113, 114, 217

Forecasting, 260-261

Generic structure logic, 11-17
  schemas, 11-12
  slots, 12-15
Grammar, 251-261

Hot buttons, 101-103, 108
Hot Buttons Worksheet, 112, 216

Implementation Project, measurable results orientation, 53-54
Insight Project, measurable results orientation, 50-51
Internal proposals, 244-250

Key repetitions, 261

Logical methodology, 9-78
  constructing, 5
  generic structure logic, 11-17

Measurable results orientation, 49-55
  Implementation Project, 53-54
  Insight Project, 50-51
  Planning Project, 51-53
Messages, 99
  developing, 6
METHODS slot, 13, 142-157
  PIP technique, 142-157
  subject slot in, 254-256
Minto, Barbara, 57

Needs component, 130-31

OBJECTIVES slot, 13
  writing, 123-41

Paragraphs, coherence of, 259-261
Parallelism, 257-259
Paramount Consulting:
  proposal opportunity, 197-209
  sample proposal, 222-243
Persuasion-Information-Persuasion, *See* PIP
  technique
PIP technique, 142-157
  assumptions of, 142-143
  at methods slot level, 145-149
  at proposal level, 159
  at task level, 144-145
  persuasiveness, determining level of, 160-163
  P-slots and themes, 163-164
Planning Project, measurable results orientation, 51-53
Process benefits, 179, 181
Product benefits, 178, 181
Project benefits:
  aligning with current situation, 31-36
  aligning with objectives and desired result, 26-28
  kinds of, 20-21
Project objectives:
  aligning with desired result, 22-26
  identifying, based on overriding question(s), 63-64
  kinds of, 20-21

placing atop pyramid, 64-67
Pronouns, 260
Proposal:
  logics of, 9-78
  preparation of, 121-196
  psychologics of, 79-120
Proposal development process, 4, 191-196
Pyramid:
  and baseline logic worksheet, 70-72
  defined, 57
Pyramid principle, 56-78
  actions:
    ordering, 64-67
    sequencing, 67-68
  activities, identifying/integrating, 68-70
  identifying objectives based on overriding question(s), 63-64
  methodology (exhibit), 62
  pyramid logic, using, 57-70

QUALIFICATIONS slot, 13
  as argument, 168-170
    structuring, 170-171
  pyramid for, 168
  writing, 166-176
Questions component, 127-130

Ratifier, 86-88
Recommendation reports, 244-250
  organizing:
    multiple recommendation, 248-249
    single recommendation, 246-248
    whole report, 249-250
Rule-bound writers, 6-7

S_1 component, 18, 36, 124-127
  buyer perception of, 89
S_2 component, 18, 20-21, 26-28, 36, 131
  buyer perception of, 89
Schemas, 11-12
SITUATION slot, 13, 36, 123-124
  and competitive advantage, 134
  components of, 124
    closing/S_2 component, 131
    needs component, 130-131
    questions component, 127-130, 132-133
    story/S_1 component, 124-127
  subject slot in, 254-256
  writing, 123-141

Slots, 12-15
  filling in/accounting for, 14-15
  relationship between baseline logic, proposed project and, 36-37
  sections vs., 14
  speaking to slots, 13
Story/S_1 component, *See* S_1 component
Subject slot:
  abstract nouns in, 252-254
  in SITUATION, METHODS, and BENEFITS slots, 254-256

Technical buyer, 84
Themes, 97-119
  counters to the competition, 104, 108
  defined, 99-100
  developing, 6, 106-108
  evaluation criteria, 101-104, 108
  hot buttons, 101-103, 108
  and P-slots, 163-164
  selecting, 105-106
  sources of, 100-104

Themes Development Worksheet, 106, 107-108, 118, 119-120, 220
Themes Selection Worksheet, 219

User buyer, 83-84

Writing style, 251-261
  abstract nouns, using in subject slot, 252-254
  active voice, 256
  changing nouns into verbs, 256
  coherent paragraphs, 259-261
  forecasting, 260-261
  key repetitions, 261
  parallelism, using, 257-259
  pronouns, 260
  subject slot in SITUATIONS, METHODS, BENEFITS slots, 254-256
  there is ... that/it is ... that, avoiding, 257
  "to be," combining *there, it, that, which, who with,* 256-257

About the Authors

Richard C. Freed (Ames, Iowa), a professor of rhetoric at Iowa State University, has studied and taught proposal writing for more than 15 years. His previous study of workplace writing won the National Council of Teachers of English Award for best book on research in professional communication. **Shervin Freed** (Olympia Fields, Illinois) retired as a partner with A. T. Kearney after nearly 20 years and continues to work actively in management consulting. For his special expertise in manufacturing strategy, he was awarded the highest designation of "Master Professional" by the International Development Research Council. **Joseph D. Romano** (Cleveland, Ohio) has been a management consultant with A. T. Kearney for more than 25 years. Having worked in both strategy and operations, in the United States and internationally, he is now the firm's partner-in-charge of worldwide training and development.